THE HALF OF IT

THE HALF OF IT

Exploring the Mixed-Race Experience

EMMA SLADE EDMONDSON & NICOLE OCRAN

WILLIAM COLLINS

William Collins
An imprint of HarperCollins*Publishers*
1 London Bridge Street
London SE1 9GF

WilliamCollinsBooks.com

HarperCollins*Publishers*
Macken House, 39/40 Mayor Street Upper
Dublin 1, D01 C9W8, Ireland

First published in Great Britain in 2024 by William Collins

1

Set in Adobe Garamond Pro
Printed and bound in the UK using 100%
renewable electricity at CPI Group (UK) Ltd

MIX
Paper | Supporting
responsible forestry
FSC
www.fsc.org   FSC™ C007454

Emma

For my mum, who now it seems, always knew who I was going to be. You once told me that children are not yours to keep but merely to prepare as best you can to send out on their way. I hope this book helps other parents to do just that.

And for my dad who stitched himself up royally with the 'dads know best schtick' – you will never get out of being on speed dial for my questions. I love you.

For all of you who needed this book. I hope you feel seen in some small way.

Nicole

To Mom and Dad,
there is no me without you.

CONTENTS

INTRODUCTION

The meeting of minds that started it all

An effort to begin with the personal in order
to arrive at the universal.

Jonny Pitts, Afropean: Notes from Black Europe *(2019)*

EMMA

A friend of mine once told me that all of her friends are mixed race. Initially, I thought – *Nah, that's not true. You're exaggerating.* But I quickly mentally catalogued her friendship circle and realized that she was being wholly truthful. She told me that this was purposeful because only other mixed-race people understood her lived experiences.

I've thought about this a lot recently because it speaks to the almost magnetic attraction I had to my friend and now podcast co-host, Nicole. I had eyed her across the modern-day bar (Instagram) and thought, *I'd like to hang out with her. We'd get on.* I had this uncanny instinct that we would be friends. At the time, I was working on a behaviour change campaign aimed at converting fast-fashion lovers to second-hand clothing and, knowing that Nicole was an influential fashion blogger, I reached out to her.

When we eventually came face to face our chatter spilled out over the table – our specific shared experiences, understanding and instant kinship kept our conversation flowing until our husbands began to ring our phones wondering where we'd got to.

Our stories overlapped and intertwined, dancing around each other without touching, sometimes mirroring, and sometimes being polar opposites – different accents, parents from different continents. And yet we were the same.

Somehow, we are the same.

Nicole and I shared stories of growing up in the US and the UK respectively – her heritage being Ghanaian Filipino and mine Jamaican British – as though we were breaking bread, gobbling down the details knowing these shared stories would fill us up for a short while, but at the same time wanting the moment to last.

That afternoon when we first met, Nicole and I talked about battling with our hair, the nightmare of going to either a white, or indeed a Black, hair salon, and the 1990s hoodwink that was John Frieda's 'Frizz Ease'. This was the universal con that summons a gulp of shame to the back of the throat of almost any person of mixed race who has been taught by society that they must tame their hair.

We talked about our parents, the impact of attending majority-white schools, the othering we have experienced from multiple communities, and of boyfriends who, we discovered, wanted us because of our visual proximity to the few melanated celebrities they saw as 'exotic' and exciting.

We bonded quickly, because although the mixed-race experience is different for us all, there is something in it that binds us. And yet within the mixed community there is also mystery, because it often feels as though someone, somewhere made an unwritten rule that no one ought to speak of our unified experience. And in truth, this is probably partly down to our own self-censorship.

For my part, I know that I have taught myself to subconsciously filter and temper words, to steady difficult subject matters that might cause offence, treating them delicately as though I were a waitress in a restaurant balancing steaming-hot plates of racial tension. I don't mean to sound as though this is in any way a hardship for me personally. It's not at all, in fact it comes pretty naturally to me. Almost as though it's innate. I've been doing this for as long as I can remember …

Mystery does seem to be a common theme when it comes to the mixed-race identity, and that's something we will endeavour to unpack in this book. There are untold stories, and often things that seem to be left unsaid.

If you're reading this and you're mixed, then you will likely know what I mean.

That night, in Nicole I found someone who was just as interested as I was in exploring the nuance in this sometimes shared, sometimes differing experience.

NICOLE

Emma and I met for a drink early on a summer's afternoon in Brixton – freelancer life meant that we could take this time off, neither of us feeling too guilty. It was *technically* work anyway, because Emma had a sustainable fashion project in mind that she wanted to get me involved in.

We lasted precisely one glass of wine before delving into our backgrounds – there was a kinship that formed immediately out of being mixed that made us at ease with one another. For me, it felt like exhaling after holding my breath for what seemed like hours. We had conversations that I had never really got to have with anyone else because up until that point I hadn't felt comfortable enough to open up to someone in this way.

We talked about hair, family, travel and careers. Our conversation just seemed to stretch out over time … we laughed at the number of people we had both encountered who would tell us that we were 'too much' of this and 'not enough' of that.

And despite my growing up in suburban Virginia and Emma in north-west London, there were common threads that tied us together in how we felt about being mixed. I sensed it was the beginning of something.

Our conversation was in some ways transformative for me. I realized there and then that for most of my life, whenever I had spoken about being mixed race I was opening myself up to other people foisting their own ideas of what that meant on to me: their beliefs about how I should 'act' or who I should 'be'.

When I met Emma, in our first conversation there was a oneness in our experiences that made me feel ready and willing to share. I knew there would be no judgement.

It was in being mixed that we forged our sisterhood, and we felt able to open up to each other in ways we hadn't before with anyone else.

The mixed-race identity and experience was something we felt not a lot of people were speaking about openly at the time. We half-jokingly suggested starting a podcast, given how much we clearly had to say, and every time we met up after that we found ourselves planning out episodes and dreaming aloud about our future guests …

We realized that if we were being honest with ourselves, we were not joking at all. Ultimately there was a wider community that had not yet connected, and a dialogue that was missing – something we felt warranted further investigation given that the mixed-race population is now the fastest-growing demographic in the US and the UK.

STARTING THE *MIXED UP* PODCAST

Cut to the lockdown order of March 2020.

Like everyone else, we were inside, anxious not only about Covid-19 but also about our work as freelance journalists and creatives. We were stuck indoors and work was grinding to a halt. We had no idea what we were going to do about paying our bills, but we had two microphones and FaceTime, so we got to work.

It was in the summer of 2020 that the *Mixed Up* podcast was born. We had already started recording episodes, and that May, George Floyd was murdered by police as the world watched – over and over again on their phones and on TV screens. It was painful to have seen Black people being killed by the police before in heinous, violent ways. And it is painful to admit that this is something that has become commonplace. But this was different. This was on the world's stage. The heaviness of that month and the months that followed was excruciating.

The brutality and coldness of George Floyd's murder being shared repeatedly was stark. We watched his grieving family. We went outside to join the Black Lives Matter protests.

Meanwhile, the energy online was frenetic – we were still stuck inside due to the pandemic, but despite being physically isolated from one another it was the loudest we'd ever felt social media to be. All of a sudden everyone was called upon en masse to share their emotions and their personal experiences in a way that was somehow more collectively vulnerable than we had seen before. People were compelled to say how they were feeling, and everyone, it seemed, was forced to talk about race.

We as Black women felt an immense pressure to show up daily online to speak about our anger, our pain, the micro- and macroaggressions we had faced in the past. How we wanted allies, but also how frustrated we were that it took such a catastrophe for people to listen to us. All of a sudden we had to put on our capes and solve the issue of capital-R racism.

In this moment there was a call to be on the side of justice, to stand together as Black people and People of Colour in the sharing of our mutual experiences, and in calling out the violence and daily white supremacy that we so often face, not only in our schools and workplaces but even in our own homes.

The trouble was that as mixed-race women we were simultaneously being told that our proximity to whiteness meant that we shouldn't speak. Or that we were speaking too much. Or not enough. The discourse in the Black community also felt divided on this issue.

At that time, this wasn't just an issue within the Black community. It wasn't just mixed-race people who had to evaluate whether it was appropriate to speak. There was scrutiny across all People of Colour and rhetoric that pitted racialized groups against one another. Everyone was questioning how far they had a stake in the conversation.

There was never any question in our minds as to whether or not it was appropriate to talk about race as mixed-race Black women – although we understand and empathize with those who felt uncomfortable doing this.

So we wanted to start a conversation.

On *Mixed Up*, we recorded an episode entitled 'Black Lives Matter and Being Mixed' because we noticed that mixed-race Black people felt that they themselves weren't allowed to express how they were affected by George Floyd's murder. It was as though mixed-race people – across the range of lived experiences, heritages and cultures – were looking for their space to talk. So the podcast – and by extension this book – has become that voice.

Often mixed-race people have felt displaced and isolated, looking for connection and community with each other, and we have been honoured to provide that space.

INTRODUCTION

Over the past few years we've interviewed mixed-race and monoracial people alike, including Afua Hirsch, Anton Ferdinand, Asia Jackson, Ben Bailey Smith, Candice Brathwaite, David Oyelowo, Jassa Ahluwalia, Jordan Stephens, Lianne La Havas, Nikesh Shukla, Tori Tsui and countless other names you will know and love. We knew we wouldn't be able to provide the wealth of experience of what it means to be mixed race or to have mixed-race children today without talking to our elders and our peers.

This is why we wanted to write this book, to provide something you could take away with you. Ultimately we were looking for kinship and community and we found it in each other, in our listeners and in hearing the multitude of stories on the podcast. Hopefully you can find your own sense of community within the pages of this book.

While this is something we wish we'd had when we were younger, it's by opening the door to conversation and accessing people's stories that we have been able to grow into the women we are today, with a richer understanding of ourselves and the beautiful, vast and varying mixed-race community at large. This book is an invitation for you to make the space to hold multiple truths at the same time, and we ask that you bear this in mind while reading. We are the living proof that racism and 'race' have to be a construct. Writing *The Half of It* and producing *Mixed Up* has been a process of finding the beauty in breaking down binaries and allowing ourselves and other mixed-race people to authentically hold all parts of their identities proudly as individuals and in community with one another.

HISTORICAL CONTEXT FOR THIS BOOK

Over the past few years while recording *Mixed Up* and writing this book, we have always found ourselves circling back to the idea that we have to know the history in order to more clearly understand and discuss the present, and certainly before we can chart our future.

Having spoken on the podcast to over a hundred people from different corners of the world about their lived experiences, we have learned details of cultural histories that we were not previously aware of. This history has compelled us to research further and seek out these stories and their backgrounds.

We spoke to Rosemary Adaser about the relentless brutality suffered by mixed-race children at the hands of Mother and Baby Institutions in the Republic of Ireland that only shut their doors as recently as the late 1990s, about how ultimately if you were mixed-race Irish you were viewed as a scourge upon the nation.

We spoke to Florence Kollie Raja about what it means to have lived through two civil wars, having fled from Liberia to Ukraine as a child, and now, again, how the Russo–Ukraine War has affected her as a Black Ukrainian – a mix that she tells us some people would find hard to believe exists.

All over the world there are stories of mixed-race people and communities that have experienced displacement or brutality: babies orphaned from the 1920s to the 1950s because of the UK's policy against the adoption of mixed-heritage babies; the Métis in Senegal, a people created by design by the French aristocracy; people who are called 'coloured' in South Africa; mulattos in Spain; creoles and mestizos in the US; and the Aborigine Stolen Generations in Australia. Once you start to dig, the list goes on.

Although we mixed-race people have existed throughout

history, there is still an unspoken misrepresentation and a wilful misunderstanding of our existence which we feel in not being able to discuss the history of prejudice, segregation and, ultimately, violence.

In the 1930s, social researcher Muriel E. Fletcher wrote the 'Fletcher Report', on behalf of the Liverpool Association for the Welfare of Half-Caste Children, which described great moral concern over the fear of mixed-race babies being born in their hundreds and thousands just before African American servicemen arrived at Britain's ports in the following decade.[1]

It was anticipated that mixed-race children would be the scourge of Britain, and eugenics theories declared that our existence would be doomed because we would inherit the worst traits of our parents – inherent physical and mental defects. We were deemed to be neither one nor the other, but decidedly worse than both. Given that, at this time, to be 'other' – Black, or indeed any other ethnic minority – would have carried with it a characterization that was 'less than human' (something, incidentally, that is still written into the American Constitution to this day), it is not difficult to imagine that mixed-race babies were thought of as monstrous.

However, we also discovered secret communities formed of people who were all known by the same ugly label, 'half-caste', and heard stories of a dive bar called the Reno, in 1970s Moss Side, Manchester, where they hung out and mixed-race children were all but conceived when their parents met on the dancefloor.

It's interesting that as we researched the history of mixed-race people, clandestine, hidden records and suppressed lived experiences cropped up again and again.

MÉTIS

Thanks to colonization, there are multiple groups of 'Métis', which is the French word for 'mixed', or 'mixed-blood'.

One of our first encounters with the Métis involves First Nations people, whose homelands are in Canada and in parts of the United States. They can trace their ancestry to both Indigenous North Americans and French settlers.

However, not all people of mixed Indigenous and settler descent are Métis. The Métis are a distinct people with a unique culture and language. The Métis in Canada have been recognized as a separate group since the Constitution Act of 1982, and in 2016 had a population of 587,545. Smaller communities of Métis live within the United States, but on the whole are largely unrecognized.

The Métis in Canada have one of the oldest flags in Canadian history which features an infinity symbol that is said to have two meanings: the joining of two distinct cultures and the representation of the immortality of the Métis Nation. There is a beauty in this, an early celebration of mixed identity, a literal 'flag in the sand' from the early 1800s.

The Métis are also found in Senegal, where a generation of mixed-race people originated from French traders and local Senegalese women, primarily in the city of Saint-Louis. They have been described as an 'elite merchant class', and were known to hold a level of power within the colonial structures. The women in particular, known as 'Signares', were regarded as elegant, refined, bourgeois entrepreneurs and played a large role in Senegal's early political and religious history. What is so fascinating about this group of Métis specifically is that they were lauded because of their European heritage – whereas there are stories of other mixed-race people throughout history where it is the root of their persecution.

In the Democratic Republic of the Congo (formerly colonized by Belgium), the Métis were children of white Belgian men and local women who were abducted from their mothers and sent to Catholic missions and orphanages. They were branded as 'the children of sin' and isolated to ensure that they would not be able to claim a link with Belgium in their later lives. Five surviving women who are now in their seventies sued the Belgian State for crimes against humanity in 2020. The suit claims that the children were abandoned by both Church and State and that some of them were sexually assaulted by militia fighters during the time of political upheaval in the country.

MIXED-RACE ABORIGINES: THE STOLEN GENERATIONS

Between the early 1900s and the 1970s, many First Nations children were forcibly removed from their families by Australian federal and State government agencies and Church missions. The children were referred to as 'half-caste', and under the policy of 'assimilation' the removal of those with Aboriginal/Torres Strait Islander and white parentage from their families meant that their lives would be 'improved' if they became part of white society and naturally 'died out'. There are estimates that in certain regions between one in ten and one in three Indigenous Australian children were forcibly taken from their families and communities during this period.

The Aboriginal Protection Act of 1869 included the earliest legislation authorizing the forcible removal of children from Aboriginal parents and gave the colony of Victoria sweeping powers over Aboriginal and 'half-caste' children, who were taken from their families and taught to reject their Indigenous heritages.[2] Names were changed, traditional languages were forgotten and children were put into institutions known for neglect, abuse and other trauma. Although some were adopted by white families, that didn't necessarily translate into safety. Not only were parents separated from their children, but siblings were separated as well. Although an apology was presented by Prime Minister Kevin Rudd to Indigenous Australians in 2008, the grief and intergenerational trauma is still palpable.

MIXED-RACE BABIES AND THE SECOND WORLD WAR

Thousands of mixed-race babies born in the Second World War were orphaned because of UK policy against their adoption. It was illegal for their Black American GI fathers to adopt them. Just under half of the children were put into homes because it was assumed they were too hard to place. These children, who were not white, were not thought of as British and yet they could not be adopted by their fathers. So where did they belong?

This segregation, this separation from our families (physical or felt), the desire to belong and the search for acceptance are all themes we have pulled from history and from conversations we are having with our guests on the podcast today.

The history is laid out for us plainly and we will make reference to it throughout the course of this book in order to provide a context within which to view and understand mixed people's experiences today.

AND WHERE ARE WE AS MIXED-RACE INDIVIDUALS IN SOCIETY TODAY?

Well that's a question we hope to answer as we take you through these pages.

From Fenty shade 300 being used (rather ungenerously) by Black Twitter as a tool of measurement to indicate where mixed people fit on the Blackness barometer, to the inside racism faced by darker-skinned Filipinos brought to our attention by the hashtag #magandangmorenx (meaning beautiful brown skin), to the disconnect we've heard from those with Arab names who, although seemingly Muslim, know nothing of that religion because the lone parent they have grown up with does not follow it – we will explore the positive, vivid conversations and communities bubbling below the surface.

Through the online platforms that are springing up, we see people who are growing more confident and who are now defining themselves and claiming their complex and nuanced identities without equivocation.

We want to create the resources and the outlet we never had, to foster belonging from reading stories that make us feel seen, and by forming the language we never had to express ourselves at the time. We want to create something for mixed-race people; for those growing up and for those tackling adulthood everywhere.

This book is also for anyone who has ever dated (or thought about dating) someone outside their race, for parents with mixed kids, and for anyone hoping to gain a bit more insight into race and identity. It turns out that it is for almost everyone.

OUR APPROACH

The purpose of *The Half of It* is to explore concepts and experiences that are part of, but certainly do not fully encompass, being mixed race. It's not possible to discuss them all within this relatively short book because the spectrum is so vast. Each experience is conditional on many different factors, from class to geographical location, to the cultural histories of those locations and how they have been affected by colonization, to whether the people in question were born and raised in one of their ancestral countries, for example. There are so many things to consider. Instead, we hope to raise consciousness around some of the challenges and topics we have discovered through our work and consider to be pertinent to the multiracial identity.

We begin with the personal in order to explain – why us? And in a way, by doing this we'll explain the need for this book. In order to support a deeper, more nuanced discussion of race in relation to being of mixed race, the book will take the form of a collection of essays, anecdotes and investigation.

At this point, after more than a hundred hours of anecdotal research for our podcast, if there's one thing we can say for certain it is that there are no right answers, and in some instances there are no answers at all but … only room for more open conversation. We would like to facilitate these discussions, which have largely been left without much introspection outside academic journals.

In an ideal world we would love you to read this book from start to finish in its intended order, so that you can get to know us a bit better before we present you with what may at times feel like challenging themes. Because before we were authors we were journalists. And our personal voices might well have proved to be our greatest asset.

Thankfully, people have returned again and again to grace us by listening to over a hundred hours of the *Mixed Up* podcast. We believe they trust us, not just because we have done masses of anecdotal and qualitative research speaking to people across the globe – from academics, mental health professionals, footballers and actors to survivors of war – but because they have got to know us and begun to recognize our personal investment in this work. That's why the book will begin with an introduction to us – your hosts for the next 300 pages: Emma and Nicole.

We realize that many of you will want to dip into the book at various chapters that interest you, but first we'd like you to understand a little about the context of our own backgrounds and points of view, accepting that you may not necessarily agree; you may not always consider them to be reflective of your own if you are a mixed-race person reading this. Conversely, there will be times when a mother, father or someone who is not mixed race for whom these topics hold interest sees themselves in the experiences here, and for us that is all part of it. Those moments when we realize that we are more similar than we are different are just as important as those when we prove to be disparate.

We encourage you to read this book not looking for things that set mixed-race people apart from monoracial people, but instead with an understanding that many of the same experiences are for us filtered through a slightly different lens.

As adults of mixed-race heritage who grew up in different corners of the globe in very different cultural set-ups, we know only too well how similar our experiences can be without actually being the same – these are the commonalities we share. We both have Black ancestry, for example, so our approach, while not exclusively focused on this, will reference it. Being Black and mixed is an important point of exploration for both of us, and so naturally it will feature as such in our book.

We both grew up in predominantly white spaces, so you will hear us refer to this and glimpse how it may have influenced our experiences.

Nicole is Black, yes – but she is also Filipina. I am Black, but I also have white parentage. How we flex in our expression of ourselves is an important part of what we want to convey about being mixed race.

Additionally, we will explore how monoracial groups can affect our experience of being mixed: how being Asian and being considered the model minority, for example, affects your sense of self. We need to look at how our parents' monoracial experiences might have filtered into aspects of our own identities as mixed people, because ultimately we must interrogate the specific cultural and ethnic contexts of monoracial groups in order to be able to define our own.

It's important to note that this is not an autobiography, and while we will sometimes use our own experiences as points of reference, as outlined above, it would not make sense to do so consistently when considering the broad spectrum of the 'mixed experience'.

We believe that much of our present is tied to our collective past; and while this is not a work of history, we think it's crucial to provide context for the reading of the text, and specifically some of the essays that refer to previous political events.

In Chapter 1 we try to give you a sense of ourselves, while exploring the idea of growing up in predominantly white environments. Clearly, this is not an experience that is exclusive to people of mixed race, but it is something that we as co-writers bonded over and later found to be an important theme based on the people we have spoken to and interviewed. Our interest in this issue may spring from an assumed proximity to whiteness which is associated with people of mixed race almost as default. How we as mixed-race people experienced some aspects of that proximity seemed an interesting space to explore and a useful context to share.

In Chapter 2 we look at the difficulties which parents might face when talking to their children about being mixed, and whether parents have the language with which to do so. What is that language? How does the experience of being mixed race as a child sometimes create challenges that are not well known or often discussed?

In Chapter 3 we look at interracial relationships and whether they are still a relatively radical act; and in Chapter 6 we talk beauty standards – a relentless theme of life for us as women.

In Chapter 11, are the letters from our listeners and the mixed-race community in which they explore the themes they wish they had discussed with their parents when growing up. It's a full-circle moment.

In Chapters 12 and 13 we look at art and food and give examples of creative explorations of identity via artists and chefs of different mixed heritage: Ana, who is Chinese-Portuguese, will introduce us to Macanese cuisine, a mixture of Portuguese and Chinese influences, and Laxmi, who is Filipina-Indian, will share the story behind her artistic take on the female form as it relates to her mixed heritage.

By bringing all of this together in this way we hope that this book will facilitate a deeper understanding of this topic and encourage awareness, reflection and conversation.

So we give you *The Half of It*.

TERMINOLOGY AND CONTEXT

We want to provide you with the definitions of some of the terms you will come across while reading this book and the context they are likely to be used in. Language is ever evolving and over time some of these terms may be deemed offensive or obsolete. At the time of publishing, these are the terms we feel most comfortable and confident using and that best reflect the world we're living in today.

Language

We are all too aware that language is an important subject when it comes to the mixed-race experience, and even the experiences of the diaspora or displaced peoples and groups all over the globe. Many of us yearn to learn a language to bring us closer to some part of our culture, ancestry or heritage, and we acknowledge that the challenges often found in accessing this language are a relevant and emotional part of the puzzle when it comes to belonging and identity. We have heard many people say that knowing the language of their parents or their ancestors can provide an additional level of validation when their identity might otherwise be questioned.

We have, however, decided not to veer too far into this subject because we don't feel that we can do it justice within the remit of this book. A separate study could be written, exploring not just how language relates to belonging and identity on an emotional level but also the etymology of language and what this can tell us about migration and ancestry.

Ethnic group

An ethnic group refers to people who are constructed as sharing a common history, language, religion and culture [...] people with the same skin colour do not always share a common culture [...] What sets them apart from white people, and is the basis for their stigmatisation by racists, is their appearance [...] not their culture. It is because racial categories continue to have both political and psychological importance that we continue [...] to use the term 'race' [when discussing people of mixed race].[3]

We are using this definition, set out by Barbara Tizard and Ann Phoenix in *Black, White or Mixed Race?: Race and Racism in the Lives of Young People of Mixed Parentage*.

Race

While we are aware that race is a social construct and that biologically we are all of the same race, we will use the term 'mixed race' throughout this book – both because it is one with which we and many of the people we have spoken to have grown up with and still identify, and because as Jamaican-born British Marxist sociologist, cultural theorist and political activist Stuart Hall put it: 'Race is both a socio-economic fact and a social construct.' It is felt keenly by People of Colour throughout the world, which means it is necessary to acknowledge it as part of how we form, describe and socialize our identities. We choose not to use the terms 'dual-heritage' or 'biracial', unless we are specifically referring to someone who explicitly identifies in this way, because they exclude many identities, given that most of us have more than two heritages. It goes without saying, however, that it is up to each individual of mixed parentage to decide which label they prefer to use, and we support their right to decide how they refer to themselves.

Racism

Racism is the discrimination against a particular racial group that takes multiple forms. There's overt racism which most would say they can easily recognize, but racism is also the discrimination against, and the systemic oppression of a particular racial group. Racism is rooted within systems of government, housing, economics, entertainment, media and culture that permeate through our society – ultimately, it's the oppression of a racial group to the social, economic and political advantage of another. We want to support the understanding of racism as it has evolved – moving us away from thinking of purely peer to peer, individual to individual interactions.

Colourism

A term first coined in 1982 by American novelist and social activist Alice Walker, often described colloquially as the 'sister to racism'. Colourism is defined as prejudicial or preferential treatment based solely on skin colour. Closely linked with racism, essentially it means favouring people with lighter complexions over those with darker complexions.

Capitalizing of 'B' for Black

We have decided to follow the lead of other anti-racist educators and organizers with this choice and have capitalized 'Black' when writing about Black people because we want to place the word on par with other recognized groupings and names of nationalities, peoples, races and tribes. Although we recognize that 'Black' is not a homogenous group in all senses, people of the African diaspora generally understand themselves as sharing an ethnic or racialized identity. Using the lowercase 'b' has been highlighted as racist in the context of an ongoing struggle for equality, particularly in the context of the historical African American struggle. 'It is an act of recognition of racial self-respect for those who have been for generations in the lower case.'

We have not, however, capitalized the 'b' in 'brown' because generally speaking, we do not feel that 'brown' has been allocated quite the same homogeneous group meaning and context by society as 'Black'. As we write this – interpretations of the term 'brown' in regard to race are variable and unique. For example, in the UK you will sometimes hear Black mixed-race people call themselves 'brown'. You may also hear someone of Indian descent refer to themselves in this way. Unless as part of a direct quotation, we therefore will not capitalize 'brown'.[4]

The Global Majority and People of Colour

The Global Majority is a collective term that first and foremost speaks to and encourages those so-called to think of themselves as belonging to the Global Majority. It refers to people who are Black, Asian, brown, dual-heritage, indigenous to the global south, or have been racialized as 'ethnic minorities'.

Where we refer to the broad range of people who sit within the mixed community, one of whose parents is from the Global Majority we may use the term 'People of Colour'. This is not a perfect label and not one that we love, but for now we are not aware of a term that better conveys the way in which this group experiences the world and is currently seen by society.

We will also use this term in order to avoid centering whiteness. This is why we will not be using the phrase 'non-white people' as a standardized term.

Monoracial

A term that is used to describe someone of a single race or ethnicity. We acknowledge that this is not an ideal or favourable term to use as it could be thought to reinforce the false idea that 'race' is a scientific fact. Nevertheless, we have used it in this book for ease of understanding as it is the term most recognizable at the time of writing.

Geography

We recognize that geography is a huge contextual factor. For example, the experiences of a Malawian Filipino living in the UK may be more similar to those of someone who is white British/Malawian mixed living in the UK than someone who is Malawian monoracial living in Malawi. People who are of mixed race or mixed heritage are received differently in different parts of the world and therefore have vastly varied experiences. For example, in regions that have been colonized, such as the continent of Africa, people may view whiteness as being applicable to all people who are not visibly Black, because Black people are the majority. In many African countries there are words like *oyinbo* (Nigeria) or *oburoni* (Ghana), which mean 'white person' or, sometimes interchangeably, 'foreigner', and you are likely to hear people who are mixed referred to in these terms.

Transracial adoption

Transracial adoption, or interracial adoption, describes any situation in which a family or parent adopts a child of a different racial background to themselves.

THE AUTHORS

EMMA

There was a distinct feeling I remember having as a small child. I was protected, happy and so very loved, but there was also a knowledge of the worry that my mum carried for me that was somehow different from the worry a parent has ordinarily about scrapes, the danger of crossing roads or talking to strangers. Our worry was quite particular, our mother–daughter bond intense and heavy. We worried about whether I would be prevented from getting into the right schools because of prejudice, and about how I would be treated when, not if, I got there.

A poster of Bob Marley – the mixed-race icon that my mum had pointedly introduced me to when I was small – hung over my bed.

I am named Emma because it is a very English-sounding name, although it is actually of German origin. It is a protective name, like a shield, one which would present someone with an idea of me that would be everything they might want to hear and feel, so I would always be in the room before they had a chance to decide I might not be everything they had wanted to hear and feel.

My mum was very protective in general, and on reflection there are many examples of this in my childhood. Like the moment my mum told me I could stop calling my dad 'David' and instead I could now call him 'Dad'. I was probably almost six years old by then and I remember I stood under that ladder for what seemed like an eternity, struggling to get the word out because it felt so odd sat on the tip of my tongue. I remember rolling it round and to the back, and then the inside of my cheek before I pushed it out into the open – 'pop', like a bubblegum bursting – and I saw him glance down from fixing the light with the biggest grin I had ever seen. I grinned back.

The thing is – my dad had been my dad since I was very small, even if he had not yet been granted the title. And I had been a daddy's girl since the beginning. I would laugh at my dad – at the Northern way he said 'ba-th' and 'gra-ss' and 'laff' and at his ponytail and beard as he fashioned my Afro hair into French plaits.

I always loved leaving for school in the mornings, my little brown hand in his huge pale one. His giant fingers holding mine in a vice-like grip just in case I should try to slip off the pavement and into the road, but I didn't mind. I didn't mind at all.

* * *

I was born in Edgware, North London, in a grey brutalist building that was commissioned in the 1960s.

As I understand it, my mum was alone in Northwick Park Hospital for the many hours of labour she endured, because (like mother, like daughter) I was stubborn as hell and in a bid to prevent nature from taking its course I refused to emerge into the cold, gruff exterior.

When I finally arrived in the late 80s via caesarean (much to my mum's upset), my birth certificate was signed bearing witness that Jennifer Anne Slade had borne a little girl. Ethnicity: 'Other', Father: 'Unknown'. And that, friends, was that.

My mum was tiny and slight, with wavy hair the colour of husk and piercing blue eyes, and she was beautiful. I don't use that descriptor breezily, in the way many people believe their kin, their flesh and blood to be beautiful. My mum was disarmingly good-looking.

She was white, and I was brown and full of chub, with an adult's head of hair, which was thick and wavy when I arrived but it would soon begin to coil its way into an Afro texture.

At that age, even swathed in a big white lacy christening gown, you would be forgiven for mistaking me for a bouncy little boy.

My mum and I might have appeared to be opposites – but we very much belonged to each other and only each other for some time, despite questions around whether I was 'in fact her baby' and the quizzical repetition of 'Where is the dad?'

There we were – the two of us against the world. My mum was determined, and in her own story she seems fearless, even in the vignette in my mind's eye of us together in the bedsit where we shared a bathroom with so many people, and where she could almost touch all the walls standing in one spot. Mine was not to question, because I was just a little bubba, and there *were* many unanswered questions. There still are, if we are being very honest – but without doubt I was protected and content.

Later, when I was around 3 years old, my mum met my dad and our twosome became three. I remember my childhood being pretty awesome, to be honest. There are countless photographs of our adventures as proof – three musketeers out stomping the rolling outdoors and climbing over turnstiles in the Dales, our red wellies matching, even if to the uninitiated onlooker, at first glance, we as a threesome did not.

My Northern grandad, my dad's dad, recently told me about the first time we went to a family party 'T'up north'. It went on late and apparently by the end of the night I was utterly conked out, as only a child of that age could have been in the midst of noise and party revellers. My thumb firmly in my mouth, I was lain across two chairs that had been pushed together for me, my little feet not hanging off the end but the edge of my party dress slipping towards the floor, as though trying to drag me off with it. An older aunt on my dad's side turned to my granny, gestured to me and asked, 'So I take it she's adopted then?' My grandad recounts that my granny replied simply, 'No, she's not' and turned away to continue her evening.

Even as a babe, when I was oblivious to the optics and to family politics, to how I was being racialized by the outside world and to the difference in the racial make-up of my family, I was already tacitly subjected to 'the questioning' – a quiet interrogation of – who I was, why I didn't appear to be the same as my family. Why are they white and I am not? Or rather, why am I Black while they are white?

And I suppose I have learned to avoid this line of conversation because it opens a can of worms and in my experience only invites more questions, ones to which I am unlikely to have the answers. People seem to feel that this is crucial information they need to know. In retrospect, it still seems odd to me that they can expect me to share something so personal (and they do ask) as part of a standardized background check so they might better 'place' me and my identity.

It seemed to me when I was younger that people would be fixated on this missing puzzle piece, intent on dragging me into sketching a proverbial family tree. A family tree of which I can't access a good 50 per cent, mind. So I've conditioned myself to swerve what can be a sticky encounter with someone I don't know well enough to warrant one.

In reality, growing into my adult life, it is something I haven't given much thought to until starting the *Mixed Up* podcast. This is probably because I don't tend to feel a responsibility to give anything of myself over to strangers or casual acquaintances. I don't have the same desire to connect with so many new people on a deeper level and I don't feel I owe other people an explanation of myself. And that's a good place to be. But when you're young you're probably not quite as hardy, not quite as self-assured, so you have to be ready for the relentless questions and moments of explanation. Or, indeed, to skirt and avoid.

While my particular family set-up and experience is not that of all mixed-race people, maybe not even most, it seems as though we likely all know how it feels to be questioned on our identity. And those of us who have grown up in predominantly white neighbourhoods but who are not racialized by the world as white will know what it feels like to be the odd one out, the one who is obviously different from everyone else in the room. And then later to head into other rooms where, on the face of it, we ought to belong because we will be among other People of Colour, but in which every now and again we get uncomfortable reminders that we may not be the perfect fit there either.

For me, this wasn't something I felt acutely while I was with my family – quite the opposite. For us it was normal, our family was normal and we didn't discuss or dwell on the idea that I was different. Don't get me wrong – I was very aware of my Blackness. My mum and I had talked about how I might be perceived differently by society. I had Black dolls and books she had hunted down that had representations of me in them. While I was still in primary school I read all of Mildred D. Taylor's books, which powerfully traverse themes of race, its political history and racism in the American Deep South. And all this without her ever really addressing the elephant in the room, fully.

It's not that I didn't know that my biological father was Black, not the man who is my 'dad', or that this hadn't been explained to me. It had. But we didn't all sit down and have conversations as a family about why I was different and what had come before. To this day I don't know what, and if, my two white brothers were told growing up.

I wince inside when people refer to us as 'step siblings' because we don't use this label or relate to it. This happened just recently when I visited my brother while he was working in Guadeloupe. When he introduced me to one of his colleagues they presumed to call me his stepsister. I was jarred and couldn't stop myself from taking offence. It's like being jabbed in the ribs. I know that because we are so visually different people lurch for a term that works for them. Met with a family set-up that is unfamiliar or unexpected, they forget to listen and sometimes feel compelled to force a label that doesn't fit. To us, we are your average siblings. A brother and sister who grew up in the same house, with the same parents, sharing each other's milestone life moments. We are independent, it's true – the three of us are always off doing our own thing – but we are also close despite the seven years between each of us.

Independence has always been a big theme in my life. My parents encouraged me to stride out on my own and try new things – perhaps that's how I ended up preparing to audition for a Guildhall jazz singing course in relative secrecy. Spoiler: I did not get in, and I am not now the next Cleo Laine despite my mighty 17 year-old ambitions.

I did, however, develop that sense of independence into a healthy entrepreneurial spirit that enabled me to have a successful career in advertising. It has seen me start a consultancy business, lead the charge in the UK in elevating the second-hand fashion retail space, become a *Forbes* 100 environmentalist, travel around the UK and Europe speaking about sustainability, behavioural change and intersectional environmentalism. And finally, in no small way I believe it has played a part in bringing me to this moment where I've felt a real pull to explore the personal and the political when it comes to identity and belonging.

NICOLE

Until I was about 10 years old I lived in Alexandria, Virginia. I grew up in a modest two-bedroom apartment with my parents, just up the road from my auntie's condo. My parents were (to me) average working-class immigrants, my dad from Ghana and my mom from the Philippines, who simply worked hard every day, not only to better themselves but also to ensure that all of my needs were met, and beyond.

All of this was completely unknown to me until I was in my early twenties. I didn't know about the multiple jobs Dad had worked to pay for my education and also build up savings for the three of us. We lived near my mom's sisters not just by mere coincidence, but, of course, for support. I was looked after by my *titas* when necessary, and the *titas* I wasn't literally related to but who were called upon after school. The support network was built out deliberately.

I think growing up as an American teenager can do that to you, especially when outside of family you're surrounded by mostly upper-middle-class white folks. You can get distracted by things that don't matter.

Teenagers can be pretty self-centered by nature. But there is truly nothing more insular than the suburban American teen. I was that teen. Or at least, that was the teen I strived to be. I yearned for the all-American girl life – the one you see in 90s teen movies.

For clarity, this was nothing like *Clueless*, there were no mansions with columns dating back to 1972. There was no computerized walk-in wardrobe. There was no white picket fence. Or any picket fence (I lived in a first-floor garden apartment). This was not the Hollywood Hills. I didn't get my own Jeep for my Sweet Sixteen. What was pretty similar, though, was growing up in the epitome of a leafy green suburbia that no one ever really leaves.

The pace was slow for me. Measured. I had a lot of good friends. I had a few boyfriends (not all at once, mind). I went to good schools. I grew up with a tight-knit family.

Don't get me wrong: I was still hyper-aware of not being white while living in a largely white suburb, at a majority-white private Catholic school and what that meant to other people, especially at my young age.

Worrying about being judged, although quite natural, feels amplified when you grow up Black in Virginia.

Like I said, I had good friends. I was never bullied or teased mercilessly. Although I'd say my life wasn't like what you might see in a Hollywood film, I guess the age-old tropes exist for a reason. Popularity really is currency, even when you are as young as 7.

On a pretty insignificant day at school I remember being deeply embarrassed about how my mom would never pack me a standard American lunch. We argued endlessly about how I just wanted Lunchables like every other kid. Dad in particular was never a fan of these. You know the one, every elementary schoolkid's dream. Essentially the 7-year-old's version of a tapas. He could spot these honeytraps for kids from a mile away in typical African dad fashion. In the exact same way, I couldn't convince him (or my mom) to get a McDonald's after school because … *why*? There was rice at home.

That's the thing about African and Asian parents – they are never wasteful. Especially when it comes to food. We are a leftover household, much to my dismay as a teenager. Mom and Dad were always advocates of fresh fruits and vegetables, home-cooked meals from the diaspora, dining out as little as possible to save money and to ensure I was getting all the proper nutrients.

Now the idea of cold baloney makes me nauseous, but back then I wanted nothing more than to make cheese-and-baloney cracker sandwiches and call it 'lunch'. Mom would always send me in with Filipino food – my favourite Filipino foods, I should add – but I was embarrassed by the fact that she wouldn't just give me a peanut butter and jelly sandwich, something that wouldn't get me looked at.

Finally, the day arrived for a peanut butter and jelly sandwich! To be honest, I don't even really like them, but they were a symbol of the all-American girl that I so desperately wanted to be. Wholesome, sweet, average … normal. So I pulled it out of my brown paper bag (you graduate to a brown paper bag from a lunchbox when you're trying to be cool, as I obviously was). And there was my PB&J *pandesal*. I could've died. For the uninitiated, a *pandesal* is essentially a Filipino bread roll. Incredibly delicious and also just a sweet bread roll. But I was absolutely mortified. Where was the PB&J in between the off-puttingly white slices of Wonder Bread that I was expecting? *Who would subject their child to these levels of humiliation?* I thought, as I explained to the entire table what I was eating for lunch. No one wanted to trade me anything for this – and you know you have a good lunch when kids are willing to do tradesies.

We all go through those moments of desperately wanting to assimilate, to fit it, never drawing attention to ourselves. Too much attention is never good. And the idea of being othered at that age never crosses your mind, until that one fateful day when someone points out that there is something different about you. Besides, when someone points out that you're 'too' different at that age, it isn't really something you are able to articulate. All you know is the sinking feeling in your stomach.

Your food smells. Or it looks weird. Or you've pronounced something in a funny way that no one understands. Or one of your parents does and you're left with a particularly nauseating feeling in the pit of your stomach. Your ears get red-hot.

You're different.

At home it doesn't matter much, though. It never tended to occur to me. Once I crossed that threshold into the outside world, that's when I was met with everyone else's idea of me – the ones that end up shaping how I see myself. The ones that most likely dictate whether I like myself or not.

Sometimes home can be a respite. It was our place for inside jokes and stories constantly retold. Like I mentioned before, my family is very close. My mother and her sisters emigrated from the Philippines to find work. It was a similar story for my dad, who moved to Florida from Ghana for university and later went up to Washington, D.C., which is where they met, at a Halloween party – the 'meet cute' that I hope to write into a film one day, but that's for another time.

I'm an only child, so Mom, Dad and I have always been thick as thieves, but I also grew up alongside my mom's three sisters. The matriarchy on both sides of my family runs pretty strong, which I love. I was heavily influenced by Filipino culture at a young age because it was such a prominent part of my home life. We all went to church together on Sundays, and then would gather at home to close out the week over lots of food (of course) and heated discussions that usually turned into arguments. But that's family for you.

I often gazed around at our table, amused at the sight of tiny Filipina women shouting and laughing over each other as their husbands looked on, knowing full well that they would never get a word in edgeways so it wasn't worth trying to interject. There is a fierceness in them I've never seen replicated anywhere.

I knew when I was a teenager that living in Virginia for the rest of my life was just not for me. I always worry about sounding condescending when I talk about this, but it felt stifling. Even in the most exhilarating highs of my younger years, through the throes of college party life and in my early twenties, it just felt textbook. As though if I stayed, at any moment I could map out the rest of my life quickly and easily due to all the parallel paths that were laid out in front of me. In all honesty, it bored me.

Initially the plan was to move to New York City and for me to go to journalism school. My goal back then was to eventually become the Black Christiane Amanpour. But due to the overwhelming cost of Columbia University tuition payments it was actually cheaper for me to move across the ocean to come and study in London instead. So I took the opportunity and flew.

Which brings me to the here and now, with over a decade in London under my belt and a multi-hyphenate career that has truly kept me on my toes.

I reconnected with my Black British family (Ghanaian, on my dad's side), and I have met the best people of my life, including Emma, who I'm thrilled to be writing this book with.

Coming to the UK has truly meant coming into myself.

1.
ALL MY FRIENDS
ARE WHITE

EMMA

It's not something I've discussed with you squarely yet as you're only just getting to know me, but I think it's a good example of the diversity that can be found within the mixed-race experience. It feels pertinent when we're talking about growing up in a predominantly white environment to share that all of my family are also white …

In and among what was essentially a joyful childhood characterized by both working and playing hard, there is no getting away from the fact that my world was white. My school was white, my friends were white, and my family is white.

Immacgate

The fear that I had as a child of being questioned was not just associated with people querying my family dynamic, it was also at times – mainly during the teenage angst years – linked to having my Blackness challenged. I'm fairly sure that many mixed-race people will, at some time or another, feel that they have had their membership to at least one of their ethnic groups debated by someone.

I relied heavily on my mum to provide me with meaningful connections to the other side of my heritage, and of course I had my insecurities in not having a direct link to one side of my ethnicity, but it was not a topic that consumed everything. My childhood was happy and full of childish adventure and exploration.

Looking back, in spite of all of my mum's efforts to prepare and protect me there were other challenges which both I and my mum had to navigate that were rooted in our differences.

Unlike daughters whose frames sprout and bend and grow in a mirror image of their mothers, I thought I looked nothing like my mum when I was little, and as the boom and bust of my teenagerdom began to pop, our physical differences only grew wider.

Nothing major, you might think to yourself, but cast your mind back to being a teen when almost everything is MAJOR. The fact I had strong, muscular, thick women's thighs that were already sprouting hair when all the other girls had smooth, thin, wispy long Bambi legs was not something my mum could actually relate to, although she comforted and reassured me. I remember being just mortified at All. The. Hair – another thing my mum almost certainly didn't have to contend with at my young age. And while now, decades later, this is something we are all talking more about and normalizing, you'd better believe that in the 80s and 90s nobody was championing their blue armpit hair.

Immacgate is quite literally burned into my memory. For those of you who are much younger than us, Immac is the cure and the curse, the hair removal cream now known as Veet.

I'll never forget when my mum introduced me to it one afternoon at my nana's house. I don't remember how old I was, but I was quite young – I think in my first year of secondary school, so maybe 11. I had been hounding my mum relentlessly to let me shave for as long as I could remember, having what seemed to me like an unreasonable amount of hair very similar in texture and curl pattern to the hair on my head … and everywhere else. So far my mum had resisted. I had not been allowed to shave a single hair.

I remember it so clearly because I recall being so hopeful: I was about to be saved from the humiliation brought on by the reaction of kids who see other kids that don't look like them, and I could feel the imminent relief about to surge into my body.

I was ready.

Apparently Immac wasn't ready for the stubborn nature of my hair follicles. Despite waiting for well over the recommended time and after multiple tries, it appeared that the process wasn't working quite as my mum was expecting it to. It didn't cleanly vanish away the hair so it could be swept off leaving a clean, creamy-pink, shiny, moisturized, hair-free leg as sold to us all in the adverts; the only way this hair was coming off was through forcibly scraping it off. And the less said about that the better.

In short, this was one of those times which highlighted how my mum's lived experiences could not always provide the background knowledge required to help me through some of my own as I grew up. She had expected this method, tried and tested by her, to be the safest and easiest for me too, but it simply didn't play out that way. Her hair, being blonde, much thinner and less stubborn than my thick, abundant Afro hair, was a different ball game.

We were working with very different bodies, different outer shells and also, with that, different reactions to them.

The body politic

'But why can't I wear them?' I wailed at the high-frequency sound vibration achievable only through the universal language of teen.

'All my other friends are wearing them,' I persisted, hanging half in the living-room doorway and half out – not only because I was strategically hiding the distinct curve of my mixed-race bottom behind the wooden frame, but also because I was hiding from my mother's answer. She, in contrast, was as comfortable sat on our squidgy rose-pink living-room sofa as she was resolutely sunk into her decision. I knew that the answer would be repeated until it was written into law, and that the more I pushed the more certainty would ring in my mother's response.

What I didn't I know at that time was why. Why I was never permitted to do the things my friends were doing and, more importantly for the specific gauntlet I was trying to run on this occasion, why I was never allowed to wear the things my friends wore.

On this occasion, it was the hot and sticky R&B summer of 2000. Craig David had been dutifully 'Fillin' Us In' all solstice long and I was desperate to be able to wear the itty-bitty jean shorts I had borrowed from a friend to attend another friend's birthday party. I was deep in the part of the teenage puberty haze when adolescent girls suddenly become aware of their sensuality, of the appeal of the coquettish curvature of their own bodies. I suddenly wanted to be desirable. I felt cute and I wanted to wear cute things that spoke to my mood. The only problem was that my mum was adamant that the fact that all my friends were wearing short, cute and tight little ensembles ('little' being the operative word here) was no reason why I should think I'd be doing the same.

It was only when I got a bit older and a bit deeper into my teens that I began to intuit that I looked different from my friends in those little denim shorts. I looked different because all my friends at that time, due to the school I went to, were white. None of them had bodies like mine. They were hair-free for a start, but that's another trauma entirely … I saw their bodies as long and lean, while my thighs were thick and my bum was big and already round and protruding, although at the time I was only beginning puberty. It meant that we looked entirely different in our clothes. Almost opposites – we were like chalk and cheese.

I could never understand at the time why my mum would say things like 'But they are not you, and you are not them' in answer to my cries of protestation to her putting the proverbial kibosh on my social status. This one was a build on the classic 'If they decided to jump off a cliff would you follow them?', and it is only now that I really understand that not only was she asking me to think for myself but that she was acutely aware of the different and specific variables at play for us: me a Black child with a body that would be perceived by the world as more grown up, one that would likely be more sexualized than my school friends. I understand in hindsight that the shorts were not just shorts: for her they symbolized a 'fear' that I would not be afforded the innocence I deserved at that age.

We never spoke about the hypersexualisation of Black female bodies, but I think once she may have gone as far as to tell me that 'I looked different from them in "hot pants"', and I remember it was pointed and significant. Even today, if I am going to wear what are commonly known as batty rider shorts to a festival or to a summer shindig, I have to ask myself if I am feeling in the mood to deal with being troubled by people, to deal with being perceived as though I am putting 'sexiness' on show.

Over the years I have often stared at images of carefree girls at Coachella clad in short shorts and tassels, their hair swinging free down their backs. And while, as an adult woman, for the most part I have a healthy enough love for my body and I am more than comfortable with its form, sometimes I have to admit I just long to wear short shorts and that be all it is.

A simple question

The nerves in the pit of my stomach were like molten lava tip winged butterflies that wouldn't settle. I sat, legs crossed, in my bedroom with the cordless home landline phone hoping my parents wouldn't notice it was gone and trying not to breathe. I held my breath because we had all agreed that *he* would never know that I was on this three-way call. I tried not to shift in my seated position while the dial tone dragged on and we waited for an answer.

My accomplices in this were more experienced than me at talking to boys. They were more popular than me and everything for them seemed somehow easier. Like it just flowed. I was confident and smart and I knew I was likeable, so I had made a beeline for them to be their friends – to be in their clique. But I was never sure if I had really made it in. They were best friends, these two, and they were the same – rebellious, fun and beautiful, I had thought at the time, and this was backed up by how the boys at our school responded to them.

Our school was nestled in the countryside in Hertfordshire and it was majority-white. We moved out there when I was 9 years old, so I had continued to commute to my primary school in Harrow which was full of all different kinds of kids – brown kids, Black kids and white kids jostled among each other in the playground.

But I had to leave early to shift up into secondary school because we had moved house and the borough in which we now lived began secondary school a year earlier, and I was excited to start there. I remember there was just one boy at first that I liked. He was sort of like me – I wondered if that was because I intuited that one parent was Black and one was white. His skin colour was similar to mine and I thought he was a kindred spirit, but he never really noticed me. Or if he did, he tried hard not to let on.

There were only about four of us Black or mixed kids in my year group. It was a good school and I loved learning, it's just that there were very few people who looked like me, and certainly no one whose family set-up was like mine. In hindsight this bred a level of insecurity about my appearance, desirability and attractiveness, despite the fact that I was brought up to be and was inherently a confident and assured child.

Somewhere along the line I developed an interest in the white boys in my school. There were boys I thought were cute, there were even some I had bants with. Perhaps that is an exaggeration – a little bit of a respectful rapport with them – but I was never the kind of girl those boys were 'interested' in in a romantic way. Put simply – I was too Black. But this was not something I could articulate for myself until I also discovered the art of the three-way call.

He answered – casual like – very nonchalant, and the three of them began chatting. I sat on the periphery, waiting for my moment. I had entrusted my friends to be my conduits, my messengers, the carrier pigeons for a simple question. They had assured me this would go smoothly and to their plan, and that there would be no hiccup.

I don't remember much of their conversation … but I do remember the waiting that seemed endless after he answered.

I remember some inane chat (even at that age I was sometimes disinterested in teenage musings). And I remember when they asked him if he liked me? If he would date me?

I remember that it was a simple question to which he delivered what seemed like a simple answer. It was so simple that my subconscious understood it immediately and yet my brain was not yet sure if it could compute.

He could not date me 'because I was "Black"' and his friends would 'make fun of him'. It seemed at the time that there was no further explanation needed. I did not ask my friends for one later because I understood.

I don't remember my white friends protesting or interrogating his simple answer and I have no idea if they understood the gravity of that moment for me, or the disconnect in the reality of my world that it brought with it. How could they? In their universe their friends were the same as them. In mine, even my family were not the same as me.

The first cut is the deepest

But it was while I was away from home at university in Bristol that I suffered my first true heartbreak. It was the first time I had felt the sucker punch of a break-up, of being left. The discombobulating confusion of realizing that what you thought was forever wasn't forever at all. The resounding sting of understanding that the love you'd given wasn't reciprocated, and that you'd been left behind. And it's a funny thing, being left behind, when you're the one that's run ahead.

* * *

When I first left for university, my best friend would send me cards and write me letters. We were (I had thought) Thelma-and-Louise close, Beyoncé-and-Kelly inseparable. So close that we had solemnly promised each other that this was the way it would be for the duration of my stint away despite the distance. And at first it was just as we'd agreed. We would send cards and letters back and forth, chattering in them about what we'd been doing, about the various thrills of being on the cusp of adulthood and about how much we missed each other. We talked often about what we would do on my return in the term-time break. For me these communications were an anchor to my home, to security and to my closest connections.

But after some time the letters no longer came, my texts fell into the ether and my calls began to go unanswered and, soon after, unreturned. I agonized over what I might have done wrong, over why I had been left out. I wondered into the night why my friend (and my friends), the close-knit group we hung around in, had abandoned me. I remember feeling heartache and betrayal – a loneliness like I'd never felt before. I didn't understand what had happened for years to come.

My twenty-first birthday may not have been the epiphany moment, but it is a good enough illustration of what had happened. That night my mum had laid on a spread and my dad had painstakingly practised making iced mojitos and strawberry daiquiris at my request. I had invited both my uni mates and my local friends, and the plan was to eat and drink at my family home and then head out to a club.

At the time I worked all my summers in retailer River Island, and as a result most of my clothes (if not hand-me-downs from my mum) were from there. I remember feeling I looked glamorous, beautiful even, in the delicate handkerchief dress I had chosen to wear over leggings with sleek black open-toe heels. Glancing around my family kitchen at my guests, it was almost too notable how few of my friends from home had bothered to turn up for me, for my biggest birthday yet. Looking back, I don't know why I was surprised, or maybe even why they were invited. The invitations winging their way over to me in the past couple of years while I'd been away had definitely dwindled. I recall that when I came home from university I often felt very lonely. There was a humiliation I dreaded in having to attempt to reinsert myself back into my own friendship group – ringing around to find out what was happening, and never being invited without what felt a little bit too much like forcing it.

And at those times when I did find myself out with my old friends from home, I remember the topic of conversation always still seemed the same as it ever was. It was like entering a time warp, where everything stood still and any reminder that things outside were growing and developing, or indeed that they moved differently, would disturb the balance. I disturbed the balance. All of a sudden I was somehow a foreigner in my own home.

I remember that all the new shiny things, the new experiences, the new cultural knowledge I came back with didn't seem welcome in this space. It was as though I had seen too much, explored too far, and it made them uncomfortable. Perhaps it made them uncomfortable that I had obviously sought out and acquired a love of jollof rice while I had been away.

I was studying Sociology and Psychology and one of the core modules I had chosen was 'Difference – Race, Ethnicity and Diversity in Contemporary Society'. I was growing my knowledge of colonialism, empire and imperialism along with the roles played by 'race' and ethnicity as sources of social identity and causes of social inequality. And I was studying all this in one of the UK's most prominent cities in the history of race relations. Not meaning to sound like a cliché, I was very much in my Erykah Badu, revolution, re-education and resistance era.

Perhaps I now had too many Black friends and too much worldly knowledge to fit into my friendship group back home. Perhaps what had happened was that they had ousted me because it was no longer a comfortable fit.

Today I often hear my peers in their thirties discussing the moments in which they recognize how frequently other people reject their personal growth, but I realize I had to grapple with this truth and resolve it for myself pretty early on.

Back then, my friends had ousted me before I had a chance to notice that I had outgrown them, and so for a long time I thought I had been left behind, when in fact I now know that I had struck out in front on a journey on which none of my party had any inclination or need to join me.

All my friends are Black

For my generation, uni was described as something that was as much about the 'experience' as it was about academic learning and gaining qualifications. What parents (who were mostly responsible for touting this idea) meant was that it was going to be a baptism of fire, experiencing standing on your own two feet and living as a grown-up, however cushioned from some realities you might have been to date.

On reflection, when I was visiting potential universities I think subconsciously I was searching for a specific kind of experience of my own. I was looking for a place to connect with a tribe I didn't have access to. I was searching for my peoples. I wanted to go to uni somewhere where I could jam with other Black and brown people, because as much as I was at home at home, as much as I loved my friends at the time and my family (always), I also yearned to explore parts of my heritage and culture that were unfamiliar to me. I didn't consciously register this, but retrospectively it's clear to me now that I wanted to be closer to Blackness. I wanted to know what it might be like to express my Blackness around other Black friends and community. I wanted to be recognized as a part of the diaspora. I didn't need this recognition from Caucasians, who most likely viewed me as Black anyway. I needed it from other Black people.

And so I went to university in Bristol – to UWE. There was a large population of Black people both local to Bristol and also those who, like myself, had come to study in the city, and, looking back, I was on a mission to immerse myself in it. It wasn't long before I had joined the 'Urban Society'. That's right – read it and cringe. The Urban Society was a concept concocted by a group of Black boys from London. It was by no means an ACS (African Caribbean Society) equivalent – but I suppose it had some of the trappings of that sort of club. I'd say now that our main consistent function was probably holding club nights that heavily featured 'Black music genres' and attracted Black ravers, or students who loved RnB, Neo Soul, DubStep, Soca, Afro Pop, Funky House and Garage music.

The two boys I hung out with whom I'd met in my halls were Naija boys from East London. The group of girls that became my clique were mainly Londoners, with different heritages – Nigerian, Jamaican, Tamil, Ghanaian – and from different geographical locations, but ALL Black or brown. And the boy I dated for the majority of my uni days and for years afterwards was a Yoruba guy from South London.

Overnight, almost all of my friends were Black. And at the time I don't think I thought too deeply about this step change in my life, but maybe anyone looking in from the outside might have found it stark.

Thinking about it now, was this by design? Was it conscious? I can't be sure, but there I was, a mixed girl whose family was entirely white, coming from an environment growing up where almost all the people I had gone to school with were white, and now all of a sudden the script had been flipped.

NICOLE

All-American girl?

When you picture an 'all-American girl' the image that probably pops into your head will be that of my best friend. Dirty-blonde, but with lemon-yellow highlights in the summer, freckled white skin, a broad smile with train-track braces – but only for a short while; enough to make them even more perfect. You've pictured her, right? That's Chelsea.

I was 'the Black best friend' in the Netflix movie of Chelsea's life. At the time, I didn't realize this at all, of course; I was too busy basking in the glow of being in her orbit. I knew what it meant for me to be associated with her. Is it possible for kids to be popular at 8 years old? Who knows, but back then I knew that somehow, despite my darker skin, I had been chosen!

I played the role of the Black best friend dutifully and proudly. There wasn't much to it, looking back. More than anything I was just happy being around her. I'd back her up if she needed my support, but there wasn't much she required my help with. She was bright, fun, friendly and charismatic at that age and I wanted to emulate that.

At our private Catholic school uniforms were the norm, so when non-uniform day came round we would 'twin' in matching outfits, down to matching hairstyles. I, of course, knew that my brushed-out pigtails would never look anything like hers, but I was dedicated to the cause. I desperately wished that people thought we looked alike.

At that age I was obsessed with the idea of 'goodness' – Catholics and lapsed Catholics will feel me on this. Catholic guilt is tough to shake off, even now in adulthood. But the thing about being Chelsea's best friend was that I knew that anyone who saw me with her would think I was good too, like her.

* * *

I was always good at making friends, and I don't say that as someone who was stereotypically popular or enigmatic. I don't think that people are naturally drawn to me, but the overwhelming feedback I've had since I was a kid is that I'm *nice*, pleasant almost to a fault. So it has always been relatively easy for people to warm to me. I don't know if that quality is solely down to how I was raised, but I have felt that ease all my life when it came to forming friendships. But what I do know is that growing up in a majority-white environment did mean to me that 'being nice' was the ultimate compliment from white people.

There have been moments in my life when I've definitely felt like a watering-down of myself, when I've kept certain aspects hidden. I felt that was needed in order to assimilate. In all honesty, I just thought that was par for the course of being mixed, of being Black around white people.

When Emma and I first met and talked about our backgrounds and how we grew up, one thing we immediately agreed on was that it felt as though the concept of 'code-switching' was somehow innate, to the point that even to give it a name felt counterintuitive because it was just so ingrained in our way of life. When you are mixed, there are some people you can be a certain way with but not others, certain friendship groups … and you become used to the seamlessness of it all. It's almost like slipping a coat on and off at the beginning and end of the day. For me it never felt like a struggle because it was just always there.

For the uninitiated, the term 'code-switching' was first coined in the 1950s by sociolinguist Einar Haugen to describe alternation between languages for those who are multilingual. It's now commonly used to discuss the ways in which minority groups try to assimilate into the white (perceived) majority by way of changing speech, behaviour and appearance.

Despite that, I know that there is still a level of code-switching involved even with my Ghanaian family and my Filipino family. There are huge similarities between the two for the most part, although I don't think I truly understood until recently how culturally similar these two places that are so far apart could be. That said, the way I am with my Ghanaian family is slightly different from the way I am with my Filipino family – that's just always how it's been. I think part of that has to do with being American, which is an added layer of fun in the shaping of my identity. But the stakes have always been low for me here because my family love me, and have loved me, regardless and I am blessed with a family that integrated and accepted one another without question, as it should be, although this isn't always the case.

Code-switching was brought back into American racial discourse in 2018 thanks to the film *Sorry to Bother You*, when LaKeith Stanfield's character, Cassius 'Cash' Green, starts a job as a telemarketer. He is struggling to make a sale when Danny Glover's character, Langston, suggests he use his 'white voice'. A survival tactic. At times a recipe for success, particularly in the workplace. People of Colour everywhere know immediately what 'using your white voice' means.

Now, although I am not mixed white, I did go to school with mostly white children until I went to university.

Let me paint a picture of high-school Nicole for you.

Likes: writing in her LiveJournal, listening to Bob Dylan and The Beatles, reading Haruki Murakami, writing on RENT message boards, going thrift shopping and rifling through used discs at CD Cellar.

Dislikes: Abercrombie & Fitch, my school uniform, going to Sunday Mass, failing algebra class, not being able to find the appropriate 'Bright Eyes' lyrics that are subtle enough to express my love for a certain boy in my class.

From my interests alone, I'm sure it's easy for you to tell that almost all my friends were white.

Looking back now, it's funny to think about when you know how much Black culture influences the mainstream and what is considered white subculture. At that time, I would've placed myself firmly in the latter – I was very much an emo kid and pop punk enthusiast of the early noughties (my parents were very baffled by this concept) – and I listened to old rock music in heavy rotation. I had (and do have) a lot of feelings, OK? But again, a quick look into the history shows that these musical influences came primarily from Black musicians – blues, rock, folk, all of it – even though now the association is that all of this is solely for white enjoyment.

At every gig I went to I was one of a handful of Black kids in the crowd, which confirmed my feeling at the time that what I was enjoying was A White Thing™. It didn't consistently *bother* me, but highlighted a point of difference that made me feel like I was odd. And at that time,

I really had no Black friends to tell me otherwise. There was no social media and there were certainly no algorithms to serve me up girls who looked like me, who were into the things that I was into. I wonder how I would've felt about myself at that age had I found my alt-Black girl team.

The nuances of being Black and being into what is stereotypically perceived to be white culture isn't something that I was aware of as a teenager, or could even articulate to myself. I think you often just boil it down to being an awkward teenager, going through puberty and being wildly emotional, or at least that's what it felt like for me. Like I said, I had a lot of feelings, and needed to express them in the only ways I knew how.

We know that Black and mixed children find their joy in so many different types of music, hobbies and interests. But I think when you are a person of colour who grows up mostly around white people you have no idea that you're acting like anything other than who you are. The number of times I was told by friends, family, even people I barely knew, as a young child and into early adulthood that I was 'acting white' has now become a cliché.

For a mixed person, being told that you 'act white' is a dog whistle. For anyone like myself, who grew up around mostly white people, it echoes like a refrain between your ears. I couldn't help but feel hurt any time I heard this. Every single time a Black person said this to me I felt it in the pit of my stomach. I wasn't doing a good enough job. I was letting the side down.

It can be common in Filipino culture to hold whiteness in high regard. So at the other end of the spectrum, this can be viewed as a compliment by Filipinos thanks to years of colonial oppression from the Spanish and the Americans. Even though I'm not mixed white, growing up in the United States is something that seems to be lauded by other Filipinos.

In an interview we did with Lizzy Kirk, a mixed Black woman who was adopted into an all-white family and lived in a small village outside Nottingham, she mentioned that the phrase 'acting white' was something she heard constantly while growing up. She is very open in the episode about how she felt perceived by both Black and white people she encountered in her childhood:

> People see me as Black because that's the colour that they see. They don't see 'Oh, she's half white and she's half Black'. Just to look at me, I'm Black. So because I have no concept of my culture at all when I was young, then obviously I'm trying to be white because that's all that I know … I knew nothing about Black culture. The food, the skin, the hair, the music … absolutely nothing.
>
> Mixed Up *podcast, Season 2, Episode 18*

I empathized with this sentiment – despite growing up within two families with strong cultures, I was ultimately surrounded by white people who were also influencing the things that I have grown to love and enjoy. I felt like I was falling short in all areas, struggling to be enough in the groups I was a part of, in the spaces I entered.

Being teach for your white friends

Essentially, those of us living in Western, predominantly white societies often have to seek to learn about Blackness in stark contrast to whiteness and the white constructs which are a constant and not something we have to actively look for. When you only grow up around whiteness, this becomes further exacerbated by the fact that your learning has to be really proactive. You have to seek out the things you perhaps were never told about or had never encountered in your day-to-day life or in your household.

After the tragic murder of George Floyd, when the Black Lives Matter protests were firmly back in the press and public consciousness in 2020, things really shifted for me, for Emma, for Black folks and People of Colour everywhere. All of a sudden, this spotlight shone on us. We were on stage. We were in front of the mic and people were expecting us to speak, eagerly waiting to hear what we had to say. I wish I could describe the feeling of overwhelm in an eloquent metaphor, but I honestly have never had anything to compare it to. It was the most bizarre, soul-crushing time.

Our white friends, our white acquaintances, were looking to us to be educated. There was so much they 'never knew' or 'couldn't believe'. The emotional toll of having conversations about race with white people who either never listened, nor cared to listen, before that significant cultural moment was burdensome. On one hand, you had a group (white people) who expected you to be the fountain of all knowledge and to bestow this knowledge on them. On the other hand, it felt like you had Black people asking, 'As a mixed-race person, are you actually qualified to speak on this?' and expecting you to 'fall back' because you weren't 'fully Black'.

As I heard the rapper and author Akala say on an Instagram Live after the murder of George Floyd and during the Black Lives Matter resurgence, a mixed person identifying as Black means that they are aligning themselves with justice. In his book *Natives: Race and Class in the Ruins of Empire*, Akala writes that he identified as Black not just because race is 'social and not scientific' and 'not because Black people are paragons of moral excellence who can do no wrong but simply because white supremacy is an unjust, idiotic and ultimately genocidal idea and because Blackness can accommodate difference far more easily than whiteness can – because its historical and ontological origins are entirely different'.[1]

All you ever truly have to share are your own experiences; that is, the same experiences that until that point in time had been diminished or dismissed outright. All of a sudden, everyone wanted to hear them. Any small experience of racism, microaggression or macroaggression was all worth listening to. Finally, the 'listening and learning' had begun. But with 'listening and learning' then came the excuses, the apologies and need for appeasement. Suddenly, every white person in my life needed to hear that they weren't racist – not like those racists over there. When you have many friends who are white, guess who's called upon to explain, pacify and educate them in these moments?

But then, here I was listening to my white uncle a year or so later, sitting opposite me, giving me the old 'I watched a programme the other day about Black children being placed in remedial schools in the 1970s … can you believe it?' Naturally, me being me, I had seen the programme.

It's the incredulity for me.

The shock.

The surprise not only about actions in the past but in the present as well. It was as though all of a sudden every day was Martin Luther King Day. No one understood why anyone wanted such a lovely man killed. Everything he'd said made perfect sense! Civil rights! Desegregation! But of course, as we know, not everyone was on board with these very basic concepts back then, and even now.

All of this is to say, it can really be your own people. As someone who has grown up with white male family members and yet not in an all-white family, it's important for me to stress how much they are still my people. I love them. And they love me. And they will say things that offend me, if not deeply annoy me. And sometimes they say they want to hear my thoughts on something when really they want to hear themselves talk. But I share with them because I want to. I have nothing to hide or shy away from just because we're family – just because I'm mixed Black and they're white.

I like to think the conversations I've had with friends and family were productive, and that Emma and I putting out our feelings on *Mixed Up* has helped not only mixed people but all people to further their understanding of race. Especially if they are in interracial relationships or have mixed kids, I like to think that there is a resource available to help them feel equipped to talk about things and, more importantly, be open to listening.

Five friends in a sedan and the N-word

'I honestly don't care if you say it. It's just a word,' I said casually, in a car full of my closest friends.

There was something in me that craved a cool nonchalance that I never had. Indifference, especially towards anything concerning race, was very much a cool-person thing back then, and in high school that was my main priority – upholding some level of coolness that certainly didn't feel inherent in me.

Somehow the N-word had come up again, which seemed to happen a lot when all my friends were white. 'NIGGER!' one of the boys shouted, in the safety of the car. He erupted with laughter, the same gleeful giggle that kids make when they get away with something they shouldn't have. 'Do you feel better now?' I asked, and rolled down the window. I needed air. The car was hot with our sweat and smoke, and my guilt for allowing this to happen made me feel light-headed. There was something about being Black – even being 'half Black' – that made me want to make my white friends feel comfortable. I didn't want to be perceived as a challenging person to be around.

For a Black person growing up in white suburbia, especially in my era (the late 1990s, early 2000s), Black culture wasn't celebrated in the way that it is today. Don't get me wrong, cultural theft was alive and well, but there has most certainly been a shift and it has become more obvious in the media and among the younger generation as the years go by.

So at an early age I felt obligated to push back against my Blackness, I didn't want that to be *the first thing* that people noticed about me, not fully understanding that that is how it's just going to be forever. When I was a teenager, that overwhelming feeling of wanting to be liked and having white friends meant that I had to pretend to be OK with racism. Naturally, I regret it now. I wish I had been armed with the language, the knowledge and the history to feel confident enough to stand up for myself. I wish back then I had felt the pride that I do now.

There is a very pivotal moment in a young Black person's life when they encounter the N-word, whether it's in reading or music or film, whether it is hurled at them or a loved one. And in that particular moment it felt like I gave a bit of myself away. At the time it was more important for me to be 'the cool girl' than to protect myself as a young Black girl – which is worlds away from how I feel now.

I often think about the moments in my teens even into early adulthood when I felt ill-equipped, I didn't feel safe enough, to defend myself or others. The times when I was too tired to say anything. Or the times when I didn't feel confident enough.

I look back on the younger me with understanding and empathy now – a lot of that inexperience and lack of confidence just comes from being a kid. But I do wish my parents had had conversations with me about this issue from an early age, as I genuinely believe it would have eased a lot of my fears around talking about race and confronting racism. I wish they had told me that I would one day have this word thrown in my face, and what to do about it. I wish that they'd taught me explicitly to enforce my boundaries and feel empowered in doing so.

When we talk about it now, there is so much they just 'assumed I would know' or pick up along the way without them having to tell me.

Ultimately it does no child any good to make assumptions about what they do or don't know.

The math ain't mathin'

My report cards were littered with the feedback and comments of white teachers who always said the same thing about me: 'talks too much', 'can be disruptive', 'needs to apply herself' – phrases that many Black children have heard and read about themselves for their entire education.

I always loved learning, reading and analysing; the texts in English lit in particular were my favourite, although math was a subject I was never confident in. Words I could understand, but numbers were a completely different language to me.

Algebra class was my own personal hell. My dad was determined for me to get through this subject and paid for another kid to tutor me during lunch. Despite the tutor, I still almost failed the class. I told my friend Jason, who sat next to me in class, that unfortunately, straight after this lesson, I would have to do even more algebra. 'God, that must be really hard for you. Being half Asian, I expected you to be good at math, but your Black side is letting you down.' It was the first time I'd heard someone say so explicitly that my being mixed with Black was something that would 'let me down'. Like an unfortunate little accident. A mishap. It confirmed my fears in what people assumed about me – that somehow my being Black was a problem.

Did you hear about Nicole?

The little mixed girl?

Oh yes, isn't it a shame that she's [whispers] *half Black?*

I never lived under the delusion that being half Filipina meant that anyone would see me as Asian, and I would never be light enough to be mistaken for a white girl. It was never a secret that I was Black, but for some reason I didn't think that it would be all that white people saw when they looked at me. I was living my own personal algebra equation and not even the right tutor was able help me work it out.

If I am completely honest, it's never what white people say about me or how they try to label me that affects me as much as when those things come from Black people. More often than not I expect to feel othered by white people; that is a rejection I have grown used to and come to accept. But when it comes from Black people, when it comes from Asian people – when I feel othered by the people from my own family, my own community, then I feel uprooted and it hurts the most.

And I write this as someone who visibly presents as Black. I've said this a few times on the podcast, but some of my biggest insecurities have been when I felt as though my Blackness was being called into question by other Black people. It's deeply personal, because all the things that I felt shaped my identity were immediately dismissed as 'not Black' – what I liked to wear, the music I enjoyed, the movies I watched, how I spoke. The majority of these things boiled down to personal tastes, apart from how I talk. And it's a very specific feeling in being mixed when you feel as though you're constantly having to prove yourself. 'I'm Black, please believe me! We're on the same team!'

Even now there is a lot of rhetoric kicking around on Black Twitter about how simply talking about being mixed, biracial, or however a person may want to identify feeds into this idea that mixed people think they're special or better than. For me, this has never been further from the truth. More than anything, I and other mixed people we have spoken to have been looking for affirmation and acceptance rather than trying to position ourselves as 'better'. And it becomes hard to talk about because we never want to admit to being othered by our own groups, right? It hurts the most when Black women dismiss my opinions or feelings outright because I'm mixed. I am racialized as Black by white society, my lived experience in this life has been that of a Black woman.

I'd say that now more than ever I try to affirm myself in my Asian-ness, because this is a part of me that so often gets erased. It's not so much noticed by wider society, even though in our household I grew up mostly around my Filipino family and culture; but I could see the assumption because it was obvious to me too that I was a little Black girl.

Filipinos in general were welcoming. Any time I thanked a stranger with *salamat*, or acknowledged their being Filipino by explaining that my mother was Filipina, there was a feeling of kinship which I always appreciated. In all honesty, the microaggressions usually came from my extended Filipino family and family friends, when they commented on how dark my skin was or on my hair texture. I did often feel like I had to affirm myself in the culture, having to ask my mom to explain to me in English what she was saying in Tagalog as, sadly, I can't speak the language. It's the same with certain foods that I haven't eaten or don't know about. But I did the exact same thing with my dad. I don't speak the different Ghanaian dialects, so I often have to defer to him for communication or explanation. I didn't grow up eating Ghanaian food that much and was an annoyingly picky eater as a child, so there is still a lot I am just trying now as an adult.

It's like being brand-new, so there's a lot of shame attached for me there – not being a good enough Filipina or Ghanaian. Being the kind of American who's often associated with being white American ... but I'm not. It's embarrassing, to put it mildly. But I think it's important to acknowledge that when you're mixed this feeling of othering doesn't just come from whiteness.

The thing about growing up as a person of colour in a predominantly white environment is that you are hyper-aware of how you're perceived. It's not just about looks – your hair, your skin, your style of clothing – it's your mannerisms and way of speaking, how you carry yourself. It's not something that's often acknowledged, even among the mixed people

I know who felt the same way, like constantly living under a microscope and trying to avoid being picked apart, poked and prodded, or even just noticed at all. It's not a constant way of being but it's there, almost like a heat signal radiating from within. The point is that you simply want to blend in but you know you're doing the exact opposite, especially growing up in a generation for whom being 'different' wasn't the Instagram influencer version of life that we see today.

I went to a house party in my hometown, a stone's throw away from where I went to high school in Northern Virginia. At the time, Virginia had just started opening things up from strict pandemic rules and we were allowed to see each other again, which thrilled me. As I set foot inside, I was immediately aware of the fact that I was one of six Black people in a full house. Not much has changed in this place in fifteen years. Late in the night all six of us ended up standing together in the foyer and we joked about being 'the only Blacks in the village'. There is a camaraderie in being the 'only'.

It's easy for me now as an adult. I walked into that house knowing exactly what to expect, given where I grew up and who I grew up around. Like most teenagers, I was riddled with insecurity and self-doubt, so a setting like this would have been all about performance. How are these white people going to perceive me? Will I be nice enough? Likeable enough? Pretty enough to be worthy of spending time with?

When it comes to race, when you're young and still growing it's a case of becoming aware of your 'otherness', and as a mixed person I find these feelings particularly amplified because they come with a lot of spinning plates: you feel like you have to appease both or all sides, and ultimately deal with other people projecting their own ideas about who you are, or who you should be, on to you. It's a lot for any person to bear.

Wait. Am I oburoni because I don't speak my language?

There have been so many moments throughout my life when I felt like things went wrong simply because of a misunderstanding. Arguments, missed opportunities, relationship breakdowns … those instances where you do have the language to communicate with someone and you simply … don't. You hold back.

But growing up as a mixed child with parents who speak multiple languages and can communicate in multiple different ways with multiple different people is a different feeling altogether. There are many instances when I'm surrounded by family members who are all speaking to each other and I just don't understand what's being said. Sometimes I can pick up on subtleties. I know when my parents are talking about me to other people (but I think that's simply because they're my parents), and I've picked up certain words and phrases that have me silently guessing alongside the conversation.

When I was growing up my parents spoke to me in English because they spoke to each other in English. Simple. They say they tried to teach me their own languages but I just ignored them. The older me is frustrated that they didn't push harder, but all of this is in hindsight.

When I was younger, I would listen to my mom speak Tagalog or my dad speak in Twi and it was just … background. I didn't try to decipher the conversation or wonder what they were talking about or who they were talking to. My head was preoccupied with who knows what else, and at that time none of it seemed important. The older I got, the more I realized what I was missing out on. '*Do you speak?*' cousins, family friends, total strangers would ask me. '*No?*' I'd say, my head half bowed in embarrassment, '*my parents never taught me.*' I made sure to shift the blame on to them; I couldn't bear any more shortcomings. At what point did it become my responsibility to make sure they taught me, or that I learned, I often wonder. My dad always says he wanted to send me to Ghana for a year but my mom was unwilling to be without me for so long.

Now that I'm in my thirties, more than anything I want to be able to speak the languages that my parents speak. Knowing that they're getting older, and being aware of what I didn't have growing up, makes me hopeful that if I have children I will be able to share that with them.

I grew up going to Ghana and the Philippines to visit my family but not being able to communicate with people fully. Not being able to hear stories or be in on the joke. Having school-age children translate for me and knowing that they could already speak multiple languages at such a young age. I was, and maybe still am, utterly self-conscious and too aware of myself in these situations.

Now I find myself looking up courses on Tagalog and Twi (unfortunately Duolingo isn't there yet) and I'm hopeful that there is still time for me to learn. I don't ever feel disconnected from my parents, but I crave that connection with others when we go back. I feel an American-shaped shame, embarrassed that other people have to accommodate my lack of knowledge. It's giving *gringo*, it's giving *oyinbo*, it's giving *obrouni*.

As of now, it's in language that I find myself feeling like a foreigner. It's where I see myself positioned closely to whiteness in a way that makes me feel uncomfortable and embarrassed. It's not something my parents have ever shamed me for, or tried to make me – or even themselves – feel guilty about. These thoughts simply never cross their minds, apart from when I ask them.

Ultimately, I go back and forth between how I feel about not speaking the languages my parents do. Time often looks like a vast expanse with endless opportunity, but it's also hurriedly slipping away from me. Now only time will tell if I can and will learn. I am lucky enough to have the connections to my family that I do, and at the end of the day the only person really placing any kind of pressure on myself is me.

2.
CHILDHOOD AND FORMING IDENTITY

Once, you told me that you were a mix. You were a bit brown and a bit white. I told you that this made you light brown and that confused you. You wanted to be our Venn diagram. You wanted to be the bridge between us. You didn't want to be more one than the other. You are quick to assert that you are a girl. A consistent thing you said throughout your entire childhood was that you didn't like the colour brown. It was too dark. Another time you told me it was dirty. Recently, you told me you wished I was white. 'Then I will be white,' you said. 'Why?' I replied. 'I want to be like Mummy,' you said before disappearing into another room, as if that was that and there was nothing more to say.

Extract from Brown Baby, *read aloud by Nikesh Shukla on* Mixed Up *podcast Season 2, '*Mixed Up *Book Club with Nikesh Shukla'*

We wanted to explore some of the experiences of conflict, development and growth that feel particularly relevant to being of mixed heritage and that might be specific to the journey of parents of mixed children. As we write this book there does not seem to be much public discourse around the journey which many mixed kids will have to undertake to understand themselves in context.

There is something specific in the experience of children potentially not having either parent have explicit lived experience that relates to their own, or to the way the outside world views them.

Clearly, given the spectrum of mixed individuals across the globe there is no way that any one personal experience we could share with you could be representative of 'the' mixed experience of childhood.

The beauty of us as a group of people is that we have such vastly different ancestries and make-ups. We will all have lived very different childhoods, due to factors such as ethnic background, exposure to our cultural heritages, our geographical location or class or how we are racialized by others, and many other factors.

Unsurprisingly, there is no definitive guide to navigating the mixed-race experience; in fact there are very few reference points at all for parents, children or curious adults. On discussing this, we agreed that while we were growing up in the UK and the US we had nothing to look to for guidance, and so presumably neither did our parents.

In the 1990s there was little visual representation of mixed-race people in popular culture, not many examples of anyone who might have looked like us in the public eye, bar Scary Spice and Samantha Mumba in the UK and maybe Tia and Tamera in the US, and certainly no one at the time who represented a more diverse mix than Black and white, or who spoke openly about straddling two worlds and two cultures in a way that could help us understand ourselves and our identities. Looking back, such representation and dialogue could have proved formative and helped us to confidently express who we were as we grew into ourselves.

Even today, when we are in our thirties, whilst there may be more people in the public eye in whom we can recognize ourselves – the

Elaine Welteroths, the Afua Hirschs and Zendayas – we can't find the kind of dialogue we describe in any sort of comprehensive form. As adult women, in some ways we are still grappling with our identities in a world that often seems to desire one or the other, and nothing in between, a world that operates in binaries. Having heard from *Mixed Up* podcast listeners who are much younger than us, we know for certain that navigating the mixed identity through childhood and adolescence is something that urgently requires its own space. It certainly deserves more careful attention than it has been granted to date.

We both found that, growing up, 'race' and specifically the nuances and detail of the experience of being mixed race or multiracial were not explicitly discussed in our households – a common reality not just for mixed children and their parents, but for those of all races. As Farzana Nayani, the diversity, equity and inclusion specialist notes, all anecdotal evidence suggests that it is because adults are reluctant to talk about race.[1] Following the murder of George Floyd and the resurgence of the Black Lives Matter movement, the curtain has been pulled back on this reality. Based on the reaction on social media and at large, and the clear unfamiliarity of the topic for many, it would appear that perhaps adults and society in general have been doing their best to avoid talking about race for as long as many of us can remember. Could it be that they have simply not felt ready to have what is a difficult conversation with themselves, let alone with their children?

Research conducted in the US both before and after the murder of George Floyd demonstrates that when it comes to ethnic minority parents, there is clearly a lot more talking about race happening. Two separate surveys of 500 parents showed that on average Black parents were more likely to talk frequently about race generally, and they did this even more so after the murder of Floyd.[2] White parents remained relatively unchanged and silent on the topic. Those white parents who did engage mostly took a colour-blind view.

Parents who identify as monoracial or 'of colour' often understand better the need to share their own racialized experiences of the world with their children, to make sure that they are prepared and aware of how society is likely to perceive and receive them with regard to how they are racialized. The research confirmed this to be particularly true of Black African American parents, who felt these conversations were necessary to avoid harm coming to their children.

In her book *Raising Multiracial Children: Tools for Nurturing Identity in a Racialized World*, Nayani discusses Dr Sarah Gaither's research, pointing out that monoracial parents of mixed children won't necessarily have much understanding of the unique experience of being mixed race when it comes to (for example) having your identity challenged or denied by others, or having to prove your racial legitimacy.[3]

RACIAL LEGITIMACY

The need to respond to the underlying sentiment faced by multiracial people and other individuals whose race may not match others' perceptions of them [...] the demand of having to legitimize one's identity by answering the question 'Are you enough of a culture or race to claim that?' [...] and the following charge – 'prove it'.[4]

Even President Barack Obama was famously forced to grapple with racial legitimacy:

Throughout the first year of this campaign, against all predictions to the contrary, we saw how hungry the American people were for this message of unity. Despite the temptation to view my candidacy through a purely racial lens, we won commanding victories in states with some of the whitest populations in the country […] This is not to say that race has not been an issue in this campaign. At various stages in the campaign, some commentators have deemed me either 'too Black' or 'not Black enough'.[5]

During an interview we conducted on the *Mixed Up* podcast with actress Asia Jackson, she asked us how we identify and what identifiers we use to describe ourselves and our lived and felt identities. We were struck by how rare it is to be asked this, and noted that until very recently, nobody had ever brought up the question of how we feel about our identities. Only since opening the dialogue on *Mixed Up* has that question become so apparent as an important one for mixed people. We don't think we're alone in finding that (probably from childhood right through to adulthood) as people of mixed race – very often others seem to believe they are entitled to label our identities before we do. Never being asked how you identify is proof of this in of itself. People simply don't feel the need to ask, and we have come to believe that this is because they find it more comfortable to assign than to enquire.

We started to unpick this in one of our *Mixed Up* episodes when we spoke to Nikesh Shukla, author of *The Good Immigrant* and father of two mixed-race daughters:

Emma: I think so often the main challenge with being mixed is that there's this collective idea that other people can project your own identity on to you, and that it's almost like other people think they own it. And so all the narrative is always around how other people identify you rather than how you identify, and I think I've felt this the most in my life over the last five years or so. There's been so much strain and friction around race openly and overtly in the public domain. I think that I've felt this in the media from all sides, and in localized conversations because of everything going on in the US, and so I feel that really strongly of late people are obsessed with dictating the identities of mixed people, but not asking mixed people how they identify.

I should ask you – putting a parent's hat on – is it about us losing ourselves and our own identities … controlling or attempting to somehow keep control of that identity of that mixed person or child so that we can have control of our own identity? Does that make sense?

It's so that we still exist somehow … I know that obviously you would want to pass that incredibly rich Indian culture on to your daughter, and that makes complete sense. And so somehow is that a fear in you about not existing, not being passed on anymore?

Nikesh: Yeah. God, that's, yeah, I really like how you phrase that because yeah, obviously you are a hundred per cent, a million per cent right.

Mixed Up, *podcast Season 2, Episode 2, 'Book Club with Nikesh Shukla, author of* Brown Baby*'*

It's very interesting to think about how this might manifest in a parent–child relationship, however well-meaning. And for us these conversations reaffirm how important it is to equip our children with the language and the confidence they need to self-identify loudly and rebuff other people when they attempt to foist their own ideas of 'who they must be' on to them based on how they racialize them, or, conversely on how they struggle to place them.

Mental health practitioner Sophie Price elaborated on why it could be damaging for a parent to dictate racial identity to their child in a way that doesn't give much room for them to explore and assert their own experience. We were discussing an article that reported on a monoracial Black mother who had decided that she categorically would not allow her mixed Black children to identify as Black because she felt they would never understand or live 'the Black experience'. She felt that their 'mixed-race privilege' precluded them from this:

It is incredibly damaging because, like you said, society is going to perceive a mixed person, if they have Afro hair or features particularly (as that's kind of one of the first things that people see [them as], isn't it), as Black. And immediately think that there is something in their genetics that is from a Black background. I think the discussion around privilege is something that often gets my back up a little bit because people that are light-skinned and perceived as closer in proximity to whiteness are often more accepted, but the privilege that white people have and the privilege that mixed-race people have is completely different.

I think that those two things can't be within the same conversation. Having a sense of self is really important when you are a child and then growing up as a teenager, particularly when life is confusing enough – you kind of add this sort of identity crisis into it. If you've been actively encouraged to deny one half of yourself that can really breed low self-esteem and a lack of clarity as to who you are [...]

I guess the thing that struck me with that is what if her children go on to have Black children? How are they going to explain to them what it's like to live as a person who is part Black, or if they have children with someone who is monoracial Black. How do they find the vocabulary to explain that and to prepare that child for their experience in the world and to get them ready for how people are going to perceive them?

How can they be expected to understand something that they've never been taught? And how will they process racism if they've not been prepared for it [...] or if their Black side has been denied to them?

Mixed Up *podcast, Season 2, Episode 12*

On the other hand, we talked to a white American mother who had agreed with her African American husband when they started a family that 'the kids would be brought up as Black and told they were Black'. As a couple they truly believed this was the safest way to bring up their children to prepare them to face racism in America. But when they put it into practice it wasn't that simple:

My husband and my plan was to raise them as Black to give them all the coping skills they would need to face the racism in America [...] It didn't work out just as we had planned. So we did have a strong plan, but what ended up happening in our raising of the kids from a very young age – when I would try to explain that concept to my kids, it didn't work in the way I was trying to do it ... I'm saying to my daughter, 'Well, you're Black,' and I really remember one time saying this to my little, very light-skinned daughter, and she (I think she was around 4 years old) holds up her arm and says, 'No, I'm not, I'm not Black.' You know, she couldn't understand. It didn't work, and with their experiences in school and in the world, well, it also didn't work when I would say to them, 'Well, you're Black.' They would say, 'No, you know, I'm mixed.' And they used to say that even before the term 'mixed' was very common. Black kids that they went to school with did not treat them as Black kids so, you know, my kind of simple recipe for them of, 'Well, you're Black' didn't work because they found that they didn't fit in with the other Black kids they were going to school with.

Mixed Up *podcast guest, Season 2, Episodes 22–23, 'An Honest Exploration of White Mums Bringing Up Mixed-race Children'*

The only way in which we can begin to equip our children with the confidence to grow into and assert their identity is by initiating the conversation, which is precisely why we started our podcast, talking not just to mixed-race people about their childhood and adult experiences but also to parents of mixed-race children. It is why we are now writing this book. We want to be a catalyst for these conversations.

WHY DO OUR PARENTS FIND IT SO DIFFICULT TO TALK ABOUT RACE?

We can all find it difficult at times to talk about 'race' and racism. For People of Colour it can feel like a heavy emotional and weighted task that can be energy-sapping, particularly when the conversation leaves us with the burden of proof. And yet these are important conversations to have, especially when it comes to the development of mixed-race identity.

Parents of colour may swerve these types of conversations because they require dipping into personal experiences, grievances and trauma, and this can lead to avoidance as a self-protection strategy.

We talked to Nikesh Shukla about the difficulty of talking to his mixed Indian (Desi) and white British daughters about race. He described grappling with presenting a truthful view of racism and the world and not pushing his jaded view of it on to them. He expressed being conflicted around wanting to be realistic to protect them, but also wanting to be able to see the world through their eyes and preserve their joy and innocence:

I'd spent four years [...] promoting *The Good Immigrant*, I was sort of [...] just done talking about trauma and I wanted to write about joy. And so I started writing these columns about how to bring our kids into the world to be joyful, especially when the world ... seemed so bleak, and I was so sad and angry about it ... the central question is how do I bring my kids into a world and raise them to be joyful and boundless and ambitious, but also realistic? ...

And how do I tell them that the world is so bleak? And how do I do it when I myself am not in the right headspace for this?' [...]

She's at that age where everyone is equal to her. And – and I found myself trying to [...] explain to her why the world might be racist by kind of going, 'Well, you know, someone might hold these views because', and then I'd have to stop myself and go, no, you're being intellectually dishonest with her because you are projecting your world on to her. You're projecting your cynicism, your jadedness, your world-weariness, your kind of lived experiences, like all of the conversations and events and stuff that you've done as part of 'The Good Immigrant' movement and all that kind of stuff. You're projecting all of that on to her. And all she wants to say is that 'racism is stupid'. And actually you have to see the world through her eyes ... I had to be like, 'Yeah, you're right. It is stupid. You're right. It makes no sense whatsoever.'

Mixed Up *podcast, Season 2, Episode 2, 'Book Club with Nikesh Shukla, author of* Brown Baby*'*

This conversation also shone a light on the painful moment when a parent of colour is faced with the result of the othering and prejudice that may be experienced either tacitly or overtly by their children outside the home. It's easy to believe that these moments might be as hard to talk about as they are to be presented with. Children may internalize hatred, colourism and prejudice that they come across without understanding what it means, and that's not an easy thing for a parent to tackle. It invariably brings up old wounds and trauma for the parent themselves, and there's also likely a realization that they can have the conversation but they can't protect their child from these moments, nor will they be in full control of how their child socializes negative messages about skin tone and 'race'.

Nikesh talked to us about navigating conversations about skin colour with one of his daughters.

Emma: While reading your book I was struck by how upset I was myself to hear about her hiding her brown doll and not bonding with it – the toy that most reflected her own image.

Nikesh: You know, that is the world I want to live in […] the world where more kids than just brown kids would have brown dolls. And therefore my kid wouldn't have grown up thinking that that doll was out of the ordinary or dirty, not something that she wanted to play with, or something that she had to hide. And yeah, like, while – Emma I'm really sorry it kind of hurt you, I'm glad it did because it really destroyed me at the time.

There was one other thought that was raised around the way we might think about race, and the way our children racialize themselves, during our conversation with Nikesh that felt pertinent. This was about what we as parents of colour might want for the way our mixed children racialize themselves. And how this selfish desire might influence the way in which we talk to them about race, or indeed the way we don't. And what that conversation is more weighted towards, or which heritage group it is focused on:

Nicole: There's a quote in your book *Brown Baby* where you say something along the lines of like, 'I don't ever want you to consider yourself white and, and then you kind of are like, is that bad?'

Nikesh: If people thought my daughter was white, would I have a problem with that? Mm-hmm ... yeah ... it was just a moment of honesty kind of going – is that, is that a bad thing to think about? ... I don't know ... how she's gonna choose to identify when she's older. And all I can do is make her proud of every aspect of her now, but yes ... by focusing on trying to make her proud of being Indian ... and brown ... am I demeaning or underselling making her proud of being white? ... I don't think I landed on an answer, but I think that's why I kind of threw it out as a question [in the book] ... because I don't know how I feel ... I think it was ... something very defensive ... that kind of erupted in that moment.

In the context of Caucasian or white parents' reasons for avoiding these topics of conversation with their children, much has been made of 'white fragility' and 'white guilt' in more recent British literature such as Reni Eddo-Lodge's *Why I'm No Longer Talking to White People About Race*, Layla Saad's *Me and White Supremacy: How to Recognise Your Privilege, Combat Racism and Change the World* and in Emma Dabiri's *What White People Can do Next: From Allyship to Coalition*.

In addition, white parents may simply not be practised in talking about 'race'. Being the dominant group in society means that they (prior to having children of colour) have often not had to give much thought to the challenges which the construct of race presents for other groups, instead benefiting from the construct and its historical structures:

I think I wanted to reflect on an experience which kind of propelled us into doing more, recognizing we were woefully inadequate in our responses. It was our son's first week at school; often [with] our son at bedtime we'll talk about what was good in the day and what we loved, and that type of thing. And often … worries and concerns come out at bedtime … it was this particular week of starting school and we had a chat, you know, we'd done our stories, snuggled down and he said, 'Mom, do you know I'm the only brown child in my class?' And I remember thinking, 'Oh God, like how do I answer that?' And I know my response was woefully inadequate. And I think I said something about other brown children that I knew in the school and it just sent me into this world of panic of, well, firstly, recognizing that response wasn't appropriate, and that I didn't have the tools to talk about this. So I think what we did was talk about how it made him feel, and he said it made him feel sad and why, and I think at that point both me and my husband just realized we needed to have more on this.

> Mixed Up *podcast guest, Season 2, 'An Honest Exploration into the Experiences of White Mums Bringing up Mixed-race Children (Part 1)'*

From talking to white mothers on the podcast it became apparent that to attempt to empathize with, or to try to understand a partner of colour's lived experience versus living it are very different things, and how easy it can be to slip into centering their own visceral reaction to the experience. This too can be a hurdle to overcome when talking about race:

Somehow I found myself, as they now say, whitesplaining … a couple of weeks ago I was on vacation with my husband and son and where we were staying it's a very rural place in upstate New York and there's a lot fewer Black people around here than we're used to where we live in Baltimore, in Maryland.

So before my husband and son were about to go out and get something, I asked them, 'Did you grab your wallet? Do you have your ID?', and my adult kid says, 'Why? Why would I need that? I don't need it.' And I said, 'Well, you've got to always have your ID with you.'

And I made some kind of comment, which is really true. It comes from my heart. Just like, 'Listen, as a Black man in America, you don't want to go anywhere without your ID.' And my kid did not like that at all. He said, 'Nobody wants to hear that, Mom.' So again, I felt like, somewhere in there, I felt like it wasn't my place.

I guess I shouldn't have said it. I don't know. It's hard for me to know what's the right thing. I stand by that statement. I feel strongly about it. I want to be educating my kids and reminding them to stay safe, reminding them where they are, but I guess it's insulting and not my place because, of course, they know where they are, and he didn't want to be reminded of that by his white mother.

… The biggest thing that I got … was a realization of what it means to centre whiteness and the damage that does, especially in a mixed home. So I think for a lot of white mums, without realizing it, we centre our whiteness a lot because I think you can have a relationship with someone who's not of your ethnicity, you can marry them and have a marriage with someone not of your ethnicity, and you can kind of go through life with those people and you can see the world through their eyes and it's one way. But then the moment you have a child together and your child comes out and your child is of a different ethnicity to yourself – for me, speaking as a white woman, there are, there are huge moments when you have a much deeper understanding of this lived experience than you ever had from seeing it through your partner's eyes. All of a sudden your proximity, in my case my proximity to Blackness, increased dramatically overnight. So when you're just in a relationship or in a marriage with a Black person, there's certain things you will experience from society. But of course, the moment you leave you're walking down the street by yourself. You go back to the comfortable life of being a white person. And then you have a baby and you're pushing your pram, and I don't know if I have the words to explain it, but it's definitely a larger moment and not a moment that you can separate yourself from in the same way, and people's reactions to you. It can be quite visceral … and they're almost like a reflex – mums in mums' groups, kind of scanning your hands to see if you've got a wedding ring on, or looking at your baby while talking to you. A little bit like you're an alien, then moving away and wanting to sit with some of the white mums of white babies. Like all of these things can happen. And I think as a result of that it's very common for us white mums to kind of centre our whiteness and our feelings and how we feel and how it hurts us and how it surprises us and how it shocks us.

And I think, obviously we are thinking of our child too, we are worried and concerned about their future and wanting to know what we can do to protect them from racism and the white-supremacist world. In doing so, I think it's really easy to get wrapped up in ourselves and in our own experience and kind of complaining to people that will listen. It's really important to remember it's not about you. Too much of my white feelings. My white feelings don't matter. Actually what matters is dismantling the system.

Mixed Up *podcast guest, Season 2, 'An Honest Exploration into the Experiences of White Mums Bringing up Mixed-race Children (Part 1)'*

And then there is, of course, still the idea held by some people that we live in a post-racial society and that racism simply doesn't exist any longer, or that if it does it takes the form of an unmistakably extreme and aggressive beast that would be easy to recognize and call out or, more poignantly perhaps, be impossible to miss. This makes racism seem like a rare and infrequent occurrence, and therefore the subject of race seems like something that doesn't need to take up a lot of space in their world and their conversations.

On the other hand, as they grow and learn about the world children look to their parents as the authority on most subjects, and this involves pressure and a responsibility to 'know', that we imagine most parents feel keenly. This comes with the potential for huge embarrassment and even shame in 'not knowing' and not having the adequate tools to tackle a topic like 'race' competently.

Perhaps this is also a deterrent to white parents. Maybe, more often than not, it is the backdrop to the common response that a child is 'not old enough to understand':

My daughter is 3, so I've not spoken to her about racism. I guess through fear of the fact that, at this moment in time, she's never said anything about anyone saying it being mean to her, about her, the colour of her skin or her hair, or nothing like that's ever been said. So I've not wanted to, I guess, taint that innocence by saying it too early.

> Mixed Up *podcast guest, Season 2, 'An Honest Exploration into*
> *the Experiences of White Mums Bringing up Mixed-race Children*
> *(Part 1)'*

As Farzana Nayani suggests in her book *Raising Multiracial Children*, it could be time to accept that it is we, the adults, who are not ready to talk about race.

WHY IS IT SO IMPORTANT FOR PARENTS TO TALK TO THEIR CHILDREN ABOUT RACE?

In very early development, children as young as 3 months old start to demonstrate a preference for faces of the race of their own caregivers, gazing far longer at those of people who match the race of their parents. Results from the same study infer that this preference does not seem to be present in newborns, which would suggest that it is a behaviour learned in the first 3 to 6 months of life.[6] By 24 months, children use race to categorize and reason about people's behaviours,[7] and by 3 to 5 years of age they choose playmates by their race, including or excluding others based on this factor.[8]

I have learned lots of things about what it might be like being an ethnic minority from being a mother to my three children, but also from being a partner to my husband. I have witnessed things such as my son being approached by another child in a playground, and then that other child saying to my son, 'Why have you got mud all over your skin?' And my son looking really confused and saying, 'But I haven't got mud all over my skin.' And then that child just retreated off to a hugely embarrassed parent and, you know, nothing more was said from that parent. And then I had to really explain, 'Maybe that child has never seen someone with beautiful skin like yours before.' And, you know, obviously, I would've never experienced that as a child and it's made me realize how important it is as a teacher, but also as a parent, to try and spread the word – please educate your children. Please make sure they are reading books with characters that feature children who look like my son, who look like my husband. Because you know, our children are constantly being damaged by the ignorance of your children. You know, these comments are obviously not made in a malicious way. They're not made to be hurtful. This child was a young child and it was said out of complete innocence. And actually, you know, noticing difference is obviously not a bad thing at all.

Mixed Up *podcast guest Isabelle, Season 2, 'An Honest Exploration into the Experiences of White Mums Bringing up Mixed-race Children (Part 1)'*

Put bluntly – it is never too early to start talking to your child about race if you want to take an anti-racist approach to parenting and, even more importantly perhaps, if they are likely to be on the receiving end of society's often misguided beliefs around race and of physical cues that can result in assumptive and rapid judgemental categorization based on an idea of ethnicity:

If parents could jump in and deal with it. Deal with their children's comments and their questions ... but I think, unfortunately, so many white teachers and white parents just feel totally ill-equipped and at risk of saying the wrong thing. They simply don't say anything at all, thus reinforcing children's misconceptions, children's misunderstandings ...

My parents – I think one of the main problems I have with them is that they don't see Nyla as a Black child and that's a problem in itself. They don't recognize that she may be treated differently or that people may have a prejudice against her or that she may have to work harder than someone who's not Black or in an ethnic minority. They just don't see that because they just see her as their grandchild and she's perfect, etcetera. And of course she's perfect, but they need to understand being a Black child and having that as the first thing people see, that is automatically gonna create judgement in some people's minds. I'm constantly having to educate them gently of the difficulties that she may have later on and, and, you know, they understand, but I think that's one of the difficulties I found personally.

Mixed Up *podcast guest, Season 2, Episode 22, 'An Honest Exploration into the Experiences of White Mums Bringing up Mixed-race Children (Part 1)'*

Delving into another study suggests that in the US, white children specifically present as strongly biased in favour of whiteness.[9]

There is even evidence to show that having explicit conversations with 5- to 7-year-olds about interracial friendship can dramatically improve their racial attitudes and propensity for avoiding racial bias.[10] Farzana Nayani reasons that not talking about race can in fact reinforce racism and racist ideas by letting children come to their own presumptions based on what they see:

If my children weren't mixed, would I talk about this stuff as early? Maybe I wouldn't. I'd like to think I would but, realistically, maybe I wouldn't. I am now one of those people who gets really annoyed with people who don't talk to their children about race, who don't have inclusive books, to open up those conversations about race with their children.

It's really important to me that children do have these conversations really early. You know, all the evidence shows how prejudice can start, you know, in infants. So it's really important to talk about race. For me, ultimately, I probably wouldn't have done it as early if my children weren't mixed, if I'm honest.

Mixed Up *podcast guest, Season 2, 'An Honest Exploration into the Experiences of White Mums Bringing up Mixed-race Children (Part 1)'*

When it comes to mixed-race identity, it would seem pertinent to consider not just how mixed-race children will socialize themselves amongst people who belong to one of their racial groups if they have no contact with the other side of their parentage at an early age, but also how they will view the monoracial representatives of their own racial groups, given that these people may not look like them. Talking about race openly, along with exposure to people from multiple racial groups, could help mixed children socialize with a positive attitude to themselves and others.

If parents separate, it's the responsibility of the parent who has the custody of the children and the majority share to still find a way to deliver on assisting their children to have a connection to all of their traditions.

Because what so often happens is that that parent often will reject it, finding hardship in having a multicultural marriage and then it breaking down; quite often what I've seen is those parents reject the culture that they mixed with and then, cut off that chapter of their life and pretend like it never existed.

But you can't do that if you have multicultural children from that marriage. And so I saw that happen in our household where my mom wanted to always erase parts of it. Of her life in Africa, and she didn't really want to talk about parts of it. Did she really understand? You know, the necessity to, uh, offer elements of African culture in our home in, let's say, access to clothes or understanding how to do my hair and those elements – because I was not taught those things.

The only way to say it is, I was brought up as a white woman by white women. And it took me a long time to re-establish and reintegrate my Black identity into my life.

Florence Kollie Raja, Liberian/Ukrainian,
Mixed Up *podcast, Season 3*

Studies have also confirmed that not only are white parents far less inclined to talk about race with their children, but that if they do they will often opt for a 'colour-blind' approach which lends itself to over-simplified justifications and ideas such as 'We are all the same.' This is problematic given that, while race is a social construct, society has historically operated, and does presently, at either a subconscious or conscious level on notions of difference and prejudice connected to racial stereotypes and the effect that long-upheld racist systems have cultivated over time.

Mixed Experiences: Growing Up Mixed Race – Mental Health and Well being (2014) by Dinah Morley and Cathy Street references research undertaken by the National Children's Bureau: interviews with twenty-one mixed-race people in the UK about their experiences as children, looking specifically at emotional well-being. Dinah Morley repeatedly notes a lack of understanding and analysis with regard to the mixed-race experience informing social health and well-being practice and policy at their time. Dinah and her co-author sought to begin to redress this with their book, which was written for the benefit of practitioners involved in early years development, social care, education, youth justice and the voluntary sector.

Although the study was undertaken in 2008, it is useful to apply some historical context when trying to form a picture of the theory and discussion among professionals, as well as an understanding of the policies, practices and resources made available to parents and social workers.

At the time, there was limited literature and analysis on of the implications of being mixed race for a child's mental health and well-being, whereas there were many studies on Black and minority ethnic monoracial groups.

We were disappointed to find, through our conversations with social workers and mental health professionals, that the landscape doesn't appear to be vastly different today.

In preparing for an episode of *Mixed Up* which focused on social care and adoption, we talked about this with both a social worker in the field and an adoptive parent of three mixed-race children who was also a professional within the care system and adoption process. They helped us get a picture of how public theory, policy and practice have been shaped over time in relation to how parenting and caregiving affects the development of a healthy mixed-race identity.

The first well-known record of mixed-race issues first being discussed in the UK was as part of a debate around transracial adoption, a situation in which a family adopts a child of a different race.[11] In this debate there was a focus on the importance of mixed-race children needing to, and being expected to, identify as Black. In the UK at the time this would most likely have focused on Afro-Caribbeans/white mixes, reflecting immigration and migration from the Commonwealth islands. The basis of this notion was the belief that mixed-race children would naturally be confused and mixed-up psychologically,[12] and scholars maintained that adopting the 'Black identity' would allay this confusion.

That wider society holds the idea that mixed-race children and adults tend to be confused about their identity is something we both agree we have been aware of from a young age.

EMMA

I recall a conversation with a Black male friend of mine, a few years older than me, when I was a teenager:

> *Friend*: 'It's cool that you're so cool even though you are mixed.'
> *Me*: 'What do you mean by that?'
> *Friend*: 'Well I find that lots of mixed-race girls are crazy … they
> just are, you know, a bit confused about who they are …
> because of their family situations. But you, you seem to
> be really grounded and stable. Really sound.'

This was said with a sense of genuine curiosity and surprise. He seemed oblivious to the idea that it could have been offensive. It was almost as though he had been waiting, as our friendship developed, to see if at some point the curtain would slip so that he could catch a glimpse of my crazy. He seemed bemused that I was, at first glance, 'pretty stable'.

* * *

This narrative of confused identity that is pushed on to many of us within the mixed-raced community has been a recurring theme in the interviews on our podcast and in our reflections on childhood, adolescence and young adulthood. And although the issue of confused identity has been consistently refuted by mixed-race scholars, the idea still appears to stubbornly persist today.[13]

The 2011 UK Census showed that mixed-race children were disproportionately over-represented in the child welfare system. It found that children of mixed parentage comprised 10 per cent of the total of children in care; the figure for the under-18 population in the UK as a whole was 5 per cent. Given this, you would imagine that research and policy would have sought to provide more comprehensive guidance for the healthy development of mixed kids – who, while obviously not a homogenous group, often collectively have a different experience to that of monoracial children and young adults.

However, speaking to an adoptive parent and foster care professional, we found that although the law was clear when he adopted his three mixed-race children in 2008, stating that race and ethnicity needed to be taken into consideration, he noted that as a white adoptive parent of Black/white mixed children he was given little guidance as to what challenges parenting a mixed child might bring, or how to nurture the mixed cultural identity.

My expectation was to learn about parenting policy and practice when it came to mixed-race children when I spoke to our social work professional, but instead what I learnt is that there was still very little to go by in 2021.

Mixed Experiences further highlighted 'that mixed-race children faced impracticable expectations from their teachers in school and racism from both Black and white pupils'.[14]* Dinah Morley describes mixed kids as 'a group most likely to suffer racism'.[15] Other studies support the idea that mixed people consistently experience racism and prejudice from both white and Black peer groups, or from the groups they should

---

* We have used language consistent with that in the study referenced here.

by birthright 'belong to'; and this speaks to the subsequent challenges mixed-race individuals can face in seeking out a safe identity from childhood through to adulthood. We imagine that many readers may find this a grating assertion, but the statistical data collected in the guide suggested that mixed-race people were more likely than other groups to experience racist abuse, including less overt forms such as invisibility in teaching materials, policy and practice.

We have no comparable data today, but we can see that in the UK mixed-race children and specifically mixed Black Caribbean children have the second to highest rate of temporary exclusion as a group (surpassed only by Irish Travelling or Gypsy Roma children).[16] Our own anecdotal evidence also tells us that people of mixed race are still grappling with experiencing prejudice from more than one group, often fielding it from both of the racial groups they 'belong' to at once.

* * *

I should add that I admit to being inhibited by a feeling that it is not politically correct for me as a mixed-race (Black/white) woman to openly mention that there may be prejudice and a sense of exclusion that comes from the Black community, but I am simultaneously reminded and emboldened by something I read on Mix-d, a support resource for mixed people and their parents. It pointed out that although outside influences can often create pressure on young people of Black mixed heritage to align as 'politically Black', the business of identity is first and foremost 'deeply personal, and should not be political'.

Honestly, for me, I think it may be impossible to decouple the personal from the political. While I have a desire to speak my own truth to popular and sometimes misguided opinions of the mixed-race experience, I still feel fiercely protective over the portrayal of the Black community. This is most definitely a political responsibility that I hold deeply. However, I still hope to encourage an honest discourse around the prejudice and challenges that can be faced by mixed-race people when it comes to belonging, forming identity, rejection and, of course, acceptance by the various cultural and ethnic groups we are a part of.

A NOTE ON MENTAL HEALTH, BEING MIXED AND CHILDHOOD DEVELOPMENT

During a conversation with senior mental health practitioner Sophie Price, we discussed Henri Tajfel's 'Social Identity Theory',[17] which proposed that a person's sense of who they are is based on their group membership(s).

Tajfel suggested that the groups people belong to provide an important source of pride, belonging and self-esteem. He argued that people tend to 'categorize' or 'stereotype' as part of a normal cognitive reasoning process which, when it comes to forming social groups, results in us dividing the world into 'them' and 'us'. When we do this, we have a predisposition to exaggerate the differences between groups, as well as the similarities within our own group, and this is what is known as 'the in group' and 'the out group'. In short, we see the group to which we belong as being different from the others (the out groups), and members of our group as being more similar than they are (the in group). But how does this affect the development of self-esteem among people of multiracial heritage, who effectively see themselves as belonging to two or more groups?

We would extrapolate that it might be harder for a mixed person to form a positive sense of self-esteem as they explore which group they feel a closer sense of belonging to, or if one or more of the groups that they believe themselves to belong to rejects them. Or indeed if they are 'misidentified' – not recognized by the outside world as being part of their 'in group(s)'.

Misidentification: 'To be considered not to be who one believes one is, to be denied preferred identities that are precious can be akin to psychological annihilation.'[18]

If, as sociologist Sheldon Stryker says, the term 'identity' can be seen as synonymous with common identification with a collective or social category,[19] then could it also be true that the hurdles faced by mixed-race young people in feeling accepted by one or more of their ethnic groups can have an effect on both their sense of self and their mental health and well-being?

In one episode of our podcast, Black and Indigenous Filipino actress Asia Jackson speaks of the conflict of not immediately finding a cultural home for her identity when she was growing up mixed:

Like many mixed people I had a confusing relationship with my identity. I didn't know I was Black until the second grade. I was living in a white community in Great Falls, Montana in the middle of nowhere. A boy in my class referred to me as the African American girl and I was like – what? What's that? Then when I moved to the Philippines I was like, OK, so I guess I'm also this, but I was bullied for my darker skin colour and my hair texture. I was like, what's going on? I didn't truly feel like I had a place anywhere. I never felt Black enough for the Black kids or Filipino enough for the Filipino kids and I'm not white, so I didn't feel at home with them. I never really felt like I had a place … It was only as I got older that I began to really embrace my identity.

We also discussed the fact that, as an adult, Asia is now able to assert her own identity, and why the distinctions she makes are important for others to understand:

So I identify as mixed, but I don't like using it as a sole identifier … I like to specify that I am Black, and I'm Asian, because someone who is white and Asian has a completely different experience to me. Also, I'm Black and you can't take my Blackness away from me. My friend is Mexican and Chinese, but he has no idea what it's like to be Black … When people say, 'You're not Black, you're mixed,' I'm like, consider this girls … 'I'm Black AND I'm mixed.'

Asia Jackson, Mixed Up *podcast, Season 2, Episode 3*

V. N. Vivero and S. R. Jenkins described what Asia grappled with from an early age as a kind of 'cultural homelessness': 'experiencing tensions that can develop when loyalty to their parents' cultural and racial identity conflicts with a need to be accepted by the outside world and/or in particular a peer group'.[20] Asia wanted to fit in somewhere when she was growing up, but struggled with the outside world trying to squeeze her into one specific category when in fact her identity was dual and fluid. She expresses a loyalty to and affinity with both the Filipino and the Black sides of her heritage, but when she is 'misidentified' it can cause her to feel a sense of cultural homelessness.

HELPING CHILDREN FORM HEALTHY IDENTITIES

Elaine Pinderhughes identifies two barriers to achieving a healthy identity: 'the continuing denigration in our society of the minority group to which they [mixed individuals] are connected' and 'the non-existence of a multicultural ethnic group to which they can feel connected, causing the invisibility of biracial existence'.[21] Pinderhughes offers mitigating factors that could be useful in helping mixed-race children and young people to form healthy identities:

1. Geographical location which minimizes othering and sense of difference.
2. Parental understanding and help with racial issues.
3. Acceptance of both parts of their racial heritage, which can be done by maintaining positive connections with individuals from both ethnic groups.[22]

One of the core learnings and moments of clarity that has come from hosting the *Mixed Up* podcast has been the realization that choice is something we can legitimately exercise. It is healthy for mixed-race children to manifest the idea that, above all, it is their choice how they identify. While many people likely agree that children should be given the agency of choice in articulating their identity, this is not always so clear-cut when it comes to mixed children, who often have a designation forced upon them by others from an early age. There is little opportunity for discussion for mixed-race children, and conversations on their identities aren't often had in private, let alone out in public. By discussing here, we hope to foster more consideration around this.

More importantly, it is a normal part of growth for that self-identification to flex and morph over time. It may fluctuate back and forth over a lifetime. Mixed children and adolescents' perception of what part of their cultural identity they feel or relate to most strongly may change on a daily or hourly basis, and that's OK. It's not devious, it's not racial or cultural appropriation, it's simply a personal reality that may differ from others that are more widely understood. As it stands today, society really seems to struggle with allowing space for this fluidity when it comes to mixed-race identity.

Something which beautifully articulates this was sent to us by a listener, and we'd like to share it with you:

Bill of Rights for People of Mixed Heritage
Maria P. P. Root, editor of *Racially Mixed People in America*

I HAVE THE RIGHT …
Not to justify my existence in this world. Not to keep the races separate within me. Not to justify my ethnic legitimacy. Not to be responsible for people's discomfort with my physical or ethnic ambiguity.

I HAVE THE RIGHT …
To identify myself differently than strangers expect me to identify. To identify myself differently than how my parents identify me. To identify myself differently than my brothers and sisters. To identify myself differently in different situations.

I HAVE THE RIGHT …
To create a vocabulary to communicate about being multiracial or multi-ethnic. To change my identity over my lifetime – and more than once. To have loyalties and identification with more than one group of people. To freely choose whom I befriend and love.

Finally, as Nikesh Shukla said in our conversation on the *Mixed Up* podcast, language is important. More important, perhaps, than we are always conscious of in our day-to-day:

> … my feeling is that, you know, language, when you're talking to mixed-race kids, language can be damaging. So I've been trying really hard to not talk to my daughters about them being half this and half that, because I want them to feel like they're whole. That they are both, in the way that two things can exist at the same time. I don't want them to ever feel half of anything.

What we have taken away from the research for this chapter is that, in order to tackle many of the potential hurdles faced by mixed-race children and young people as they struggle to belong and to carve out their identity, we need to foster conversations, not just about race but also about the distinct experiences of being mixed race and the specifics of a child's ethnic backgrounds and their 'cultural meanings'.

These conversations, this open dialogue, could instil confidence in young mixed people to develop an assuredness around who they are, and furthermore help them nurture a wider environment in which mixed-race children do not feel intimidated by friends, family and strangers alike into identifying in ways that might later prove harmful or untrue to their felt and lived selves. It is very important, particularly for our children, that as a society we begin to accept the fluidity of the mixed identity as truthful in each stage or epoch of its journey, as opposed to something we deem performative or insincere when it does not fit with our own idea of what or who this child or person should be. There's no room for a binary approach to raising mixed-race children.

3.
INTERRACIAL DATING AND RELATIONSHIPS

'I Love You' is a complicated phrase to say to another person. Modern language describes it as a sentence, but anyone that has been in love knows it's more like a dissertation.

(Suli Breaks, spoken word artist and writer)

EMMA

It is fair to say that we are in some ways the product of our parents' approach to our upbringing. We can be heavily influenced by cultural ideals passed down to us; our sense of self is nurtured and shaped by our parents and their experience of the world, its politics and of course, the way in which they approached the journey of love.

When we think about our mixed identities and how multiple cultural understandings must coexist to create the unity that make us whole, we must consider everything that constitutes who we are. So it follows to start at the very beginning – the relationships and marriages we have been born out of. In order to understand the mixed experience we must first paint a picture of what it really means to embark on and be in an interracial relationship.

In order to grasp both the beauty and the potential challenge of interracial dating, we need to appreciate the landscape – which is a complex one. So let's get real with it. It's going to be truthful and most probably a little bit gnarly. Buckle up as we get into dating dramas, the business of meeting family members and the life-changing revelations that mixed-heritage relationships can present. When all is said and done, we are talking about hard work. But to be fair, my nan always did tell me that the best things usually come from hard work …

If I reflect on this – I grew up thinking that the most beautiful relationships are supposed to involve at least some work, and honestly, after many years of experience, I now feel like the very best relationships are those you respect enough to keep working at them indefinitely. The best ones, the most loving ones, are a life's work and they teach you things you never knew about yourself …

In the end it's not just 'love'. Love can't exist in a vacuum. But instead it's love *and* a whole lot of learning, maybe even research; a readiness to understand that which you have not traversed and a willingness to come outside yourself and your own experience that will be required.

DATING DRAMAS AND WHERE THE DATA FROM DATING LEADS US

Perhaps in the modern day the well-known idiom 'The course of true love never did run smooth' should be adapted to add some warning colour: 'Three swipes right, a whole load of fetishization, some serious screening tactics, a few racist frogs later … and you still might not have found true love.' We jest, but this seems to be a fairly accurate characterization of what many People of Colour experience when running the gauntlet of today's dating scene.

Around half of 16- to 34-year-olds use dating apps; 45 per cent of those who do so have tried this way of finding a date before the age of

21, and in 2017, 39 per cent of heterosexual couples reported meeting online.[1] Because of Covid-19, interactions with new potentials at the bar were severely limited for a time and this became the prevalent way in which people sought romance, human contact, or their forever lobster. According to Business of Apps, many people converted to online dating during the Covid era: to be exact, 323 million worldwide now use dating apps.[2]

So what can the data tell us about the dating experiences of those who (like our parents did) become romantically involved with someone belonging to a 'race' that is not their own?

Although the mixed-race population is the fastest-growing demographic – the stats still suggest that overall, people still have a preference for a partner of their own race. Sadly, the data also indicates that racial stereotypes borne centuries ago are still very much at play today. Living in a post-racial society we are most definitely not, despite the naive cries of protestation from those who would like to believe it.

OkCupid data shows that 82 per cent of non-Black men on the app have a bias against Black women in some form. Its founder, Christian Rudder, noted in an OkCupid blog post that user data indicated that most men on the site rated Black women as less attractive than women of other races and ethnicities, while further studies showed that Black men and women were ten times more likely to message white people than white people were to message them.[3]

Some would assert that this proclivity is not rooted in prejudice and instead is simply an indication of a person's 'type on paper'. In reality, when we couple this with a wealth of anecdotal experiences of fetishization (both on- and offline) which women and men of colour have reported, we can trace these predilections as far back as the beginnings of colonization, and the politics of war. Whether now held subconsciously or otherwise, we can map them right back to a hierarchy of desirability and attractiveness created to uphold notions of People of

Colour being less than human in order to support white Europeans' unconscionable operation of slavery.

When Europeans first came across the African continent in the fifteenth century, it was common for travellers to characterize Africa and its people as wild, animalistic and overtly sexual. Books like *Heart of Darkness* (1899) by Joseph Conrad would continue to replay these prejudicial tropes centuries later.

Perverse mythology which became widely believed to be true included the hyper-sexuality of Black men (you are probably familiar with the stereotype that persists today in regards to the Black man's penis being larger than that of other men) and of Black women being the instigators of sex. They were almost always characterized by European scholars and colonialists as highly sexual, but certainly not beautiful; the African body was frequently described as darkness (the evil or the foul) in contrast to whiteness (the origin of light, purity).

> I haven't dated since the 1980s – when I was at boarding school in Lincolnshire and I was one of only two non-white girls in the whole school. I do remember plenty of conversations where I overheard the boys talking about sex with brown girls being crazy. That kind of fetishization is still around.
>
> *Jules, mixed Black Jamaican/white British,* Mixed Up *podcast,*
> *Season 2, Episode 22*

During Victorian times, when a woman's femininity and chastity were inextricably linked to her presentation, Black women were forcibly exposed, stripped of their clothes and beaten publicly, while white women were religiously protected, their modesty treated as paramount. And if, as the American author bell hooks asserts, 'colonization devalued the Black woman's body with permanent effect',[4] then it is not hard to read between the data set to see the root cause of the prejudice, racism and fetishization that manifests itself in interactions on dating apps today.

Black features were often likened to those of animals, our hair, for example, being described as 'a covering of wool' and our lips as similar to those of monkeys.[5] Stereotypes of sexual prowess or danger in Black men via the mythology of the 'Mandingo Warrior' or the 'Black Brute' have been absorbed by popular culture in articles, speeches, films, and books such as *Uncle Tom's Cabin* (1852), Thomas Nelson Page's *Red Rock* (1898), Charles Carroll's *The Negro a Beast* (1900), D. W. Griffith's *The Birth of a Nation* (1915) and Tony Calvano's *The Sin Smugglers* (1965) – on into the rhetoric of Enoch Powell's 'Rivers of Blood' speech and the eugenics theories still being touted in the 1950s and 60s.

In 2022, research from Bumble dating app showed the groups most likely to experience unsolicited fetishisation and microaggressions during online dating were men and women from mixed-race backgrounds with 50 per cent of women from mixed-race backgrounds having experienced fetishisation.[6] This tracks back to the many representations of oversexualisation and availability that originate from stereotypes and characters like the 'Tragic Mulatto' outlined in Chapter 7.

With such tropes prevailing into recent modern history, it is not hard to see how the prejudice, racism and fetishization that manifests itself in interactions on dating apps today are connected to tropes created over a century ago.

In 1920, E. D. Morel, editor of *Foreign Affairs*, wrote about the 'barely restrainable bestiality' of Black troops stationed in Europe after the First World War and how it had 'led to many rapes'. And that this was 'particularly serious as they were the most over developed sexually of any race'. In the US, these brutish caricatures have been pervasive throughout times of slavery. Charles Carroll specifically believed that 'mulatto brutes' (mixed men) were the rapists and murderers of his time.[7]

These damaging notions continued well into the modern day, whether through Blaxploitation movies that featured an on-screen 'brute' caricature or the villainization of Black men and boys as sexual predators. Only recently have we seen the Exonerated Five (previously the Central Park Five) walk free after they were falsely accused as young boys of rape. The US sociologist Allen D. Grimshaw noted that the 'brute' caricature gained in popularity whenever Black people pushed for social equality.[8]

This less than human characterization made it easier for Europeans to justify the enslavement and inhumane treatment of Africans for profit, and for white supremacy across the globe to continue to position Black people as 'less than' and 'other'.

Asian men have not fared well from stereotypes that have been developed to push political agendas in the West, either. Historians trace stereotypes about Asian men back to around two hundred years ago. When Asian men came to America in large numbers providing cheap labour in the 1920s, they were barred from marrying outside their race, confined to specific 'Asian' demarcated areas and prohibited from purchasing property. There was a widespread fear held by American men that these Asians were taking their jobs; subsequently many were also barred from doing industrial work and forced to take up roles that were thought of as traditionally feminine, such as laundry and cooking. Coupled with this emasculation was widespread propaganda known as the 'yellow peril', which purported that Asian men were dangerous rapists to be feared by white women. This was part of a political move to keep Asian men subjugated.

In 1882 the Chinese Exclusion Act was passed, meaning that no Chinese people could immigrate to the US for the next ten years. Most other Asian groups soon followed, so that eventually only Filipino immigrants (who were still considered part of the American colonies) could arrive in America to stay. For those Asian men already in the US, with no Asian women to court, this meant a burgeoning bachelor society.

> The emasculation of the Asian male has a very long history. Many Asian Americans are still horrified by older images such as writer Sax Rohmer's books about the sinister Dr Fu Manchu and Mickey Rooney's buck-toothed Mr Yunioshi from *Breakfast at Tiffany's*, perhaps the character Asian Americans most commonly identify as a racist icon of an earlier Hollywood. Some of a younger generation cringe at the sight of the nerdish Long Duk Dong from the 1984 teen classic *Sixteen Candles*.[9]

More recent propaganda around the Asian male in America still takes its influence from the Vietnam War. Scholars have written about the connection between that war and the development of an Asian American identity, but these concepts may have first been theorized in *Gidra: The Monthly of the Asian American Experience*, the self-proclaimed 'voice of the Asian American movement', a revolutionary monthly newspaper written by students of the University of Los Angeles between 1969 and 1974 which covered issues facing the Asian American community. In the June/July 1970 issue, *Gidra* published one of the first articles to report on the anti-Asian xenophobia of the war. The article, written by Norman Nakamura, who had recently completed a tour of duty in Vietnam, described rampant racist attitudes and behaviour towards Vietnamese women, children and the elderly. Nakamura wrote that this behaviour was not only widespread, it was given the green light, because US soldiers were taught that the Vietnamese were not people but 'only gooks – an epithet that plagued all Asians at the time because American society did not seem to distinguish between groups'.[10]

HOW DOES HISTORY TRANSLATE INTO MODERN-DAY DATING PREFERENCES?

So what are the consequences of racialized gender stereotypes and how do they play out in modern dating?

Data collated in Rutter's OkCupid post showed that 90 per cent of non-Asian women excluded Asian men from their preferences and that Asian men received the fewest unsolicited messages from women across all demographics.[11] To add insult to injury, Asian women are purported to end up marrying white males by a ratio of at least 2:1 over Asian men.[12]

The same OkCupid research demonstrated that Asian men were ranked as 12 to 14 per cent less attractive than average by white, Black and Latina women.[13] And research by New York's Columbia University found that they were least likely to get a second date, and that an Asian man would have to earn an additional $247,000 for white women to consider dating him over his white contemporary.[14] The OkCupid data concluded that, in summary, Asian men are almost always least preferred by women from all other races.[15]

Harmful historical stereotypes of the Asian man and woman seem to be alive and well today, perhaps even perpetuated by dehumanizing media such as video game play. Thien-bao Thuc Phi studies video games as 'transformative works', examining how Asian men are presented in them. He concludes that 'Asian men in particular are difficult to find in roles outside of martial arts games or historical period games such as the *Dynasty Warriors* series, *Tenchu*, or *Genji*',[16] suggesting that they only exist in the mainstream imagination if they are situated in the feudal days of China or Japan, consequently erasing their existence from present-day America.

He notes: 'In fact, the one place where Asian American men regularly make appearances is as yakuza or triad thugs in some urban-themed games with contemporary settings, restricting these characters to background at best, and stereotypically villainous at worst.' He describes his journey through *Shellshock: 'Nam 67* and explores themes in the game. He highlights that these Vietnam War games are effectively the only ones that feature Vietnamese people, thus reinforcing the old roles that the West has created for them in popular entertainment and film: as prostitutes or the 'gook' who get shot. He recounts how, firstly, the premise of the game seems to be to destroy the Vietnamese protagonists, who are of course depicted as the evil enemy. Secondly, none of the hero avatars that can be chosen – as you might expect – are Asian. Thirdly, and rather crudely, part of the game presents the opportunity to be solicited by and to exploit Asian women characterized as prostitutes. Fourthly, the inherent portrayal of the Asian man is ultimately cruel, woman-hating and almost inhumanly evil:

> Later in the game, after some of my crazy platoon mates executed some Vietnamese civilians for fun, our Southern Vietnamese guide tortured a Vietnamese woman who is revealed to be a spy for the Vietcong, and as if to suggest that Asian men are even more brutal than any other race of man, he tortured her breasts with his knife before cutting her throat.[17]

Thien-bao Thuc Phi testifies how visceral the difference is between sitting through an American movie depicting the Vietnam War versus the psychology of playing a nine- to twenty-hour video game in which you shoot only at Asian presenting men – especially if you yourself are Asian or indeed Vietnamese.

It's worth noting how damaging over time the dehumanization, emasculation or minimization of representations of yourself might be to self-esteem, and how this might play into dating and matters of romance.

We have not seen many Asian men playing the handsome protagonist who gets the girl historically, and not even until very recently in modern films, TV and popular culture. The *Guardian*'s Ann Lee describes Asian men as, until lately, depicted only as sexless; as 'effectively having been neutered by Hollywood'.[18] She refers to films like *Romeo Must Die* (2000) starring Jet Li and Aaliyah, who were romantic interests but who never saw a passionate embrace because in fact it was left on the cutting-room floor. More recent examples include *The Edge of Seventeen*'s (2016) Erwin, who is more wet than smouldering, and Jimmy O. Yang in *Love Hard* (2021), who, it appears, initially has to be cast as a catfish for the directors to make the story of him eventually snaring the girl believable. It's only very recently that the likes of Henry Golding (*Crazy Rich Asians* [2018], *A Simple Favor* [2018]) and Simu Liu (*Shang-Chi* [2021] and *Barbie* [2023]) have been awarded the assertive or desirable protagonist role, and it's interesting to think about how all of this manifests and how it may have become internalized when it comes to Asian women's preferences away from the men who presumably look most like them and most akin to those they see in their families, their homes and their communities.

Jason Chen's 2016 Facebook and Twitter study looked at what the three top stereotypes for Asian American men were and they came back as: good at maths, small genitalia and good with computers. What's more, 50 per cent of Asian men had heard someone saying in their presence that 'they don't date Asian men'.[19]

Another study looking at 2.4 million hetrosexual interactions showed that Asian women were preferred by most men,[20] but for one of our contributors, Klarissa, it begs the question – is this just another example of fetishization?

With dating apps, one of my big worries was being fetishized. There is a lot of fetishization that goes on for Asian women and I was really worried about it. So initially I didn't put either of my races. I didn't get a lot of hits at first. Once I did I started getting messages, I feared – does somebody just want to date me because they are really into Asians?

Klarissa, Mixed Up *podcast contributor*

THE REALITIES OF MODERN DATING – SCREENING TACTICS, SELF-PRESERVATION AND LEARNINGS

In one of our episodes of *Mixed Up* we wanted to validate our theories around how historical prejudices impact one-on-one interactions within dating, so we explored, anecdotally, how these preferences play out.

The following anecdotes are grouped into dating, relationships and family. Our hope is that reading them is almost like being a fly on the wall to difficult conversations, the highs and the lows across the trajectory of relationships, from parents-in-law consistently denying the existence of racism in the presence of their grandkids to the compromise and harmony required to nurture your relationship with your partner and bring up your kids as a united front.

Dating

I have to worry about how they will react to me as a Black woman. It's the same feeling of walking into a room and realizing you're the only person that looks like you in there. It's not as simple as a girl meets a boy on an app. Even if I don't want to lead with it, I don't have a choice in the matter. It's going to be the first thing a guy sees when he sees my photo.

Food is a really good indicator on how to weed out some of the bad options. I might drop in stereotypically Black or Southern food, just to see what they say.

I've had one guy Google banana pudding after I mentioned it and there's nothing very alarming about that, but it's the guy who thinks he's being funny when he cracks a joke about watermelon – that's the guy you're hoping is not the guy every time you interact with someone on these apps … Then there's the ones that think having a Black woman as their 'type' is the same as liking brunettes. When the guy starts sounding super-proud of himself because he's dated a load of Black women. Or acting as though you should fawn over him as a Black woman because he has dated a long line of Black women.

There's a gross expectation that if you're a Black woman you're somehow up for anything – there's a type of guy who hyper-sexualizes from the jump and gets offended if you get offended if they talk about the size of our lips in a photo, or ask if you can twerk or if you have child-bearing hips …

The reality of using these dating apps is that most of the men that appear on them don't look like you. It makes you wonder if this is already rigged against you.

It's also not good if they don't acknowledge your race. Because people who don't see colour don't see you.

(Sherell, Black American)

I was dating this guy who is British and American. As I was walking back into the house I heard his grandmother say, 'I am so glad you didn't bring the coloured girl'. His parents said, 'We don't talk that way about other people. Ngoni is a part of the family'. I chose not to take it as a negative thing because the parents spoke up. I was happy I heard what she had to say about me because he did tell me before 'that my grandmother is a *bit* racist'.

The first time I met her she was nice to me, so I was quite happy that I heard what she had to say about me even if I was taken aback. To actually hear her talk about me was hurtful, but I prefer to know someone doesn't like me because of the colour of my skin rather than lie about it.

When you're dating someone from another race it takes introspection because you don't want to pull your partner into a situation where your family members might have a problem because I think it can be awkward. It's great to sit down with your partner and find out if that's going to be OK for them.

(Ngoni, Black Zimbabwean)

In Brazil there are lots of mixed-race people. I did see myself reflected quite often. Being mixed race wasn't really a desirable thing. Everyone's dating tastes were very Eurocentric. Everyone was crazy for the lighter people. If you had light eyes you pretty much had everything in Brazil. I wasn't particularly attractive. When I moved to the UK, the tables turned. All of a sudden I found out that I was 'exotic'. I did get a lot more attention from boys I fancy. I quite like a white boy. In Brazil, they wouldn't really look at me.

(Hendy Mendes, Mixed Brazilian)

I've ended a relationship with a white guy over racial gaslighting. If your partner doesn't understand how they are invalidating your experience, that's a problem, if they expect you as the person of colour in the relationships to let comments about People of Colour slide, that is a major, major issue. The signs that a person is prejudiced can be in the minor things.

When you're in an interracial relationship you have to accept that you will likely have to check the other person if you're the person of colour.

(Anon)

What people have learned from their interracial relationships

Because we have been brought up in different ways it means that we can support each other in areas where we may struggle ourselves since different cultures have different ways of handling situations. I think we have been able to look at different ways of looking at situations, which I think is really nice and really important. Nice to learn from both sides.

(Izzy, Chinese Indian)

One of the by-products of being a partner in an interracial relationship – he was woke long before any of his friends and family were and I listened to him when he's in the other room having these passionate arguments with members of his own family, and friends of his who haven't caught up. I think if you're in an interracial relationship you understand by proxy a lot more about that person's experience in other ways that people can't, because they don't spend enough time with you to witness the same things as they happen. I feel for him sometimes because I can feel his frustration … but it's just so interesting how much empathy he has because he's seen so many different versions of it also through travelling the length and breadth of Kenya and witnessing real poverty, and I'm happy for him that he's had the privilege of seeing what he's seen because a lot of people have never left the Northern Hemisphere, so in some ways is it their fault?

(Anon)

How did I maintain aspects of my cultural heritage? Well I basically gave him whiplash – I showed him one version of Kenya and then a completely different version of it, basically to give him an understanding of what life is like outside of the privileged bubble that he grew up in that I was co-existing in with him.

(Anon)

The first date I went on with my boyfriend was actually to go out for dim sum, and the first thing my mum said to him was, 'I heard you ate chicken feet'. After, when he met my dad, it was also the first thing my dad asked him – chicken feet is now a bit of a meme in my family

I really like that my boyfriend is really interested in my background and likes doing the things I like doing, like going for dim sum, and he's interested in my family history, and I realized that is actually so important. I've never had that before.

Coming from two different backgrounds means you can bring so many things to the table for your relationships to grow in a way that makes people understand.

(Izzy, Chinese Indian)

You learn the most from people who are not like you. I went to church, whereas his parents wanted them to choose religion for themselves. Whereas with mine it was like there was no choice in the matter. Which isn't good or bad, it's just a different perspective.

(Anon)

Family, meeting the parents and getting married

I met my husband in 1986. The biggest lesson we have taught our extended family is that we have endured, we are still together … maybe the fact that we are from different backgrounds and upbringings, there is a shared world view that keeps us together and we have so much more in common than not. Things are different for us because we are not like other couples, we don't know any other couples like us, we are unique.

(Jules, mixed Black Jamaican/White British)

My husband's paternal grandmother reminded me of the *Little Britain* sketch where this lady can't understand the Indian woman in the slimming group because that's exactly what she used to do to me, she would turn to my husband or his mother and say, 'What did she say?' and ask them to relay … It was comical, in a dark way.

(Hendy Mendes, mixed Brazilian)

When we got together, and when it became clear that we were going to stay together, our families did have misgivings. My family was from Jamaica and my husband's family was born in India and moved to England in the 1960s.

It never occurred to me that my husband's mother might want to arrange a marriage for him, but that was naivety on my part.

My mum and dad, they really liked my husband so that helped, but they had misgivings: would I have to convert to his religion, how would that affect our children? We never discussed these things but they told me so after we got married, actually.

Interestingly, recently I've had more discussions with my mum than ever before about race, mixed race, which we never talked about before. Perhaps Coronavirus and the BLM movement has instigated more of this. She said she had a similar conversation with her dad that I had with my dad – think about the kids, what kind of a life might they have, what difficulties might they encounter.

(Jules, mixed Black Jamaican/white British)

RAISING KIDS, MIGRANT IDENTITY, GOING BACK HOME AND CONNECTING THE KIDS TO THEIR HERITAGE

Raising children in an interracial relationship is actually quite tricky, bringing two cultures together. My parents were African and extremely strict and my husband's family were quite relaxed. There are things I won't allow at all. It's so important that you study really hard.

I am Black and my husband is white and he's never experienced racism at all, and when, for example, my children reached a certain age I told them the world will see you as Black and you need to be prepared. People will say bad things to you. He said, 'You don't want to perpetuate these racial myths.' I said, 'Babe, it's not a myth.'

One of my children was only young and she was told Black people were the worst and she wouldn't be played with.

When she was older – and what happened with George Floyd became a thing and she wanted to go and protest – and finally my husband got it. He realized racism exists and it's going to be a big thing.

The chat with your children about how to handle the police and how to be respectful. It's weird talking to your 5-year-old about being stopped by the police. My husband thinks it's wrong.

[And with sons who will be] Black men who I am hoping will be successful ... the world will treat them abhorrently in some instances and that's just something he is getting to grips with mentally.

(Anon, Ghanaian woman)

My mother. She had an amazing journey and she's been through real hardship – they thought she was a Russian spy when she arrived in West Africa because she wasn't able to enter in a normal way. And she walked through the jungle while pregnant with me to get into Liberia ... this is the interesting thing about multicultural marriages. I don't think we ever know what we're getting into. I didn't know what I was getting into when I entered a multicultural marriage outside of my own cultures. Even though I'm mixed race and think I'm so international, I didn't know what I was married into when I entered another religion and culture.

And I don't think my mom knew, nor my father necessarily [when she did], but my mom thought they would stay in Europe. So that was a sort of naivety of hers to believe that. Eventually, my father wanted to return back to West Africa. I didn't think she saw that coming, but she did follow him. So she must have really loved him, and she did go over and those were defining years of her life, but she speaks so fondly of them. There's certain things that you know not to ask and, and there's certain stories that she will never tell you. This conversation about the responsibility of parents entering multicultural marriages is how do you honour traditions if the parents stay together, how do you create a balance? And sometimes I think, as much as you might see a multicultural marriage from the outside, what actually happens is sometimes one culture can dominate in that house, and I've seen that in many multicultural marriages. And then if parents separate, it's the responsibility of the parent who has custody of the children to still find a way to deliver on assisting their children to have a connection to all of their traditions.

Because what so often happens is that that parent often will reject it; in finding hardship in having a multicultural marriage and then it breaking down, quite often what I've seen is those parents reject the culture that they mixed with and then cut off that chapter of their life and pretend like it never existed. But you can't do that if you have multicultural children from that marriage. And so I saw that happen in our household where my mom wanted to always erase parts of her life in Africa, and she didn't really want to talk about parts of it. Did she really understand? You know, the necessity to offer elements of African culture in our home, in, let's say, you know, access to clothes or understanding how to do my hair and those elements. I was not taught those things.

And so that's a responsibility that I think sometimes people don't understand. And so that's something I've been very mindful of in my new chapter moving forward. The only way to say it is, I was brought up as a white woman. By white women. And it took me a long time to re-establish and reintegrate my Black identity into my life … and although my mother saved my life, my biological father searched for me for years and he was never reunited with me. And years later I learned that he had looked for me and that he had, you know, died really sad that he was never able to find me. And so it has repercussions and consequences, but, as you say, you're gonna have compassion for this because this is like, one woman. And I remember Mum saying, there was a point where she didn't even know what to do, and she, what she did is she remembers sitting on the, on the step in front of her house in Liberia in the middle of the night and just looking up at, and it was a full moon, and just actually speaking to the universe and saying, 'I don't know what the next step is, what, what should I do?'

'Cause I have to surrender at this point and I'm just going to do whatever I have to do next. And it's going to be brutal and it's going to be harsh and it's going to harm and hurt some people, but I'm going to have to make a decision that's right for my daughter, and as a mother, and I'll pay the consequences for this. You can only have compassion.

(*Florence Kollie Raja, mixed Black Liberian/white Ukrainian*)

That feeling of belonging is something I'd never really talked about. We should have these conversations, they are important for your kids as much as they are for you. It surprised me to find that my kids had very different feelings. I was surprised to learn that one son identifies as Indian and my other son just as British and doesn't feel he needs to categorize himself any other way.

(*Jules, mixed Black Jamaican/white British*)

I try to take my son back to Brazil often … someone said, 'Oh my god your son is so beautiful' – Brazil still has this colonial hangover of being white is beautiful. This guy said he would be though, thanks to that 'gringo' blood, or he would just be some little 'neguinho' Black boy … the nerve to say my son is only beautiful because he has European blood in him.

(Hendy Mendes, mixed Brazilian)

A particular challenge in my life was learning about his [Indian] culture and his parents and how they were around my kids. His mother didn't believe in saying no to my kids. It caused some problems. Let me say everything turned out OK. As a young mother at the time that was difficult to take. We get on great now – we live next door.

(Jules, mixed Black Jamaican/white British)

At the Kenyan wedding all the decisions were taken away from us, there was a committee of aunties, and I had to keep reminding my other half that in Kenya the tradition is that the wedding is really more for the parents […] at times you feel like a prop and there were times I felt like a guest at my own wedding.

(Anon)

It felt even more real because when the conversation around Black Lives Matter increased in society and started to increase in homes, it actually put my marriage under pressure as well. It wasn't that I increased my Blackness in any way. My Blackness has always been there, but when I actually openly discussed those subjects with my ex-partner in the home, it was really quite a shock and a surprise to me how uncomfortable he found those conversations. Which actually, I think with time, led me to realize that people will project on to mixed-race people. Quite often they want to pick the best parts from them. And they don't actually understand you in your entirety. And that can be friends, and it can be family, it can even be parents.

And it can be partners. So I have this multicultural marriage – myself, being of mixed origin and uh, my ex-husband being also mixed [culturally] in his own right because he is Indian but grew up in Africa and then came to the UK. I think he had accepted a version of me, and when that version leaned a little bit more towards a slightly different side of my identity there was a very great sense of discomfort in him because I think he always thought I sort of shaped to Indian culture. And I think that's the double-edged sword of being mixed race. I was so good at fitting into groups that there's like an assumption because you've got that, that kind of world outlook and so people have this comfort with you straight away, they project on to you who they think you are, without actually realizing who you are. And so, that [practised ease around people] is a great skill set in life, and yes, it means that I have wonderful, even more mixed-race kids than even I am 'cause they've got even more mixed cultures in them. And I had a beautiful marriage and I got to get to know another culture …

What it means actually in the long run is that some people will get you, some people won't. What Black Lives Matter did actually show is people's discomfort as to discussing race and discussing the Black agenda, but I didn't realize how much that discomfort sat in my own home. So that was a little bit of a surprise.

(Florence Kollie Raja, mixed Black Liberian/white Ukrainian)

The first BBQ I went to in the UK was a bit of a disappointment … it's burgers and sausages, and where I am from it's quite a big deal – rib-eye steaks …

I remember I went to my mother-in-law's BBQ and she took a chicken breast straight out of the packet and just slapped it straight on to the BBQ. I was horrified – you can't do that, not even a bit of salt – a bit of a shock to the palate!

(Hendy Mendes, mixed Brazilian)

I could talk about my mum all day. As an adult, we've talked a bit more about what that was like because she said, you know, obviously now your dad [activist and civil rights campaigner, who became known in 1960s London as a godfather of Black Power activism], everybody knows the story, but at the time people didn't know if he was guilty or people weren't sure if he was this shady character that was being made out in a, you know, there's no smoke without fire kind of feeling.

And, it was very, I think, very isolating for her from that standpoint. My dad always had very well meaning, very politically active people on the right side of history, around him, white and Black. You know, I kind of noticed that about his stories, that a lot of white people came to advocate for him.

But I think my mom's role is very complex in his story and in hindsight I just grow every year, I just grow in appreciation for how isolating that must have felt for her. And my relationship with her, you know, like every mother–daughter relationship, is complex, but in terms of sort of identity it was only recently that she, that we kind of openly acknowledged how different our experiences were, because of the colour of our skin. Lucy Ann – just thinking about her, my smile is from ear to ear and I do think that, that her experience is relatively untapped or discussed. She was raising, you know, four mixed-race children, with the love of her life and the father of her children looking at constant persecution. And my mum and dad didn't need to be married for me to think that their love story is probably the most beautiful one I've been able to witness. And it wasn't perfect and it was messy, and it was all the stuff in between. But yeah, just that appreciation of relationships is so hard as it is.

(Lenora Crichlow, mixed Black Trinidadian/white British)

REFLECTIONS ON THE JOURNEY AND A CONCLUSION

All this is not to say that the parents of mixed-race people are special or superior in any way for choosing the path they have, but that perhaps they have been on a special journey of sorts; because if you deep all of the propaganda and negative noise and even geographical or socio-logical hurdles they have had to filter out in order for us to be here, in order to still be together in those cases – it's pretty astounding.

In a *National Geographic* article, 'Visualising Race, Identity and Change', Michele Norris, curator of The Race Card Project, notes a phrase she has heard repeatedly: that in matters of romance, 'the heart perhaps is the last frontier.' She goes on to unpack this as the idea that 'a rainbow generation would lead us to a promised land where race is at least less prickly than it has been in the past.'[21]

Despite some of the more recent frivolous and silly rhetoric around mixed-race people being the face of the future (for more of the same see the *National Geographic* article above and the countless social media accounts and posts fetishizing interracial love and children) that directly or indirectly paint mixed people as a desirable hybrid, if we examine how many of the negative and malevolent characteristics associated with

People of Colour still pervade our media, tech and personal mindsets, interracial unions, could – to this day – still be interpreted as a radical act.

4.
ADOPTION, THE CARE SYSTEM AND BEING MIXED

I had quite a difficult experience because of my race pretty much from the moment I was born because decisions were made for me that affected the rest of my life based on the mix that I am – based on the race that I am.

My whole childhood, teenage years and adult life I've struggled with my identity, and a sense of belonging … in reference to race, in reference to family, in reference to location, in reference to everything, I would say.

My mum is white British, my dad is Black British – his parents are Jamaican. Her parents were racist.

So when she had a baby with a Black man her family disowned her and cut her off. She didn't have any money – all her privileges got cut off. She tried … but she was on her own and my dad was very absent and elusive. We would go for months without hearing from him, or seeing him. Basically she decided it was all too much for her so she couldn't look after me herself any more.

She didn't instantly decide to put me into care … there was a period over a couple of years where I was in and out of foster care

… She would give me up and then she would say – 'No I want her back.'

They [the care authorities] put a picture of me in the Black newspaper *The Voice*. They decided that if you had any Black in you – then you were Black. They said that I was a Black child and I needed to go to a Black family.

(Anon, mixed Black/white British)

Over time, while we were producing *Mixed Up*, adoption and the care system emerged as a core theme of the mixed-race experience. We found that we were consistently receiving messages from mixed-race people who had been adopted or who had spent time in care.

In retrospect it's not at all surprising that a narrative of displacement, disconnect and in many cases rejection would be compounded by having no obvious route back to your racial or ethnic heritage – a heritage that, for anyone on the outside looking in, you might appear to wear on your sleeve due to the colour of your skin, your facial features or hair type.

We have heard some emotional accounts of how growing up as an adopted child or in the care system can play a huge part in forming identity, and there seems to be a particular disconnect felt by adoptees or cared-for children of mixed-race heritage. We wanted to find out why this is such a common thread.

FRUIT OF THE POISONOUS TREE

Emma

A friend of mine is mixed and adopted, and she was in and out of care between the ages of 3 and 5. She would tell you first-hand that her experiences – of being separated from her mother, and of foster care and adoption from the age of 5 – have had a profound effect on her sense of self, her life experiences and the forming of her identity. Essentially, her adoption has been a spectre in her life and has deeply influenced how she feels about whether she belongs in the environments she moves through. This is still true today in her thirties.

After over two decades of knowing her, I have heard so many stories and seen so many instances of people attempting to dictate my friend's identity to her. When she was put up for adoption (as the chapter's opening quote illustrates) it was a specific requirement of the care authorities that the adoptive parents be Black.

Throughout the time we've been friends I've personally witnessed people trying to tell her that she is more of this, or not enough of that to qualify for being Black, or to be recognized as mixed race at all. I have also heard of moments in her life when she has been mistaken for white, and other moments when she has been told by Black people that she should make no mistake – 'she is *not* Black'.

But, as the opening quote demonstrates, what might play out as a continuous stream of microaggressions in any mixed-race person's life ordinarily, could take on a more life-defining character when it relates to decisions made that will determine a mixed child's future, their separation from their birth parents and their journey through care and adoption.

THE CARE AND ADOPTION SYSTEM AND MIXED-RACE CHILDREN – A CHEQUERED HISTORY

The idea that feelings of rejection, displacement and racial imposter syndrome might be exacerbated in the case of a mixed adoptee seems immediately obvious. But it wasn't until we heard the 'Fletcher Report' mentioned on Nora Fakim's *My Mixed Up World* radio show that we realized that there was a historical thread here that needed to be unravelled in order for us to truly understand why adoption and the care system are a recurring theme in the stories of many mixed individuals' life experiences.

Once we started to dig a little deeper, we discovered a murky history of entanglement between the politics of racial segregation and immigration and the social question of the mixed-race child as a 'problem'. Since as far back as the 1920s, mixed children have been used as symbols for political ideas and as so-called evidence for the validity of far-right notions.

On 16 June 1930, the *Daily Telegraph* printed a piece about the 'Fletcher Report' portraying mixed people as a 'social menace'. Other headlines published during this period included 'Menace of Mixed Unions'. The report in question – which was nationally commended for its insight at the time – deemed mixed children as an ungodly, undesirable problem: the children of sin and, worse still – the evidence of sin manifested. 'It' was something that must be dealt with in order to restore a healthy balance to society.

To give a little bit of contextual background, the 'Fletcher Report' was a 'research' project undertaken by Muriel E. Fletcher, who was tasked with investigating the social economic plight of what she called 'half-castes' in Liverpool. The research was conducted on behalf of the Liverpool Association for the Welfare of Half-Caste Children and the report was backed by Rachel Fleming, a prominent eugenicist, along with other pseudo-scientific intellectuals.

At the time, many of these individuals were concerned that Liverpool had a 'colour problem'; the report came off the back of these fears and became one of the most pivotal to be published in the history of poor race relations. It was entirely focused on mixed-heritage children and their family structure.

Eugenics theory: A heinous theory that viewed humans in terms of being 'inferior or superior' in stock. Eugenics is the scientifically erroneous and immoral theory of 'racial improvement' and 'planned breeding,' which gained popularity during the early twentieth century. Eugenicists worldwide believed that they could perfect human beings and eliminate so-called social ills through genetics and heredity.

Fletcher attempted to use eugenic techniques to study the physical and mental quality of what she called 'half-caste' children, and while eugenics theorists believed that selective breeding would improve the physical and mental quality of humans, implicit within her report was the idea that the children of African and white British/Europeans were an anomaly. The babies of interracial relationships were erroneously branded as genetically abnormal. Consequently the report is said to have had major negative ramifications for the mixed-race experience, cementing sexual taboos and a fear of mixing brought on by racial mythology.[1]

Scientific racism: Ideology that appropriates the methods and legitimacy of science to argue for the superiority of white Europeans and the inferiority of non-white people whose social and economic status have been historically marginalized.[2]

The 'Fletcher Report' refers to 'half-caste' intelligence as being 'more inferior than the lowest, ragged white child [Fletcher] observed', and notes that 'all the circumstances of their lives tend to give undue prominence to sex [...] and those mothers of a better type regretted the fact they had brought these children into the world handicapped by their colour'. The report not only depicts mixed-race children as destined to be outcasts in society, but also cast out by their white mothers.

Essentially the report was concerned with reaffirming the prevailing viewpoint at the time that the history of Black presence in Liverpool had caused a major social problem and that existing immigration policy ought to be strengthened. It boiled down to a stigmatization of Black/white sexual relationships, the offspring of which were branded as less than human degenerates prone to illness and promiscuity – an argument that could be used as a reason in itself to prevent immigration.

Fletcher goes on to stigmatize the women who have relationships with Black men as having 'chosen a life that is repugnant' and labels them as prostitutes or mentally weak. In *Multiracial Identity: An International Perspective* Mark Christian asserts that the legacy of the 'Fletcher Report' continues to feed into stereotypes of mixed-heritage Black people today.

After some investigation, it seems fair to conclude that where we find imperialism and colonization (and in some cases the religious institutions it has left behind), we also often find that mixed-race children were seen as evidence of the awful outcome of racial mixing and as a reason to intervene in the changing shape of a nation.

Mixed children were painted as the product of an unsavoury union and ultimately used as the argument against immigration and racial mixing. Part of this demonization and seeing it through was excluding or removing children from society, warning by extension what could happen to you or your children should you decide to 'fraternize' with the idea of blending two worlds that had been kept relatively separate to uphold the notion of white supremacy.

I mean, I would, I would argue that not being adopted … the issue was that nobody wanted a mixed-race child. It wasn't about a policy, that came much later. The women having mixed-race children, well, having a relationship, having a child that either they didn't want, or when they realized their families were gonna reject them, they had to give up. They put them into care and then they remained in care because no one wanted them. No one wanted us.

Dr Melissa J. Wagner, Mixed Up *podcast, Season 2*

It seems impossible to begin to understand why mixed children were given up by their parents or abandoned to the care system without examining the historical tendency to point to mixed-race children as a political symbol of unsavoury change. The rhetoric of the past has very much influenced the present when it comes to the experiences of mixed people and their ending up in care.

THE MÉTIS

Another example of this is the story of the Métis, which had been shrouded in secrecy until as recently as 2018 when the Belgium government officially recognized the segregation policy that had been employed against more than 15,000 biracial children born in the Congo (now the DRC) between 1946 and 1950. The children were stolen from their Black Congolese mothers by the Belgian State because they posed a serious problem for white Europeans, who had upheld a hierarchy of white supremacy and segregation for centuries. These mixed-race children – babies of white Belgian men and Black Congolese women – are known as the Métis.

At the time of their birth a marriage between a white man and a Black woman was not legally recognized by the State, so these mixed-race babies were labelled children of sin; children of prostitution. In reality, for the colonisers they posed a living, breathing threat to a regime that positioned white Europeans as racially supreme. Their very existence challenged the basis of the racial theory on which colonization was built and by which it was maintained; and so via a rule of law issued in 1952 the authorities worked with the Church to forcibly abduct the children, whom they considered the property of the Belgian State. They were put into a care system run by the Church, sent to Belgian orphanages or fostered. Their mothers were portrayed as unfit to parent them.

Archivist and historian Delphine Lauwers characterized what happened to the children as 'the targeted segregation of biracial children born during Belgium's colonial regime'[3] to avert the potential danger of a future force for revolution should the children stay with their African families. She described what was done by the State as a 'theft of identity' as the Belgian government attempted to cut off mixed children from their origins by changing their names, birth dates and by obscuring records.

Children who recall the day when they were forced to leave their homes and their families because they were mixed race report arriving at the mission only to be treated as less than human, suffering depraved conditions, hunger and sexual abuse. Most are still struggling to understand what happened to them and battling with the displacement and isolation of not being able to regain family connections and ties to their ancestral homes.

THE MIXED-RACE IRISH

Meanwhile between the 1930s and 1960s, almost 6,000 miles away, Ireland saw a surge of African students from Ghana, Nigeria and South Africa arriving to study in its universities.

As a result babies were born out of wedlock from relationships between the students and Irish women. Given that interracial unions and pregnancy outside of marriage were not accepted by Irish society at the time, many white women were forced or persuaded to move or to leave their children in institutions and orphanages because of the racism and stigma associated with mothering a Black, mixed-race child.

Many were physically attacked and condemned for having interracial relationships:

> You're eight months pregnant and you are cleaning an institution from top to bottom. You're underfed. You're not given any meds during the pregnancy because the whole idea was that you as an offender have to suffer through your labour. So no medication, not even an aspirin given to you during pregnancy, during the birth itself, shunned by the other people in the hospital, other people being told not to go near that corner because there's an unmarried mother, a penitent in that bed with her [brown] baby.
>
> The treatment by the Catholic Church and State was barbaric. And it wasn't just the Church. It was doctors, it was the legal profession, it was the police, it was social workers, it was teachers. Every part, every arm of society was involved in making the lives of single pregnant women as miserable as possible.
>
> *Rosemary Adaser,* Mixed Up *podcast, Season 3, Episode 9*

Anecdotal evidence from the Association of Mixed Race Irish (AMRI) reports that most of the mixed children who have now, as adults, spoken out were sent – like the mixed children of the Congo – to Catholic institutions where they suffered racial, physical and sexual abuse at the hands of the people who were supposed to care for them. And sadly, it was widely believed by the nuns that these mixed children were unadoptable; unlike the Irish white children who found themselves orphaned, mixed-race Irish children were abandoned in homes, often never even offered up for adoption and left to languish, led to believe that they were shameful manifestations of their parents' sin:

It was very brutal for all the children. But I think because we were visible, we were more inclined to get the kicking than other children who could hide by sheer numbers. You know, in a sea of white, you've got one brown face, you're gonna notice the brown face … it was emotional: blackmail threats, anger, swearing, hectoring, bullying, ignoring responses, denial of requests for distress relief, just the children feeling endlessly overwhelmed, silent, compliant, biddable. It was a wearing-down process over the lifespan of that child from the time they entered that institution to the time they left. And the idea was to make us biddable, to groom us, if we were lucky, to become servants in middle-class households … if we were very lucky, some kind middle-class family would take us in and we'd be their servant, their nanny, nappy changer.

It was, extremely rare [that mixed-race babies were adopted], predominantly because of the model applied by the Catholic Church. Now, in the Catholic Church in the middle of the twentieth century, one in twenty of their families was engaged in missionary work. The missionaries would come back and the discourse was that Africans were savages in need of taming. So therefore, those Irish women that had babies with Africans, they were considered the lowest of the low. They were hoes, and the fathers were just considered savages. And so those women had committed double jeopardy here. First of all they weren't married, and secondly they had mated with a member of the slave class. One of the hallmarks of these institutions is actually the death of babies, because babies were neglected. They were neglected. It was cheaper to have them die than to actually feed them so the death rate among the infants was horrible. For the case of Black and Black mixed-race babies, we were as a matter of course hidden from would-be adopters. I'd say, Black mixed-race

babies and Traveller children commanded no value whatsoever.
The white babies were sent to the States and came with a
guarantee of whiteness, and that was stated at ministerial level …
when assuring would-be parents in America, they were told there
can be no doubt that the taint of colour will not be in any of the
babies we send you … it was State policy.

Rosemary Adaser, Mixed Up *podcast, Season 3, Episode 9*

The State had devolved all power to the Church, and the Church purported that these children were not worthy of adoption. Mixed-race children were simply not considered to be suitable candidates and so rarely put up for adoption – instead they were most often put into what amounted to workhouses (industrial schools and institutions).

Rosemary Adaser, founder of the AMRI, describes the sexual abuse as well as the relentless racism she faced in the industrial school she grew up in. In the *Guardian* documentary 'Ireland's Forgotten Mixed-race Child Abuse Victims' Rosemary describes being told that she could not bathe until the last of thirty other girls (who were white) had used the water because the nuns said she was dirty. She told of having to clean the toilets in the middle of the night and not being allowed to wash her hands before she returned to bed because they said it wouldn't matter anyway because of the colour of her skin.

In her book *Don't Touch My Hair* Irish-Nigerian writer, academic and journalist Emma Dabiri has written about how it was not rare to find that mixed people of the generations above her had suffered similar upbringings:

Mixed-race people I met, certainly those who were any older
than me, had grown up in institutions […] According to the
alumni of these abhorrent facilities, this 'special attention' seems
to have extended to racist assaults which served to compound the

physical, sexual, emotional and mental abuse many of the children were subject to.[4]

THE STOLEN GENERATIONS

Similar occurrences of the inhumane removal of mixed-race children from their families can be traced all over the globe and were taking place well into the 1970s in Australia, where Aboriginal mixed children were still being removed from their parents by the Australian government.

This campaign of abducting children was ongoing roughly between 1905 and 1967 and was based on the cynical idea that Aboriginal people could be dying out. Having seen the Aboriginal population decline dramatically under the impact of new diseases, repressive and often brutal treatment, dispossession and social and cultural disruption and disintegration, it was believed by the white population that the Aboriginal population was doomed to extinction.[5]

In 1915 A. O. Neville was appointed 'Chief Protector of Aborigines', a role created by the Australian government seemingly with the sole purpose of controlling the Aboriginal people. He presided over the policy of removing mixed Aboriginal/European children from their homes to 'breed out the colour in them', which advocated that mixed children be removed from Aboriginal society so that they could be 'trained to work in white society'. It was believed that over generations they would eventually be subsumed into white society.

This policy was known as the Half-Caste Act (enacted in 1886), and it allowed the forcible removal of mixed-race children from their parents. This was positioned as providing the children with better homes than those affordable for typical Aboriginal people, where they could grow up with 'better prospects' – to work as domestic servants. The Northern Territory Chief Protector of Aborigines, Dr Cecil Cook, argued that 'everything necessary [must be done] to convert the half-caste into a white citizen.'[6]

We know now that the legacy of these horrific abductions – when children were forced to divorce themselves from their heritage, culture and language, and also in many cases suffered abuse at the hands of residential school custodians – lives on in survivors who have spoken out on the atrocities they witnessed and how it has detrimentally affected their mental health and their ability to form loving relationships. Devastatingly, in many cases what they suffered has also affected their willingness to continue to live.

BRITAIN'S GI BABIES, TIGER BAY AND THE ERA OF MORAL CONDEMNATION

Although they are rarely featured in historical accounts of the Second World War, roughly three million American troops passed through Britain in the period 1942–1945, and it is thought that over 200,000 of these were Black men.

There is evidence to show that right from the off the British government sought to control and restrict contact between white women and Black GIs for fear of 'the procreation of half-caste children', which would create 'a difficult social problem' according to the Home Secretary, Herbert Morrison.

To the discomfort of British Army officials and the government, many romantic unions were formed between white British women and the Black GI officers and around 2,000 mixed-race babies were born. The babies were considered to be illegitimate and the US and British Armies would not permit the couples to marry. According to African American journalist and former GI Ormus Davenport, the US Army unofficially had a 'gentleman's agreement' with the British Army which became official policy. The agreement said: 'No negro soldier or sailor will be given permission to marry any British white girl!'

The babies of these unions were considered to be illegitimate and labelled degenerate because mixedness was thought of as a 'handicap akin to physical deformity' since the children ... are neither one thing nor another and are thus badly handicapped in the struggle for life',[7] and their mothers were branded as immoral, loose, over-sexed and unpatriotic. It could be argued that in this instance the privilege of whiteness is exposed as being quite conditional. They were often pressured to give up their children by family, Church authorities and the 'Mother and Baby Homes'. This stigma continued into the 1970s, and those babies put into children's homes as a result were rarely adopted.

The presence of Black and brown people in the UK is often characterized in historical accounts as starting during the Windrush era, but in fact there were considerable pockets of immigrant communities in the 1900s, 1920s, 1930s and 1940s, from London and South Shields to Liverpool's Toxteth and Cardiff's Tiger Bay, and the aftermath of the Second World War saw arguably the most concentrated arrival of mixed-race babies.

In a period that was termed the 'era of moral condemnation', government guidance advised British women not to marry Hindu, Muslim, Chinese or Black men, and some in public office, undoubtedly spurred on by the prominence of eugenics theory at the time, even called for the introduction of anti-miscegenation laws mirroring those in South Africa. With prominent eugenicist Marie Stopes recommending the sterilization of 'Half Castes' at birth and mixed families facing State-organized interference and restrictions, including the issuing of identity cards, curfews and orders to report regularly to the police, interracial families were terrorized and their mixed-race children demonized.

After the Second World War the Foreign Office even went as far as to forcibly repatriate 1,000 Chinese sailors who had settled in Liverpool after coming to Britain in 1912 to work on the steamships. In a covert meeting in Whitehall on 19 October 1945, the government set about what they described as 'the usual steps for getting rid of foreign seamen whose presence here is unwelcome'.[8] Many of the seamen had married British women and had children and their families were never told what was happening. As the *Guardian* reports, 'most of the Chinese seamen's British wives would go to their graves never knowing the truth, always believing their husbands had abandoned them'.[9]

There seems to be a pattern here whereby society and its governing bodies have viewed mixed-heritage children as the strange product of an undesirable union, a problem to be dealt with; and in extreme scenarios, as we have seen, they have been used as an opportunity to prove a political standpoint.

UK/WESTERN ADOPTION POLICY AND THE ENDURING RELATIONSHIP BETWEEN THE RACIAL CLASSIFICATION 'MIXED' AND THE RESIDENTIAL CARE SYSTEM

During the 1970s, a particular strain of social work theory expressed a strong conviction that transracial adoption could be considered a form of genocide. The thinking was that by adopting children of colour into white homes there was a very real potential for 'Black' culture and future Black families to be killed off. The Association of Black Social Workers and Allied Professionals (ABSWAP) led this school of thought, and although it originated in the US it soon became prominent in the UK, where social workers grew increasingly reluctant to put children into adoptive or foster homes that they felt didn't reflect their race.

Transracial adoption: Transracial adoption, or interracial
adoption, describes any situation in which a family adopts a
child of a different race.

John Small was a member of the ABSWAP, an organization which in
the 1980s contributed to a radical shift in the ideological base of social
work practice. He was also the author of the chapter 'Transracial
Placements: Conflicts and Contradictions' in *Social Work with Black
Children and Their Families* by Shama Ahmed and Juliet Cheetham,
which reflects what was at the time a new ideological position under-
pinning the recruitment of Black carers and the placement of some
Black children with them. Attention to identity was incorporated into
practice guidelines for all children,[10] and legislation mandated that
due consideration be given to their race, language, religion and
culture.[11]

This ideology and policy pushed back against the 'cultural deficit
model' and prior Eurocentric assertions that Black Afro-Caribbean
family units were not fit to care for children and that it would be advan-
tageous for Black and brown children to be placed with white families,
and focused heavily on the idea that white parents could not possibly be
equipped to guide children of colour safely through childhood in a
racist society.

It was thought almost impossible that a white parent would be able
to understand and indeed combat how harmful racist messages might
be imbued through media and societal attitudes. It was believed that
white adopters and foster carers would not make an effort to comprehend how people and children of colour are truly affected by racism,
how they are racialized, and how structural prejudice and negative reactions to them outside the home might affect their experience and
development. But, most poignantly perhaps, it was suggested that transracial adoption that sent Black children to white homes would foster

cultural hegemony and strip them of their cultural identity, killing authentic Black identity, sowing confusion and preventing survival techniques from being passed on. With the turn of the century it became clear that children who were very young were being left in the care system because a match that was deemed suitable could not be found.

In 2012 Michael Gove, Secretary for Education and former Secretary of State for schools, children and families, outlined the then current government requirement that when you're matching a child with a family you must take ethnicity and race and faith into primary consideration, asserting that this should not be at the cost of children being left in care. Gove wanted to remove this requirement, and in 2014, through the Children and Families Act, he got his way. The guidance was now clear that children could be placed with prospective adopters who did not share the child's ethnicity, but instead the focus would be on who could best meet the needs of the child throughout childhood.

So while in 2023 mixed children are among the groups adopted at higher rates, reports continue to show that they are over-represented in every category of the care system – 'Children in Need', 'Looked After Children' and Children on the Child Protection register – with mixed children being on the Child Protection Register at double the rate they present in the population.[12]

Although policy and times are changing, there is evidence that paints the picture that ideology which depicts mixed children as problematic has stuck. Ideas that pathologize mixed children as problematic and as a dilemma for positioning and placement both ideologically and literally can be traced as far back as the stories of the Second World War babies born of relationships between Black American GIs and white British mothers and the government's dilemma over what to do with them. In the post-war 1940s the so-called problem was apparently of such magnitude in Britain that the Home Office proposed sending mixed-race babies born of American GIs and white British women during the war to America to be adopted by Black families:

> Policy and welfare concerns from the post-war era until today have consistently debated the question of what to do with the children of interracial relationships. The value of the brown baby as a symbol of racial harmony bears no relation to the statistics, which present the mixed children of a white mother and a Black father as most likely to enter care under the age of one year.[13]

Researchers and academics have also referenced the attitude, and in some cases prejudiced belief system, of social workers who are unable to think about mixed relationships in a positive way as another reason for increased admissions of mixed children into care, particularly those from white lone-parent families.

The origin of the portrayal of interracial relationships as dysfunctional and white mothers as societal rejects and non-legitimate mother figures for their Black mixed children is also not difficult to trace as a contributing factor to the high number of such children in care, as well as their adverse experiences. The idea that white mothers are not competent to parent children whose race is different from their own has become pathologized by social workers, to the extent that mixed children with lone white mothers are taken into care in 59 per cent of referrals, as opposed to white children with lone white mothers at 49 per cent.

MY MOTHER, THE RELUCTANT SOCIOLOGIST

Emma

When I first began reading sociology journals and the documented history of mixed-race children placed in care and about their mothers, I felt instinctively that this idea that white mothers were incapable of raising their mixed children was a clear theme. It triggered a memory of a conversation that I recall having with my mum when she was doing her Sociology degree through the Open University. I remember it vividly: she told me that when I was little there were some people that suggested to her that I be given up to the Black side of my family to bring me up and that she would somehow not be equipped to raise me, despite being my mother.

I felt that her fear around this topic was not perceived and paranoid but somehow real and valid, although at the time, I could not have put two and two together that she herself was aware of academic social theory, which would have been popular around the time of my birth.

All of this culminates in a disturbing state of affairs that gives rise to the question of whether white mothers are equipped to parent their own mixed children. After doing further research into academic thinking and policy regarding transracial adoption, fostering and placement, I felt sure that there was something in this. Something that deserved dedicated space here in this chapter.

Transracial adoption ideology presents an issue for children of mixed-race parentage for a number of reasons.

It is not possible to determine the heritage of a child based solely on their appearance; in fact more than a few reports and journal articles we've read resort to grouping all children of colour – Indian, Caribbean, African and Sri Lankan mixed children, for example – under the umbrella term 'Black'. We know that this was a common term of reference for People of Colour across the board until relatively recently, and essentially if you were not white you could be labelled 'Black' by societal bodies or institutions.

However, grouping a child in this way does present an immediate difficulty in how to place them. It may mean (particularly for a mixed child) that they could be placed with a family that is visually a good fit but culturally not so in terms of the child's true ethnicity and cultural identity, or indeed the child's experience with their previous primary caregiver.

This system is also problematic even when a child's ethnic mix is more clearly identified and used as a guide for their placement with a family. For example, a child who is Chinese and white British would likely (due to transracial adoption concerns) be viewed as best placed with a Chinese family, and a Black African/white British child would be determined as best placed with a Black family, regardless of that family's ethnic origin. The issue with this is that a mixed child may, for argument's sake, culturally identify just as much white as they do Black, or just as much white as they do Chinese. Before finding themselves in the care system, they may also have spent their formative years with their white caregiver and white family members and have very little knowledge of Black or Chinese cultural norms and traditions. They may actually identify more strongly with the cultural aspects of their early life and, given that (unlike monoracial children) their heritage and ethnicity are likely to be a mix of two or more demographic groups, it seems over-simplistic to eyeball them and categorize them by the race that is more visible at first glance.

Professor Lucille Allain describes how social workers perpetually referred to a child as Black, insisting that she was in denial about her 'Blackness' even though she was in fact of Indian and white British origin.[14] Allain notes that every time the care services tried to place her with an Indian foster family she would run away in an attempt to get back to her white biological mother, saying that she found the foster environments quite alien to her, strange and uncomfortable. Of course, this could be due to the obvious emotional trauma of being separated from a caregiver. But it could also infer that the cultural elements which were assumed to be appropriate for her were, at this point, foreign to her given her prior life experience. Who is to say that it was better to force her to adjust to a cultural landscape that was completely new to her at this stage when she had just as much claim to her white heritage as she did to her Indian one?

We see in my friend's testimony below that it was this challenge that she faced when she was put up for adoption, the only acceptable adoptive family (in the eyes of the social workers and care system) being a Black one. She felt as though she was expected to 'be Black', but she did not really know how to 'be Black'. She had no cultural references to lean on and as a result she felt much like the odd one out in so many ways at many junctures of her upbringing:

Because I was put into a Black family and I had to experience another family's culture and traditions and experiences I was told to conform rather than being able to find myself, I didn't have a choice, I was told, you're Black, you're being adopted by a Black family – we go to church on Sundays and so on. I was put in a Black newspaper to be advertised to Black people for adoption.

Speaking to other mixed people like me – they feel I am just as much white as I am Black so why would I rule out an entire part of myself … I think it's had a negative impact on how I understand myself and my identity. Purely for the fact that I was told that I was Black and I had to be adopted by a Black family so then I had siblings that were Black and I felt like the odd one out growing up. I don't think the idea to put me with a Black family was a good one. I think it was a bit unfair. I think that basically I'm just as much white as I am Black, so why would you then just completely rule out one race and tell me that I'm Black and I have to identify as Black and be raised as Black, because I'm not Black, I'm mixed race? … I don't know if they would do that now, but back then it was different.

I didn't want to tell people as a kid that I was adopted. Kids have no filter so they just say anything. So they would say things like, 'How is that your brother, he looks completely different from you? He's Black, you look white', and I had to make up stories and say he is my brother but my dad isn't my real dad and my mum had an affair and we don't talk about it … I hated people saying he's not really your brother, because he was my brother.

If I had grown up with my [biological] mum and dad then I would see it every day. I would have started off straight away knowing that I was mixed race. If I had had that experience growing up, I would have always been comfortable with myself.

I wished that I was darker when I was younger so I would blend in.

My [birth] mum wanted me to be adopted by a white person but she was told no …

(Anon, mixed Black/white British)

It seems that as the mixed-race demographic grows and post-racial theories become more widely established in pushing for an understanding of race as fluid, multiple and relational, the current paradigm by which transracial adoption is discussed and assessed may become redundant.

Race is created and reinforced by people through social practices, and it is true that race holds very real social meaning for people's experience of life despite what we know about it being a construct and not a biological reality. When it is used as the driving factor in assessing the validity of a potential relationship between caregiver and child, particularly where a mixed-race child is concerned, it serves to demonstrate a lack of understanding of the mixed identity and experience in all its unison, plurality and difference across the spectrum.

One thing that is starkly obvious to us is that the pathologization by society and social bodies of the 'problematic' nature of mixedness, of the incapability and illegitimacy of the white mother to parent her mixed child, and the demonizing of the mixed person have their roots in cynical and rather sinister historical policies connected with control, restriction and the eradication of difference. We may not witness them playing out so overtly today, but when we look closely at the care system we see the legacy of a campaign started long ago to deter interracial relationships and race-mixing and the negative stereotypes and ideology it left behind.

5.
LIVING OUR LIVES IN FULL COLOUR

One of the earlier episodes we recorded on *Mixed Up* was called 'Living Our Lives in Full Colour', not long after we had both watched the documentary about Rachel Dolezal on Netflix called *The Rachel Divide*. It was somewhat of a trigger for us to see a conversation that felt very specific to mixed-race people about identity and belonging being co-opted and hijacked to become a sensationalist story.

When we mention the name 'Rachel Dolezal' you more than likely will know who we're talking about. The image of a white woman with a curly wig (maybe braids) and overly tanned skin will pop into your mind – a white woman who, for many years, pretended she was Black.

Her story was particularly visceral because it was one of the first times that we can recall in recent history when the fluidity of race was being debated in such a public space. But there *she* was, Rachel Dolezal, a white woman – on every morning talk show, every newspaper, every radio show – speaking about how she should be allowed to choose her race.

Stay with us, because this is a concept that makes a lot of people nervous. The idea of fluidity or duality in race is something mixed people are innately familiar with. But it was painful to watch as, yet again, something that we have only spoken about among ourselves, in our private circles and our safe spaces, had become a national spectacle because of Rachel Dolezal.

Mixed people have not had the freedom to own their own stories of fluidity and of choice. We aren't able to identify ourselves or take ownership of this topic that is so inherent in our community in a way that has authenticity and nuance.

Rachel Dolezal came into the public consciousness in 2015, when she became infamous for posing as a Black woman and moving through the ranks to being the president of the local chapter of the National Association for the Advancement of Colored People in Spokane, Washington. Rachel tanned her skin and often wore braids, wigs and weaves, and she self-identified as mixed race on forms and documents over the years. Her white parents came out publicly in the local news and to local police (who were investigating her reports of a hate crime at that time) that she was their daughter. With the scrutiny and backlash that followed, she was dismissed from her position as an instructor in Africana Studies at Eastern Washington University and was removed from her post as chair of the Police Ombudsman Commission, acknowledging that she was 'born white to white parents' but maintaining that she self-identified as Black.

She was using the term 'transracial' to describe herself, and to communicate this idea of her transitioning from her former white self to being a Black woman. And when we investigated the term 'transracial' we found that it was already a legitimate reporting descriptor used to describe children who are adopted by parents who are racialized differently to them. The children are known as transracial adoptees and the families are then known as transracial families.

The transracial adoption stories that are out there are closely linked to those of mixed people, especially ones who grew up in white households. For those of us who don't have the lived experiences of transracial adoptees, what may spring to mind are images of blended families that tend to be celebrity tabloid fodder, the Jolie-Pitt family, for example, and likewise Madonna and her children. Often mixed people are held up as some kind of paragon of racial utopia, as a sign that we as a society have moved on from the racism and prejudice that has been woven into the very fabric of our modern world. The same goes for those who are within the transracial adoptee community whether they are mixed or not, and ultimately this is a mischaracterization and an idealistic form of one-dimensional storytelling.

If, like us, you were not aware of the term 'transracial' before Dolezal brought it into the wider public consciousness, another example of a transracial adoptee family depicted in popular-culture storytelling appears in NBC's *This Is Us*, which aired in 2016, which you may recognize. It follows the generations of the Pearsons (a white American family), and within it the storyline of Randall Pearson (played by Sterling K. Brown) as the family's Black adopted son.

After further research we learned that Rachel Dolezal did in fact grow up in a transracial family, with adopted Black brothers and sisters, surprisingly co-opting the term to suit her own narrative. Sadly, because of her actions, she has erased their stories (and other transracial adoptees) in the process with the media frenzy and the mockery of her use of the term that ensued. The term now almost sounds ridiculous solely because of its association with her, as the transracial community tries to claim it back. It's important to recognize that while transracial adoption stories and outcomes will vary, just as all adoption stories do, transracial adoptees can face legitimate and unique challenges that can have long-lasting negative effects on their childhoods and the forming of their identities. Living with racism from adoptive family members, a lack of diverse community or ties to the adoptee's cultural heritage can contribute to them feeling fractured or displaced.

MIXED PEOPLE'S RACIAL IDENTITY CAN BE FLUID

Despite the controversy surrounding Rachel Dolezal, her arrival in the public consciousness raises some relevant topics when it comes to mixed people and identity. We often talk about fluidity, how identity is frequently a journey, that it is possible to inhabit more than one racial identity at once and how that is both valid and an important context for others and their perception of us.

The frustration here lies in the fact that a white woman gets to wake up and decide that she is Black, based solely on feeling. In the documentary she even poses the question 'Who are the gatekeepers to Blackness?', not acknowledging that, as someone who cosplayed as a Black mixed woman her whole adult life and has mixed children, she is engaging in the most ostentatious display of white privilege, unable to see the impact of her actions on Black and mixed-race communities.

Our interviews tell us that it is fairly common for mixed people to feel they are simultaneously being judged for who they are while also having people (strangers or otherwise) label them or mislabel them. It can feel like there are few opportunities to talk about this without being dismissed or implicitly accused of exaggerating the issues, and we can only come to the conclusion that stories like Rachel's contribute to the stereotyping of mixed people and the diminishment of their stories.

The Dolezal saga plays into the idea that mixed people can't be trusted because they are 'confused' about their identity, meaning that they don't have strength of conviction in who they really are. We continue to be stereotyped as people who take up the mantle for causes only when it serves us, along with other false narratives. So many of us lack the agency to put out our 'felt' identity versus what people think they see when they look at us, and that should be something we get to take the lead on when it comes to conversations about race and identity.

A more recent example of this co-opted 'transracial identity' is that of the British media personality Oli London, a white man who was thrust into the public eye after he appeared on the documentary series *Hooked On the Look*. Oli has gone through multiple plastic surgery treatments since 2013 to look like BTS singer Jimin and was open about his goals to 'transition' into being Korean. He appeared on *This Morning* to announce his intention and debut his full racial transition surgery and described 'feeling born in the wrong body', likening this to many of the same sentiments we hear from those in the transgender community.

It's important to approach everyone's story with empathy. There is truth in what Rachel and Oli have said about themselves, in that there are so many layers to us humans and so many contributing factors to how we may identify. This is something we come back to again and again when we talk about identity – that there is always nuance.

However, it's also important to highlight that these are the types of stories which the mainstream media tend to focus on. In Oli's case it was the theatrics around his surgeries and how much money he may have spent on his 'transformation'. And as much as he was a 'fan' of Korean culture and 'loved and respected' Korea as a country, it should have been possible for him to recognize when he was feeding into racist tropes and stereotypes, that it is not possible to embark on these surgeries and modifications and popularize them without stereotyping Koreans at the same time.

It's similar to the coverage and discourse we've seen about mixed-race people in the public eye – looking at them almost through a lens of piqued interest, as something to 'figure out' or 'get to the bottom of'. The media jump on the almost 'freakishness' of the issue, and there is a lack of care as to how language and terminology can affect this group of people.

KOREA AND TRANSRACIAL ADOPTION – *HONHYŎRA MUNJE*

When you look into the history of transracial adoption, there is actually a strong through line of mixed-race Koreans (and naturally other groups with dual identities).

Mixed children were the trigger for international adoption, starting in Korea. Over 200,000 children were sent abroad to the United States, Europe and Australia in the six decades that followed the Korean War, of whom over 40,000 were mixed. During that time, Korean President Syngman Rhee reportedly referred to mixed children as 'refuse' the country needed to rid itself of, and 'the mixed-race children issue' became a campaign platform for President Rhee at that time.

In the history of both North and South Korea is a nationalism rooted in a homogenous ethnic and racial identity that emerged following Japanese colonization, commonly spoken about in academic circles then ramped up in political ideologies and dictatorships during the Korean War and the time that followed in the 1960s.

A wave of Korean and mixed Korean babies were adopted by white American parents, and now there are more Korean adoptees in the United States than any other group. In 1953 a large group of mixed Korean children were orphaned after American soldiers left Korea following the Korean War. The South Korean government worked directly with an American man, Harry Holt, who began an evangelical Christian-based adoption agency after adopting eight Korean children of his own following the war. Korea's first welfare agency, Child Placement Services, was established in the 1950s expressly to remove mixed-race children from the country.

Yuri Doolan is a historian and assistant professor at Brandeis University in Massachusetts. He was born on a US Air Force base to a white American father and Korean mother in the 1980s, spending his early childhood in Korea before his parents separated. Yuri, his mother and younger brother then settled in Ohio. His first book, *The First Amerasians: Mixed Race Koreans from Camptowns to America*, which reveals the US government's involvement in removing thousands of mixed-race children from US-occupied South Korea into adoptive American homes during the 1950s and 1960s, ultimately looking into the origins of transracial adoption:

> In this period, before the Korean War, there already were so many children born to US servicemen and legitimized by the US military. Families that actually hoped to be intact biological families. The war just exacerbated all of this, with single mothers trying to take care of their own children without their GI husbands or partners. And the war only exacerbated that it also only created more content, intimate contact, more rectory children. Still, Americans remain pretty indifferent to it and it wasn't until the mid 1950s, I would say, when the population became so discernible, and it was such a large population of mixed-race children that Americans started being kind of criticized on the international stage for their imperial behaviors and practices. And that's when America started to care and try to resolve this huge PR crisis. And how they did that was they went into the camptowns, where many of these mixed-race families were the mothers and the children, and convinced the mothers to give them up for adoption to predominantly white American families back in the US. And that was the creation of the first permanent international adoption program in the United States. And it's also like, where we get the first, so as to say, transracial family as well.

While acknowledging the pain and rejection that some South Korean transracial adoptees have felt, Yuri believes it's important to interrogate the existing narrative that it is because Korea is widely known as a homogenous society, and challenges the idea that it was solely the Koreans' decision to remove mixed Koreans from their mothers; he believes it is important to acknowledge the wider influence and impact America had on the country at that time:

> The thing to remember is, the existing narrative really is the same narrative Americans created to justify taking children from Korean mothers and placing them into American families, which, as I mentioned earlier, was a way to redeem the image of the US intervention. Because the Americans have created this problem of separating Korean American families, and racist use of immigration policies and immigration laws have also contributed to that. We really have to think about that narrative we're prescribing to.
>
> It suggests to me that there might be more to the story, and that the kinds of narratives we have today were actually shaped by those American humanitarians. And so we need to actually deconstruct them.

At that time American humanitarians were also, in large part, heavily involved in Christianity. There seems to be a religious thread that runs through the adoption and adoptee community, and it's one we have also heard from Rosemary Adaser, growing up mixed Black in Ireland as a survivor of the Catholic Mother and Baby Institutions. Yuri comments:

> A lot of the first organizations that were involved in placing mixed-race children into US families did have religious leanings: some were missionaries, and among the organizations involved in

the beginning you had the Seventh Day Adventists and the United Presbyterians and the United Presbyterian Mission, you had some Catholic organizations, and even Harry Holt, who is kind of considered 'the father of Korean adoption'. He wasn't a religious missionary himself, but he had evangelical Christian sensibilities. They actually would place them in born-again Christian homes over homes that met better financial and emotional criteria, to be able to handle adoption of this kind. Definitely a Christian religious element to it and it all played into the Savior narrative. A part of it was also saving these children from Communism, and Communism is bad news because it's the enemy of Christianity, and so they all fed into each other.

(Authors' interview with Yuri Doolan)

Becky White, co-creator and director of The Halfie Project, looks into the experiences of mixed Koreans all over the world through podcast episodes, video interviews and a newsletter, asking questions about identity. We connected with The Halfie Project in the very early stages of our podcast and had the opportunity to speak with Becky about *honhyol* (mixed blood) and mixed Korean identity:

During and after the Korean War, in the 1940s, 50s and 60s, the first generation of *honhyol* experienced such painful lives as they were seen as the living embodiments of Korea's suffering and the country's inability to protect itself from outside forces. *Honhyol* were now physical symbols of American nationalism, camptowns, women using their bodies to escape poverty, etc.

In reality there is evidence that many mixed Korean children were born from loving relationships between Korean women and American GIs, but there is such little research done about the lives of mixed Koreans that the stereotype of the first mixed Koreans being children of prostitution is still the most prevalent. They became the poster children of American saviourism and the first to be adopted to the US, rather than given a chance to become part of a new post-war Korea.

The Korean government designed this powerful idea of Korean blood purity and nationalistic pride in order to keep the country together and survive the hardships, which we must acknowledge ultimately led to the Korea we know and admire today. The first mixed Korean children were the sacrifice made to bring Korea through tough times. This concept of blood purity still lives today.

In my own lifetime I have experienced everything from complete rejection to cautious curiosity, and now I think the pendulum has swung so far, to glorification. There are more and more mixed Koreans appearing on TV, as K-pop idols, as models, etc. But even this is just praising mixed Koreans for their looks (again, primarily those who are fair-skinned) and not truly accepting us as just fellow Koreans who have lived a different way.

We have heard many times that mixed Korean children are the prettiest, the best genetically, the luckiest, have the best of both worlds etc., but marriage with a non-Korean could lead to their mixed child having a hard life. It's a strange clashing of ideas – are mixed Koreans the best? Or are they having a hard time? Which one is it? I think we're still working it out as a society.

(Authors' interview with Becky White)

WHAT ABOUT THE MIXED TRANSRACIAL EXPERIENCE?

The real stories of transracial adoptees have been almost completely erased because of the sensationalist narratives surrounding Rachel Dolezal and Oli London. Unlike Black and Asian people, they've been able to exaggerate the caricatures of race and monetize them. Being in the public eye, they are wheeled out in a way that trivializes genuine feelings around identity and displacement. Many adoptees – especially those of earlier generations – have been urged to abandon their cultures rather than celebrate them. Being encouraged to assimilate and to fit in with your adoptive family is something that transracial adoptees have had a lot of experience with.

Yuri comments:

Some of the first people to critique Rachel Dolezal's use of the word 'transracial' were adoptees themselves who had become cultural producers and scholars of the dominant rescue narratives around international adoption. They came out to remind everybody that there was already a term that existed in critical adoption studies called 'transracial' that referred to the process of these interracial families. The process of overlapping racialization that occurs, they already had a term, but it was being taken out of context and in a sensationalist way.

(Authors' interview with Yuri Doolan)

What has happened here is the co-opting of very real identities and identity struggles. Transracial adoptees and mixed people have never had the opportunity or the language with which to express themselves in ways that have been supported, nurtured or even, up until this point, noticed at all. What we in these groups have always sought is to be able to discuss the fluidity of our identities, the fluidity of race, and be allowed to choose our own identity, especially as mixed people – so often the world is doing that for us. Seeing white people afforded that space instead is crushing.

It was interesting to discover that when you are a mixed-race child adopted by white parents, particularly if you are mixed Black and white, this is also considered to be a transracial adoption.

In doing the research for this book, we found that in some reporting the terms 'Black' and 'mixed race' are used interchangeably, specifically when writing about children in the care system; and it seems to be the same in the US with the descriptors 'Black' and 'biracial'.

Looking at the history of mixed children in the care system, if you're mixed you are likely to be transracially adopted. The likelihood of you being adopted by two mixed parents is slim; the likelihood of you being adopted by one Black and one white parent, for example, is also slim.

Lizzy Kirk, whom we spoke to on the podcast, is an example of a mixed Black woman who was adopted by a white family:

> I was adopted when I was – I think I was like 6 weeks old when I was adopted. Obviously, I always knew there was never a question of not being told I was adopted because I was the only Black person in the family. I lived in a very small village and I didn't really meet another Black person until I was like 14, 15, 16 years old? … So I've just got used to being the odd one out basically.

There is a common thread of 'feeling different' and an erasure of identity for mixed-race people growing up adopted, simultaneously living in the only way they know themselves to be but also trying to understand and connect to the parts of themselves from which they may feel distant or disconnected. Lizzy also told us:

People see me as Black because that's the colour that they see. They don't see, 'She's half white and she's half Black.' They just look at me and I'm Black. So, because I had no kind of concept of my culture at all when I was young, obviously, I'm trying to be white because that's all I know ... It was really confusing 'cause people see me as Black, so they expect me to be Black ... I knew nothing about food ... the hair, the skin, the music, absolutely nothing. So I lived my life up until I was, like, 16, 17, I just tried to live as a white because that's all I knew, but no one saw me as a white person. Then when I moved to Long Eaton [Derbyshire] I was suddenly surrounded by all these Black people who are immersed in their culture ... I remember when I first moved to Long Eaton and I was so intimidated by them, I was accused of being racist to Black people.

Mixed Up *podcast, Series 2, Episode 18*

Rick Allen's story is different, as that of a mixed Black Korean man who was adopted by a Black American family when he was a baby. Most stories you read about transracial adoptees concern white or majority white families; however Rick's early life experience was with a family that looked like him and raised him as a fully Black child who felt he had no reason to question his life and upbringing until the age of sixteen.

He was born in Incheon, South Korea to a Black American GI and a Korean mother in 1980. His parents were unmarried and his father returned to the States. Rick was 'instantly surrendered' to St Vincent's Home for Amerasian Children (also known as Father Keynes). He was not there very long before he was adopted by his two Black American parents:

My father's a Black man, my mother's multiracial. She's fair-skinned, but like Black, some white, some Native American. And they were at the time living in Seoul, because my father was in the Marines. And he was stationed there. And so they adopted me and just before me they adopted another half Black, half Korean girl from the same place as me. We're not genetically related, but she's my sister. We moved to the US just a few months after my adoption. And I lived, like, a normal life, I never really thought anything was unusual, until I was 16 years old. That's when I found out about [my adoption] and, shortly thereafter, that I was half Korean. That really changed a lot of my brain chemistry where I suddenly had this missing life experience.

Rick's adoptive parents were going through their divorce when he was 16 and he was living with his mother when she asked him to scan some legal documents. In those documents he discovered that he and his eldest sister were adopted and his youngest sibling was the biological child:

Growing up, we were into a lot of Black stuff and I didn't feel like that was, like, that was like missing, you know? So the Korean half was this pot that was completely unfilled. And it actually took me some time to really start filling it, to really feel like that's what I wanted to do.

Rick describes this process of immersing himself into Korean culture and discovering more about himself as a 'gentle avalanche':

It wasn't everything all at once. Things started trickling in and then suddenly it was like a flowing stream. Transracial adoptees, specifically, are on different timelines when it comes to how or when we talk about and dive into the culture of our birth. Because for some it's, like, super-late, and for some it's really early. I don't know where I would be if I had known [earlier]. If my parents had sat me down when I was 5 and said, 'Hey, this is who you are. You're adopted.' Would I have wanted to then do it? It's impossible to answer questions. I think the way this all unfolded is why I'm here now.

Rick's parents went into the adoption process knowing they wanted to adopt mixed-race children because they were underserved and under-privileged.

We wouldn't have had the same rights when it came to things like on a schooling level. And this is why there was a home [an orphanage], at least one home that was just mixed kids, and that's where we [my sister and I] were.

(Authors' interview with Rick Allen)

Research has been conducted into, and reports written on, the United States' racial identification processes that were brought in and then institutionalized by South Korea at this time, as Yuri mentioned – in particular the segregation of mixed-race children that Rick describes, and the pathologization of mixed Black children as 'social handicaps', ultimately forcing the hands of Korean mothers to give them up.

HOW CULTURAL APPROPRIATION HARMS MIXED-RACE PEOPLE

Rachel Dolezal did an interview with TMZ defending Oli London and saying that what he does isn't cultural appropriation. She said:

> Cultural appropriation is very different from just being authentically yourself. So being true to yourself is a very different journey and experience than stealing somebody's culture in order to profit or gain from it. There's a different thing there, and I think sometimes people are confusing those two.[1]

There is a false equivalence to Rachel's argument. Cultural appropriation is very different from being authentically yourself, but she's completely ignoring the fact that what she and Oli have done has been to profit from marginalized people's cultures and repeatedly cause them harm by invalidating their stories.

Dolezal was given a book deal and published her book, *In Full Color: Finding My Place in a Black and White World*, in 2017, rewarding the controversy that swirled around her in 2015. She profited from it and undertook multiple speaking engagements, none of which she would have had without this very public cultural appropriation.

Most importantly, at the end of the day this is all costume. It's cosplay. Whether or not you have had surgery, you can essentially take off your 'guise' should it not suit you, should it no longer be trendy or celebrated in the mainstream, while the rest of us have to continue as we are.

White public figures like Rachel Dolezal have modelled themselves off the ambiguity and are able to get away with it. And 'ambiguity' is a word that is always associated with mixed-race people, giving rise to the fallacy that they themselves can also take off their costumes – society doesn't like any levels of uncertainty or unticked boxes.

There are so many mixed people to whom we have spoken who cannot relate to the 'desire' or 'trend' to be perceived as racially ambiguous that white people in mainstream media have taken on. In the conversations we've had on our podcast and within the pages of this book, we've found that what most mixed-race people want is, ultimately, to be seen as their whole selves and to be identified by the groups they belong to. Rick said:

There's often an assumption about [transracial adoptees] being whitewashed and often it is something that the adoptee him- or herself is struggling with, because many of us were adopted into, like, white homes. And, and, you know, we live in a lot of situations in [majority-] white worlds. We're surrounded by white people all the time, and expected to fit in, and that is just like a downhill slope of trauma. Because, you know, then at some point most of us break free from that.

And then now we're, like, living in [between] because we don't know how to be Korean or Chinese or Black because there's no one around to teach us. We oftentimes have to deal with a cultural reckoning as transracial adoptees. And most of the people in our lives don't know what to do with it.

(Authors' interview with Rick Allen)

Rick said that seeing Rachel Dolezal and Oli London for the first time made him realize that co-opting and misappropriation of race, and specifically race-related issues, was always out there, and that he recognized it more as time went on. Cultural appropriation and cosplay further stigmatize the mixed-race community as duplicitous, deceitful and confused when it tries to refer to fluidity and ultimately delegitimizes its stories. These stereotypes only further intimidate mixed people into censoring and refraining from voicing the discrimination that they may be facing, and certainly prohibit the healthy navigation of identity growth and change over time.

Rachel Dolezal and Oli London's actions and the media fanfare around them make a mockery of the mixed and transracial community's lived experiences and ultimately derail a conversation which needs to be had – and from which the wider world would benefit.

6.
BEAUTY STANDARDS

'Were you ugly or were you a POC who grew up in a predominantly white environment?'

NICOLE

I remember coming across this question on my TikTok 'For You' page one day and simultaneously bursting into laughter but also feeling like everything had suddenly clicked into place.

I grew up never feeling beautiful, even in moments where I was supposed to – my birthday parties, my homecoming dance, my prom, my graduation … As touched on in Chapter 1, growing up in a majority-white neighbourhood and majority-white school meant that I felt ugly most of the time. And even if the feeling wasn't just 'ugly', the comparison to my white friends meant that I would almost always lose out every time because I inherently knew that how I looked, even at my best, paled in comparison to how beautiful they could be.

It was a different time in the late 1990s and early 2000s – but I imagine if you rarely come across anyone who looks like you, or you rarely have moments when your beauty is affirmed and celebrated, or if you don't celebrate yourself, then that will have an impact on your psyche and your self-confidence.

Writing about beauty and 'attractiveness' is a tricky area: despite how subjective it is, there are mainstream ideals of beauty that we have had ingrained in us from childhood – what we have grown up watching on our screens or even had articulated directly to us by friends and family.

It feels wrong to place importance on something that feels frivolous, but as writer and theatre performer Travis Alabanza told us, gender and race are linked to power:

> All of our choices about gender are linked to race because it is linked to power. We know that we're more powerful, the more successful man or woman we are. We can access more power, dependent on the more, quote, unquote, 'beautiful' we look, and we know that beauty isn't separate from whiteness and race.
>
> Mixed Up *podcast, Season 3, Episode 2*

WHICH IS IT? 'RACIAL AMBIGUITY' OR 'BLACKFISHING'?

I never thought I'd see the day when being labelled as 'racially ambiguous' would categorize you automatically as more attractive to men or the wider media.

Growing up in the 90s, being mixed and being perceived as 'palatable' was never something that entered my consciousness. Especially at that age, when you are a child, that is not something that you're thinking about. I'd even say that in the 90s this wasn't a concept that I'd heard of, even as a child or a teenager and young adult. It certainly wasn't something I could perform for attention or 'wield' to be seen as sexy.

We are now living in a world where white women are buying darker shades of foundation in order to make sure their faces match their tans. The amount of YouTube 'get ready with me' videos on the subject are endless. It's both fascinating and slightly disturbing to watch how this has evolved over time.

We are also living in the era of the mixed race 'Instagram model', a stereotype rife within the influencer community that views mixed-race, light-skinned women as attention-seeking and allowed to ascend through presenting as 'racially ambiguous'. We've even begun to see white women cosplaying with this so-called 'racially ambiguous' aesthetic in order to notch up their beauty credibility; the Kardashian-Jenner clan immediately springs to mind.

But of course, being an early adopter of the Internet – my constant social media use means that I remember the day when the term 'black-fishing' was born on Twitter. Wanna Thompson, a writer and cultural critic, noticed this trend of white women donning what is now perceived as the modern-day blackface. Emma Hallberg, a twenty-something Instagram model, featured in Wanna's thread and became infamous after a few Black women who were following her realized that she wasn't Black or mixed race at all; she is in fact white.

The thread featured images of Hallberg with a significantly darker skin tone, in stark contrast to what she looked like when she was several years younger. The difference was very noticeable. That, combined with the overall aesthetic that she adopted from Black women – wigs and weaves, acrylic nails, heavy monograms – meant that you could quickly see how her followers could make the assumption that she was someone who was at the very least of mixed origins. After receiving a barrage of criticism from her followers and the general public, she quickly garnered media attention. In an interview with BuzzFeed News in 2018, she denied using self-tanner or spray tans, saying she never 'claimed or tried to be Black or anything else'. Hallberg also said 'I do not see myself as anything else than white [...] I get a deep tan naturally from the sun.'[1]

Australian rapper Iggy Azalea also came under fire on social media for blackfishing when screenshots of her music video 'I Am the Strip Club' were shared. In it her skin tone looks significantly darker than usual and she is wearing a black wig; when criticized on social media, she cited the room being 'dimly lit' with red lighting as the reason.

Jesy Nelson left Little Mix to start her solo career in 2021 and appeared back on the music scene with her debut single, 'Boyz'; she was met with strong criticism not only for using Black men and dancers as props in her video but for blackfishing overall.

After that music video aired we were surprised to find that many of our white friends thought Jesy was mixed. Meanwhile, there are already two mixed-race women in that band, Leigh-Anne Pinnock and Jade Thirlwall, both of whom have been open about the backlash and criticism they received within their industry and even from their own fans about their racial identity. Leigh-Anne specifically brought out her own BBC documentary, *Leigh-Anne: Race, Pop and Power*, having felt she had not been given the space to speak publicly about her experience of being mixed race while being in one of the most popular girl groups.

And this doesn't just stop with skin tone and hair texture. The BBL (Brazilian butt lift) is one of the fastest-growing cosmetic surgery options globally. The goal is to have a rounder bum and tiny waist, a body type most commonly associated with Black women and now made famous in the mainstream by the likes of Kim Kardashian (who, however, denies having had her bum augmented).

Hourglass body shapes, loose curls (but also straight hair), tan skin (but not too dark), long nails – this is what we know comes from the Black aesthetic and the 'video vixens' back when they used to air music videos on MTV. Even the style of clothes, now referred to as 'BBL fashion' – all cut-outs, bodycon and contour – came from Black women but were popularized in the white celebrity mainstream. The overall goal seems to be to look racially ambiguous, to be able to pick and choose the bits of non-whiteness that are deemed desirable by society's ever-changing standards.

The wider impact of this is that mixed-race people too – women in particular – have been called out for blackfishing because of how they look. In 2020, a mixed Black girl, Rachael Brown, was accused on Twitter of blackfishing because of her skin tone and her blonde hair and the story was picked up by the wider media during the time of the Black Lives Matter resurgence. She had to publicly explain her heritage; something that would have looked obvious to most is now being conflated with white people getting a heavy tan.

Surveying the landscape of beauty and aesthetics, it seems as though the common physical markers of our ethnicities have become popularized through 'beauty trends'. This is a further example of how 'blackfishing' impacts the wider mixed-race community with stereotypes of being duplicitous or deceitful – being able to put on a costume, or to 'perform' an ethnicity.

But this type of beauty appropriation doesn't just happen with the Black aesthetic.

The 'fox eye' make-up trend became increasingly popular in recent years after being seen on the likes of models including Bella Hadid and Kendall Jenner. The look is essentially based on the traditional cat-eye winged liner, but also involves pulling one's hair and skin back to elongate the eye shape – looking very similar to those of East Asian heritage. This trend went viral on TikTok and became popular enough to be offered as an option by plastic surgeons for a more permanent look.

Anita Bhagwandas, award-winning journalist and beauty editor, who has been working in the industry for over fifteen years for major titles including *Glamour*, *Allure* and *Stylist*, is also the author of *Ugly: Giving Us Back Our Beauty Standards*. She said she had often noticed the racialization of beauty trends appearing among beauty influencers as well as on the beauty pages of magazines and online:

> This has definitely been a shift in the last five to ten years and I think it's because of social media – in particular TikTok … trends happen before those following or creating them realize they're actually culturally insensitive or appropriative.
>
> Cosmetic surgery and aesthetics has become much more popular in the last decade, but it has always prized Eurocentric beauty and Caucasian features as the pinnacle of what's attractive. More recently surgical trends like the 'fox eye' appear to recreate a monolid shape (that many from East Asian heritages have), and it's a case of the cosmetic surgery industry jumping on trends to capitalize and not caring about appropriation.
>
> The issue always is that these features might have been the subject of bullying or taunts for somebody from that heritage, but a white person who got a 'fox eye' wouldn't be party to the same abuse.
>
> *(Authors' interview with Anita Bhagwandas)*

While the aesthetics of our bodies become pushed out into the mainstream as 'trends', these same aesthetics are often the ones we are shamed for by our peers, possibly those close to us, and even people we don't personally know. Meanwhile, white beauty standards are simultaneously imposed on mixed people as the beauty standard. However, when you have multiple backgrounds, it can become an exercise in ticking boxes to look like the groups that you already belong to.

WHAT DOES IT EVEN MEAN TO LOOK 'AMBIGUOUS'?

Emma Breschi, a Filipino-Italian model and actress, told us that it is almost standard practice for her to be 'told' who she is and what she looks like during castings for her work:

> The weirdest part about being mixed is everyone else has their own idea of what they believe you are ... if that makes any sense? The amount of castings or jobs I've gone on, and had a white person tell me what they think I am, versus accepting what I actually am – which is a mixed-race woman.
>
> It's always: 'Wow, where are you from? I can't quite put my finger on it ...'
>
> To which I would say: 'I'm half Filipino, half Italian.'
>
> 'Ah, see I would have never said that, you look more Indian to me.' Or 'Really? 'Cause I would've put you down as Middle Eastern' Or 'Cor, I would've never thought Filipino, you look more Latina to me.' Or 'Filipino, what is that!? Oh really, is it Asian?'
>
> No wonder why I've got a severe identity crisis at times!
>
> I think it's also interesting how certain people, even within POC groups, will tell me what I am or what I'm not.
>
> I've had some people in the industry try to police me in how I even choose to identify myself. When I say I'm mixed race, they're like – 'Well you're not because you're basically white.'
>
> *(Authors' interview with Emma Breschi)*

BEAUTY BASED ON YOUR LOCATION AND YOUR LOCAL COMMUNITY'S BEAUTY IDEALS

Jenni Rudolph is a singer-songwriter and the co-founder of the LUNAR Collective, a community for Asian American Jews. Jenni is Cantonese and Jewish American, and she shared with us her experience of growing up being seen solely as a Chinese girl and looking different from her sisters, and how that impacted how she felt about her own beauty:

I grew up in Huntington Beach, California, which is not only a very predominantly white area but also historically has ties to white supremacism and neo-Nazis, and white power rallies are hosted there.

The culture is very icky and not my thing, and very not conducive to having a very confident, proud, mixed multicultural identity ... I didn't really have a connection to being Asian aside from appearing Asian and denying it when people would ask me ... [I didn't pretend] I wasn't Asian, but just kind of not wanting to be Asian and trying to shut down people's assumptions.

People would see me, and then they would see my white dad, and be like, oh, are you adopted? And what kind of made that worse is that I have two younger sisters ... and the two of them have always been very ethnically ambiguous-looking. So I have many years of photos where my skin is like ten shades darker than them. So I can understand, looking at these photos, why people would be confused on how we're related.

This brought up a ton of feelings of shame and internalized racism. For me, when I was young, I really did not want to be Asian.

Mixed Up *podcast, Season 4, Episode 3*

Jenni talked about colourism and how she internalized negative feelings about how dark her skin was when she was younger. How she wished for curly hair and lighter skin. This brings us full circle to the beginning of the chapter, because undoubtedly the white, Californian, right-wing community Jenni grew up in would have influenced her perspective on her own beauty, which in her view was certainly far from any mixed aspirational ideal. Your geographical location and environment can completely change how your 'beauty' is perceived and how you experience it.

Zuleika Lebow is Jamaican and Ashkenazi Jewish – her father came to the United Kingdom as part of the Windrush Generation. He was an academic, a Marxist scholar and author, and one of the founders of the Black Unity and Freedom Party as well as the radical journal *The Black Liberator*. She spoke about what it feels like to be told she is both 'white-passing' and 'racially ambiguous' as a mixed Black light-skinned woman with ginger hair and freckles. She said both of those things come 'with intense privilege as well as harassment':

The phrase I have heard the most is 'You look exotic', and what is interesting about that phrase is that it is a blanket statement that is highly culturally relative. In Jamaica, Brazil or any other country where there is a lot of mixing I am not remotely 'exotic'. I happen to be a mixed Black woman with pale skin and reddish hair, which is unusual but not anomalous.

In the UK it's very different: I am questioned about my heritage, I get stared at by people trying to work out where I am from, I receive intrusive questions, people try to touch my hair and don't believe me if I say I haven't had a curly perm or that it's not a wig, I have been asked if I bleach my skin and what products I use to get it so white.

Zuleika says that she gets comments from both Black and white people, and is conscious of how class affects how she is received and perceived:

> Saying all this, I move through the world very differently to my siblings with darker skin and I am well aware of that privilege. There's also an intersection of class here that is important to mention; the way that we interpret race in this country [the UK] has so much to do with class and behaviour. Both of my parents being university-educated and being middle-class has a lot to do with the way I move through the world and impacts the way I present to others, including the way I speak.
>
> When I was younger, I didn't necessarily have the language to articulate any of this, and I didn't completely realize the privilege and responsibility that come with benefiting from colourism as a mixed person.
>
> A lot of the issues I had were the opposite: not being recognized as Black or feeling like I had to prove my Blackness a lot, wishing I was darker-skinned so I could be more recognizable as a mixed Black person. It took me until I was about 26 to begin to be comfortable with the idea that how others perceive me isn't my business, and that recognition (or lack thereof) of my Blackness or Jewishness should not affect my relationship with my culture. I am still healing from a lot of the rejection I experienced from both sides of my heritage in that regard, but I think seeing more content creators who are mixed and who share similar experiences helps a lot.
>
> *(Authors' interview with Zuleika Lebow)*

Zuleika makes reference to there being a very specific context that dictates how her beauty or aesthetic is received and therefore how much she might be admired or harassed, based on where she might be in the world, based on which community she finds herself in. Because, of course, there are both local and global beauty standards at play.

Layla Hatia is a Muslim woman of Gujarati and English descent who grew up in Gloucester in a very close-knit Gujarati community:

> I was the result of a very controversial relationship between my mum and her secret English boyfriend. As many of these stories go, my biological father didn't really stick around to see me grow up. I was raised in my grandparents' home alongside my aunts and uncles. It was a huge deal back then, I was very obviously not a fully Indian baby. My mum's indiscretion couldn't be hidden with a lie, it was obvious for the whole community to see. What was incredible is how my grandparents did not let that deter them and they raised me in their home with love and pride.

Being fairer-skinned with light hair, Layla says that people often assume she is fully white English, Turkish, Irish or Iranian:

> As a child and a teenager I was often sent to the 'white people table' at an Indian wedding, which normally consisted of the bride or groom's work friends, to check they were OK and didn't need more food. I hated it, but the people around me didn't understand why I would hate being the white people's envoy. To me it reinforced the feeling that I wasn't like everyone else, I was different and it was the first thing people could see. To them it was funny and just a way to palm off a crappy job on to a younger relative.
>
> I identify with my Muslim Indian heritage. I have very little to do with the English side. Yet I am 'white passing' so I'm afforded the associated privilege. It's very confusing even as a 35-year-old.

When it comes to beauty and growing up in a predominantly Gujarati household, Layla describes what it felt like being a child and wanting to look like the rest of her family. And how even in the present day, looking 'white passing' makes her feel like she often has to explain her presence:

> I have a really strong memory from when I was probably 6 or 7 years old, sitting quietly in a corner trying to felt-tip my red hair black. I was desperate to look like the rest of my family.
>
> Honestly, if I could look more like my family I would. I'd like to walk into a mosque/wedding etc. and not have to explain my presence. It's a weird one because I understand British society and how members of my family face prejudice for the colour of their skin or for being clearly identifiable as coming from a Muslim background. Even Indian culture itself prizes fair skin – close members of my family face discrimination for not being fair enough. Yet I still wish people would identify me as Indian and Muslim. It's a paradox.
>
> *(Authors' interview with Layla Haita)*

In communities of colour it's not uncommon for there to be a focus on 'favouring' those with a lighter skin tone, and there can of course be benefits for mixed-race people who have fairer skin or who ultimately look like they would fall within the Western ideal of beauty. Anita Bhagwandas comments:

> The message it sends is that you'll never be beautiful unless you're white – and it erases People of Colour from the conversation. It's also hugely insensitive when people still live with the trauma and the inherited trauma of being persecuted for the colour of their skin – we're still impacted by the effects of slavery, colonization and partition.

The message that is being passed down, not just through the mainstream media but also through inherited generational community ideals, is a heavy burden for women – who, we could argue, feel they are often in a state of performance in terms of femininity, beauty being its cornerstone. So when beauty trends shift and cherry-pick these racial elements – hair texture, skin tone, the contour of the eye, the fullness of the lip – mixed women are left right there at the intersection, being accused of putting on a costume.

Mixed-race women are often placed smack in the middle of notions of performance or 'passing' because of Western beauty standards, the conflation between being mixed and being 'exotic', and the hierarchical value that whiteness and proximity to whiteness holds in our society. There is an inherent interest in and curiosity about our appearance – why do we look this way? How is it possible? Even before we are born there is speculation about our hair texture and skin colour, all of it up for public debate. But the reality is that most mixed-race people grow up feeling as though it is impossible to live up to any one beauty ideal.

DIFFERENT CULTURES WITH CONFLICTING BEAUTY IDEALS

I was constantly told to stay out of the sun so I wouldn't get too dark and had my nose pinched by my Filipino family so that my nose bridge wouldn't 'grow too wide'. But then I was also told by my Ghanaian family that I didn't eat enough and that I needed to grow into my body, not be too skinny, while being told by all of wider society that my body was too big and that it needed shrinking down. At times we come from cultures that have completely conflicting beauty ideals, rendering it impossible for us to fit into the metaphorical box.

I internalized these areas of lack – these areas where I was not enough of one thing or another, parts of me where I was too much – to mean that I was ugly. In a society that is consistently trying to reduce you down to being one thing and when you are shown that you are outside of the beauty ideal, it's unsurprising to make that connection within yourself.

Growing up in between these aesthetics, how you feel about the way you look is shaped by how other people perceive you, by your environment. Who praises you? Who makes you feel ugly? There are multiple factors, which may also play out against the backdrop of a largely Western-skewed view of what is attractive and pleasing.

These women's stories show that, whether or not there is love and support from your family and encouragement of how you look, there can be external factors that plague your perception of your own beauty and attractiveness.

Dr Melissa J. Wagner told us about how she was made to feel ugly in her own family and how she never felt beautiful growing up in a predominately white household and society:

> I was never made to feel beautiful by my mother. I was never made to feel beautiful by any of the white people. I knew there was something wrong with me. I grew up, you know, feeling very, very ugly. And then, you know, it got to this point and of course, well, like my mother couldn't deal with my hair, so she chopped my hair off and I was, I dunno, 4, I think.
>
> I never felt, I never felt good-looking. I mean, maybe I'm not, I don't know, but I mean, I never grew up feeling that I looked right, and that was primarily [from] white folks.
>
> Mixed Up *podcast, Season 2, Episode 8*

Melissa's experience of being made to feel ugly by her mother, never feeling attractive or 'right', is a result of growing up in the late 1960s and early 70s, when people did not trust interracial mixing and rhetoric was being pushed out that Black and brown people migrating to the UK were polluting England. Those Black and brown people were invited to come for economic reasons, and the result is the mixed-race children whom political figures like Enoch Powell were condemning at the time.

Fast-forward to today and there is an abundance of anecdotal evidence of women who want 'mixed babies', almost as though they are a trend in themselves, or an accessory to be bought. I've seen the hashtags on social media, which I understand on the level of wanting to find families that look like yours; but they have evolved into entire Instagram pages dedicated to mixed babies where images of your child can be featured. There is something voyeuristic and perverse about scrolling through these accounts: not only do they show an endless stream of children, but I notice that in some instances their faces are put through the same whitewashed filters (which automatically lighten your skin and narrow your nose) and apps in order to enhance their features or to make their attributes appear more European. If this is what we are seeing happen to babies, it's no wonder that mixed-race adults feel fetishized as well.

The contemporary idealization of mixedness sets your value purely on how you look, your proximity to whiteness being what society values most of all and perceives your beauty to derive from.

* * *

I only joined Tinder for a brief summer after a bad break-up, back when it was the only dating app available (look at me showing my age!). There I was subjected to a barrage of hyper-sexual, racist messages, fetishizing me in ways I had never had to encounter before. There were the subtle references to my skin tone, but also the overt messages like, *Never having been with a Black girl before, is it true what they say?* And if the conversation ever got far enough for them to know that I'm also mixed Asian, they immediately wanted to know if I was submissive.

More recently, as I embark on another journey into the depressing world of dating apps, I'm open about my mixed heritage because I am proud of it. I hope that it can be a sign of kinship to both Filipinos and Ghanaians alike, to mixed-race men in general or anyone who has ever been to either of those countries. But, unfortunately, being open to it means being fetishized and my mix becomes 'the reason' I am beautiful to men – and I know this because they tell me. *No wonder you're so attractive. Mixed genetics is the future of our species.* Yes, that's an actual message from a man.

It's exhausting and demoralizing, and to be brutally honest, at times it can prey on the deepest insecurities that I have had about myself. All I ever wanted to feel was proud of myself, feel beautiful, feel seen, feel wanted – and when you are fetishized or eroticized in this way you find it hard to understand what else anyone sees about you. You start to believe that is the only thing you have that's valuable, the only thing you have to offer.

This is a topic that many of us who identify as women can relate to. However, we have also had men on our podcast give us their perspective. Ben Bailey Smith, aka Doc Brown, told us that he was fetishized as a mixed-race young man growing up:

> You become an object of fascination … people want to sample you like you're some kind of free flavour of ice cream on a coupon day at the ice cream store … and it's way worse for mixed girls, especially with some of the language we use around them, it's very objectified in the worst way.
>
> But I can say, before I was in a relationship I've had more than one occasion where things were getting hot and steamy and I had to fucking walk away because of certain things that were said in the moment … 'Oh, I've always wanted to try one of these!' I'm not one of these.

I've also had, 'Oh, I've always been scared of an actual [Black man]' ... like I'm some kind of entry-level Black.

Mixed Up *podcast, Season 2, Episode 20*

Historically, Black men and women have been sexualized because of their physical attributes and stereotyped as being 'well endowed' and 'good in bed'. This is something we also touch on in Chapter 6.

In series 4 of *Love Island* there were two white contestants, Ellie Brown and Georgia Steel, who said that their 'type' was mixed-race men. This was startling: it was a dog whistle moment when once again someone's personhood was minimized. It's what Ben describes above: your level of attractiveness is seen only in terms of the parts of you that are 'other' or 'exotic' because they are different from what society deems the standard. So often this is dismissed as a preference or a type, but there is nothing complimentary about being chosen because of a reductive and lurid stereotype.

It's a given that we all want to be seen as beautiful. However, no one desires to be fetishized or sexualized to the point where they are no longer recognized as human beings: this is not something mixed people aspire to, especially in adolescence.

As Rosemary Adaser told us:

There's this idea that somehow because we have some mixedness in us, there's an element of privilege. Therefore, if we do get the odd bit of racism, well, frankly we should shut up about it because it's never gonna be as bad ... It irritates me because when I'm walking down the street, nobody says, 'Oh, there's that pretty little mixed-race woman.' What they see is a Black woman, first and foremost, to a racist. Any kind of colouring in your skin is seen as Black.

And what I suppose for a lot of mixed-race people it is about recognizing that. Perhaps for some other members of the Black community – racism is real, but it's just as real for us. *It's just as real for us.* And there is colourism, even within the mixed-race community, there is colourism … if you're very fair-skinned, then you're going to have an easier ride than somebody with a darker skin tone. And I'll be honest with you, I think that is the case. That is the case, but that still doesn't mean that that light-skinned girl is not experiencing very perturbing actions directed at her, perhaps even more so precisely because she's light skinned with 'good hair'. And certainly when I came over to London in the seventies as a Black Irish woman, I got as much abuse from Black people in London as I did from the Irish people. And that was specifically about my mixedness.

Mixed Up podcast, Season 3, Episode 9, Black History Month:
Rosemary Adaser on Surviving Ireland's Mother and Baby
Institutions and the Untold History of the Incarceration
of Mixed-race Children.

COLOURISM RESULTS IN SKIN BLEACHING

The impact of colourism has resulted in the emergence of skin-lightening and skin-bleaching practices and cosmetics across the globe. In particular, beauty products are marketed to countries in Africa and Asia where people have been conditioned to believe that the closer to whiteness you are, the more beautiful, the more successful you will be, the more opportunities you will have.

There is a long history of skin-lightening practices that dates back to ancient times across the different continents. The popularity of these products increased by the twentieth century, and while white people in the United States and Europe were enjoying beauty trends like tanning beds in the 1960s, African and Asian countries were being marketed skin lightening.

Looking back through history, it quickly becomes clear how parts of the world that were colonized by Western nations have been afflicted by the beauty standard. Countries like South Africa, for example, with its clear history of apartheid, have been moulded by the segregation of People of Colour as well as their hierarchical ranking within those groups, meaning that even the slightest difference in shade can benefit you or make your life more difficult. Likewise in India, while the caste system is rooted in ancient Indian beliefs and has its part to play, the modern constitution was shaped by the collapse of the Mughal era and the rise of the British colonial government in the country, which handed down white European beauty standards.

Since starting the podcast and writing this book, we have often felt as if colourism has been a tool used by white supremacy to keep us women divided within a hierarchy of aesthetics – and that this is a direct effect of colonization.

Tabitha Corsin is a Tamil beauty content creator and model. While she is not mixed race, she speaks to the experience of being a darker-skinned Asian woman who has grown up experiencing colourism within the South Asian community:

It's something that has affected me for most of my life, I would say. Growing up as a darker-skinned Tamil woman in particular, I've definitely been bombarded with many comments telling me that I'd look even prettier if I was fair-skinned, or that I was 'pretty for a darker-skinned girl' – such a backhanded compliment, which I now see is actually an insult. I've also had plenty of 'skin-lightening' solutions and unsolicited advice from those around me to help me 'not get any darker'; some of these would include discouragement from going out in the sun in case I'd catch a tan, or advice to not wear so many bright colours as they wouldn't suit me.

Having darker skin has always been such a negative in South Asian society – as well as among family members. I also feel like having the South Asian media/advertising/cinema industries pushing this narrative has definitely affected how I saw myself growing up.

A study done by the International Women's Journal of Dermatology (2023), to look into the attitudes of colourism and usage of skin lightening products among American women of colour found that rates of skin lightening vary globally: 27 per cent in South Africa, 77 per cent in Nigeria, 40 per cent in South Korea and China. The report found that skin lightening and bleaching are a threat to consumers because of ingredients leading to adverse health consequences with long-term use and a lack of medical input. Mercury, hydroquinone and steroids are the most harmful ingredients often found in skin-lightening merchandise around the world.[2]

* * *

Having shopped in Black hair shops (most often not owned by Black people) to find my hair products, there have been times when I have received samples of skin-lightening products in my bag mixed in with other sample products. I remember being shocked the first time, thinking that surely this was something that didn't happen now, in the present day, and that products like this, specifically targeted as skin-lighteners, had disappeared from the shelves; but unfortunately that isn't the case.

When I've visited family in Ghana and the Philippines the skin-lightening products are rife, and at times it's hard to tell whether there are actually ingredients in the products that can contribute to actual skin bleaching, or if the branding and marketing are just using the phrases 'white', 'bright' and 'pure'. I felt at risk just trying to buy a face cleanser because the majority of the products on the shelves had that same messaging printed all over.

While in the United States these creams have been regulated by the Food and Drug Administration since the 1930s and are less commonly used there and in Europe, their popularity has boomed in the Asia-Pacific region. The global market for skin-lightening products is an expanding and largely unregulated multi-billion-dollar global industry with women constituting 80 per cent of the market worldwide.

Skin-bleaching products are most popularly used in the form of creams (side effects include skin irritation, blue-black discolouration and blindness), but now come as injectables and digestible tablets (side effects include kidney and thyroid disease). They are being sold today and can easily be purchased online. Skin-bleaching creams that contain ingredients including mercury, hydroquinone, and/or corticosteroids which have not been prescribed by a doctor are banned in the UK and the United States because of the serious side effects.[3]

What comes to mind when reading about these skin-bleaching products, seeing what primarily women of colour are purchasing, what is being illegally brought into countries like the United States, the United Kingdom and across Europe, is the intersection of sexism, racism and capitalism. How we are taught to believe that we can only be beautiful if we are lighter. How this breeds self-hatred. And how, if we just purchase this product, it will change everything; our lives will be easier because we will be seen as more beautiful – even if that product could potentially damage our internal and external organs and ultimately our lives in the process.

POPULAR MIXED-RACE BEAUTY ICONS AND THE FOCUS ON WHITENESS AS A PREREQUISITE FOR BEAUTY ACROSS THE MEDIA

When you do a Google Image search for a 'mixed-race woman' you come across a clear pattern of predominantly mixed women who represent a Black and white mix, which we feel has become the generalization for what people mean when they talk about mixed-race people. We know that being mixed can cover a broader range of heritages. It is simply impossible for any of us to look exactly the same, but this has become the standard that has been set in people's minds.

In terms of mixed-race beauty standards, it's hard to see how there could even be a standard to live up to, given just how broad the spectrum is. However, the mixed-race women we have grown up with in the media, particularly in the 1980s and 90s, including the likes of Thandiwe Newton, Halle Berry, Lisa Bonet and Mel B, had many thinking that being mixed embodies being Black and white.

The lack of diverse representation among mixed-race people in general also had us trying to fit in within our own 'standard' of beauty and falling short – especially those of us who don't have any white parentage to speak of.

When speaking to some of the mixed women who are not of Black and white heritage, we also questioned some of the ideas we hear in the mainstream about mixed-race beauty being what we should aspire to. What are we unwittingly limited to by only seeing Black and white mixes held up as examples of beauty on our screens? What does that standard of beauty look like within your ancestral home?

When we spoke to Claire Yurika Davis, who starred in the first series of *Next in Fashion*, we asked her about beauty standards and the idolization of fair and light-skinned Asians:

Because the thing is, yeah, when it comes to East Asians, East Asians will accept you if you are half Asian, but you better be white Asian. Otherwise you're not getting in the club at all. And I've always talked about this 'cause it's annoying.

Especially in the fashion industry, you'll get, you know, people who have done a piece and I see loads of my friends in this article or whatever, like '10 East Asian Creatives That You Should Follow' or something specifically about Japanese people. And there's someone who's got like one-sixtieth Japanese through marriage or some bullshit and they're featured on the front page and I'm like, 'Hello?' Like you didn't even think that I was also Asian, even though I've told you.

The face of being Asian aesthetically needs to be white for these people ... Because I think that for a lot of Asian people, it's much easier to accept somebody and be on the side of somebody who is light-skinned, white passing or fully Asian-looking than someone who isn't because they're like, 'Well, you are definitely not in the club. You don't look like us.'

Mixed Up *podcast, Season 1, Episode 3*

Ultimately there seems to be a level of fascination behind your 'beauty' or 'attractiveness' that is linked to your mix, and mixed-race people's beauty is consistently reduced to proximity to whiteness, perpetuating this awful cycle. Anita Bhagwandas told us:

I'd felt ugly as long as I can remember. I was first fat-shamed at a children's party aged 4, was told my friend couldn't play with me because I was brown, and like many children of colour experienced a stream of macro- and microaggressions growing up. So for me, beauty was always about trying to be as pretty as I could. I'd spend all my money and time looking for ways to be pretty, as determined by the teen magazines I read in the 1990s where everyone was thin and white – as were all the pretty, popular girls at school and the celebrities everyone aspired to.

I was sold Eurocentric beauty ideals – like straight hair and blue eyes – as the only standard to aspire to; there weren't really any other options. I couldn't buy any make-up for my skin tone growing up in Wales; I didn't get a foundation that matched my skin tone until my late teens. I'd have to try and mix my own. When I tried to buy cosmetics the people on counters were rude, and you were made to feel othered and less because you had dark skin. All of this meant that I never felt enough in terms of beauty, but that transferred to other areas of my life too; like dating and the eating disorder I ended up developing.

(Authors' interview with Anita Bhagwandas)

Ava Welsing-Kitcher is a mixed Ghanaian British beauty editor and brand consultant who spoke to us about hair and beauty. In an industry dominated by white people and Western beauty ideals, she talked about colourism and how whiteness is a tool used to measure mixed-race people's beauty:

I just always imagine what would Blackness be if we hadn't had the Eurocentric standards to govern it by ... And it's just, it's so amazing and disheartening that we are meant to fit into these little boxes and these little categories, and that's what our worth is defined by.

Mixed Up *podcast, Season 1, Episode 6*

We have also interviewed mixed actors across all genres and from multiple countries about their experiences in the casting room before they appear on our screens and perform in some of our favourite stories. Actors like Asia Jackson and Lenora Crichlow have been open with us about their struggles in being cast in projects, which comes with an added layer of difficulty because of their mix and casting directors being not quite sure where to place them.

Lenora Crichlow spoke to us about a casting experience when she was told that she was only good enough to play the role of the 'best friend':

> I would get lots of comments about how I show up for auditions and what it is to look sexy and appealing. Then I was in an audition where I was told to read for the lead, so I did. And I did a good job. I'll toot my own horn here, it really spoke to me. It was one of those ones that I really enjoyed and the casting guy said, 'Um, it was really great and we really like it.' And then he kind of turned to the lady who was manning the camera and said, 'But you know, I don't really think they're going that way. You know, for the lead, it's good that you are so confident … and you're so beautiful. And we just think your mixedness would be better suited to the best friend.' And I was like, wow, he said that out loud. I think the tape [was still] rolling … The only thing that qualified me for the best friend was my mixed-raceness and he just said it … It was like a formula. That I would be the best friend of an earnest white woman. And just cheer her on.
>
> Mixed Up *podcast, Season 2, Episode 24*

Hearing Lenora's experience about being typecast as the 'best friend' felt relatable, meta even. Having been that best friend and feeling relegated to a supporting role in my own life when I was younger. When you are surrounded by majority-white peers, beauty is currency. If you are seen as beautiful and attractive in their eyes, the more popular you become, your status rises. Everyone else is just on the fringes.

It's important to note that there is also no guarantee that any mixed person is going to be light-skinned, or white presenting, or have a looser curl pattern. Somehow this has become our own stereotype to live up to within the community – a common stereotype and misconception.

What you will look like is something that people talk about from the moment you are conceived, the moment you are born. Your parents will hear about it, and then you will too when you are a child, through your adolescence and all throughout your womanhood: what the beauty standard is going to be for you and how much or how little you will be able to live up to it.

BUT WHAT'S BEAUTY WHEN IT'S AT HOME?

Afua Hirsch, award-winning British broadcaster and journalist, spoke to us about her experience of bringing her infant daughter to her home country of Ghana and how she was surprised to receive comments about her child's complexion:

> The heartbreaking one for me was when a young woman in Ghana (when my daughter was a little baby), said to me, 'Is this your daughter?' And I said, 'Yeah,' and she said, 'Oh, you didn't do well at all.' And I said, 'What do you mean?' And she said, 'Well, you know, you're light-skinned, your child should be more light-skinned than you. You know, each generation should get closer to, to white.'
>
> That really broke my heart, firstly because she was saying that about my beautiful little newborn. But also because she looked

like my daughter. And so the kind of self-loathing that she would have to have to regard that as a failure on my part – that I brought into the world another girl who looks like her … you know, that interaction just embodied so much of the violence of the empire for me and its ongoing implications for us all psychologically.

If you do come to Ghana with a very light-skinned baby, people will really compliment that baby. And, you know, people say, 'I would like to have a child who looks like that.' It's hard. It's really hard to hear, but also, you know, it's the symptom, not the cause, it's the symptom of the deeper inequality that still exists. So, you know, attacking the person doesn't actually solve the problem, even critiquing the person doesn't solve the problem, they're reflecting something that is very real.

Mixed Up *podcast, Season 3, Episode 12*

Afua's experience speaks directly to the idea that you aren't necessarily going to be born 'light-skin' just because you are mixed.

As mentioned earlier in the chapter, the impact of colourism has meant that we are constantly comparing our beauty and our value to one another and even reducing it to skin tone. The devaluation of darker skin has come to mean the uplifting of lighter skin as a direct result of colonization and the effect that it has had on our own communities, which are meant to be our safe haven.

In terms of what makes us feel beautiful, what makes us feel at home, there are hair and beauty rituals that are also passed down to us that are culturally significant – they give us a feeling of connectedness and comfort, even though they are aesthetic and superficial; they make us feel like we are home and that we are surrounded by our loved ones.

Layla Hatia shared one of her earliest memories, that of her grandmother putting kajal on her eye line, and how as a child it made her feel special. And the ritual of sitting in between her grandmother's legs as she put Amla oil in her hair:

> There were quiet moments of connection. The application of *mehndi* was another one of these moments. *Mehndi* is generally reserved for special occasions like weddings or Eid day, so it comes with a sense of excitement and anticipation. That anticipation is wrapped into the whole experience, waiting your turn to have *mehndi* applied in an intricate pattern, waiting for it to dry, carefully applying tea tree oil to help bring out the colour, going to bed with plastic bags on your hands to stop the *mehndi* flaking on to your sheets. Waking up excited to see how deep the colour is and if the pattern survived smudging in the night. It's a tradition that has passed through the generations, and now, instead of waiting for a distant 'aunty' to do it, I wait patiently for my younger cousin to apply *mehndi* to all the women (and some of the boys) in my family before special occasions. Women sit together late into the night sharing stories while *mehndi* is applied. These moments are often the best part of the celebration you're preparing for.

There are moments in these rituals from our cultures that are outside Western beauty standards and allow us to nurture our identities and shape our own beauty standards and aesthetic ideals. They can almost become our tools, so to speak, which allow us to wade through the negative impacts of a beauty standard that is so focused on whiteness. These rituals enable us to connect with a more rounded sense of self and allow us greater expression through our hairstyles, our clothing and our make-up.

And while writing about beauty may seem like a trivial pursuit, one that sounds frivolous and superficial and is often dismissed as insignificant, the racial and sexual focus on mixed-race people leads to fetishization and sexual violence, which we previously discussed in Chapter 3, Interracial Dating and Relationships, and again in the next chapter, The 'Tragic Mulatto' Myth.

7.
THE 'TRAGIC MULATTO' MYTH

In the early nineteenth century, a trope was born in American literature that became known as the 'tragic mulatto', where a character who was mixed Black and white was often presented as depressed, suicidal and reckless – either endangering themselves or behaving in a way that was deemed 'promiscuous'. According to the trope's characterization, their behaviour apparently stemmed from their own internal conflict that they would never fit in, mirrored by being shunned by society. At the time the racial lines were so divided that neither their Black nor their white sides could fully accept them for who they were and they were depicted as 'doomed' characters who could not survive.

We find this trope of the 'tragic mulatto' meaningful because of how it has been weaponized against mixed women in the past and how it persists throughout modern portrayals of mixed women in the media today. When we discussed writing this book in its early stages, we felt it was important to call out and draw attention to the stereotype for precisely this reason.

THE ORIGINS OF THE 'TRAGIC MULATTO' TROPE

Scholars credit the author and abolitionist Lydia Maria Child with the creation of the 'tragic mulatto' trope in her short stories 'The Quadroons' (1842) and 'Slavery's Pleasant Homes' (1843), which are considered to be anti-slavery literature. A 'quadroon' was the term used to refer to a mixed Black person who was considered to be a quarter African.

In 'The Quadroons' Child chronicles the life and death of a mixed-race woman, Rosalie, and her daughter. Their lives are fundamentally marred by being not only mixed Black but also the descendants of former enslaved people. Rosalie is technically unmarried to a white man under the miscegenation laws of the time, but they share a mixed-race daughter, Xarifa, who also suffers a tragic fate. Rosalie's 'husband' decides to marry a white woman out of political ambition but wants to keep seeing Rosalie as his mistress; she refuses and later dies of heartbreak after losing him.

Despite falling in love with her harp teacher, whom she plans to marry and move to France with, Xarifa discovers that her mother's freedom papers have not been recorded, which means that she is still legally the property of the original slave owner's family. She is then auctioned off and sold to a man who wants her as his lover, but she refuses. What follows is more devastation in the form of rape and suicide – a pattern that repeats itself often in stories about the 'tragic mulatto'.

The stories are centred around biracial women, in particular those who can 'pass' as white or are 'assumed' to be white, which is something we will explore in more depth in Chapter 9. Whether or not the woman is 'actively' passing as white or just accepting of the fact that people view her as white, and therefore able to elevate her social standing or class, it doesn't matter because none of it will save her in the end. Usually there is a brutal reveal in which the white husband, partner or lover of the 'tragic mulatto' character discovers she is not who he believed her to be. She either loses everything, is brutally murdered or commits suicide.

It's important to note the gender dynamic here – the origin of this trope was written by a white woman, in novels written primarily for other white women with mixed-race women as the protagonists.

The women characters are often described as being fetishized – because of their perceived whiteness or proximity to whiteness – or alternatively eroticized because of their Blackness. The 'tragic mulatto' is pathologized through her depression or self-loathing, which manifests through alcoholism or 'promiscuity' and apparently stems from seeking approval from both sides of her heritage. Being able to 'pass' as white only leads to even deeper self-loathing and guilt from being accepted by a community that would reject her outright if it knew that she is also a Black woman. At the same time she is depicted as desperate for the approval of the Black community, despite knowing that being fully immersed in her Blackness would mean giving up the 'safety' apparently afforded to her through her whiteness. Ultimately, for the 'tragic mulatto' there is nowhere truly safe in society.

PROPAGANDA FOR MISCEGENATION LAWS/ONE-DROP RULE?

The stories by white writers read as propaganda for miscegenation laws, and later movie directors and producers used these women as an example of what 'one drop' of Black blood could do to a person – the emotional turmoil, the perpetual unhappiness, societal scourge, degradation and ultimately an untimely end.

Child's intention with her abolitionist short stories may have been to comment on anti-slavery and women's liberation, however – intentionally or unintentionally – she birthed a stereotype that is used even to this day to characterize mixed people, who because of their mixed heritage are depicted as suffering from mental illness and perpetual confusion, which means they can never accept themselves and are constantly seeking approval from others. Although the stated objective is to aid race relations and bring Black and white people closer together, what this trope does is actively sow more division and create a legacy that continues to discourage interracial relationships and positions the mixed identity as defunct.

Another well-known origin story of the 'tragic mulatto' is that of Peola in the 1934 film *Imitation of Life*. Peola is the daughter of a Black housekeeper and is so fair in complexion that she is perceived to be white. One day she is antagonized by the daughter of the white family they work for, teased and tormented because of her Black mother, and as a result Peola then rejects her Blackness from a young age. The older she gets, the more that rejection comes from society and contributes to her own self-loathing. She is desperate to be seen as white, she wants to marry a white man and be able to live a life free from the societal stigma of being Black. She decides to leave her family home and tells her mother, 'Don't come for me. If you see me in the street, don't speak to me. From this moment on I'm white. I am not coloured. You have to give me up.' Her mother dies of a broken heart and on her deathbed Peola is seen begging her for forgiveness.

The character of Peola was so reviled by both white and Black audiences at the time that her name was being used until the late 1970s as an insult against light-skinned mixed women as the female equivalent to 'coon' and 'Uncle Tom'.

The following line in the 1959 reboot of the same name particularly poignant: 'How do you explain to your daughter that she was born to hurt?' Although the storyline is slightly changed and the characters' names are modernized, the question supposes that mixed children are born to suffer, and the general view that being mixed or of mixed Black heritage immediately tars you is gut-wrenching.

In researching this particular trope, and in all of our discussions on the podcast about mixed identity in general, we often deliberated publicly and privately about how this was a conversation that mixed women took on or were centred in in modern times, and it is plain to see that the 'tragic mulatto' trope is the reason for that. It cannot be coincidence that the conversation around race and identity is gendered in this way. It is often women who are depicted as cunning and duplicitous, ready to deceive – so it is unsurprising that these stereotypes are easy to foist upon lighter-skinned mixed women who are sometimes perceived as white.

It is mixed women again who are given the characteristic of seeing themselves as 'better than' or having 'airs of superiority' because they are able to pass as white, and a stereotype that was written into literature has somehow been applied to light-skinned mixed women everywhere, regardless of whether they can 'pass' or not and in spite of their actual lived experiences.

It seems as though the fate of the 'mulatto' woman is sealed in this trope, whereas mixed men are portrayed slightly differently. In the film *The Birth of a Nation* (1915) a well-known scene in cinematic history despite its offensive nature, the 'mulatto' male character of Silas Lynch is portrayed as psychotic and violent – a far cry from the light-skinned, mixed male stereotype that we see today which characterizes mixed-race men as far more soft and feminine in comparison. Both male and female tragic mulatto tropes signal what racial mixing and the abolition of slavery would mean in American society. He is portrayed as manipulative, an alcoholic who is not only drunk on liquor but drunk on power. However, in spite of this he rises up the political ranks and provides freedom for enslaved Black people, a positive course of action within an inherently racist movie.

The difference here between the portrayal of mixed women and mixed men – specifically biracial, mixed Black and white men – is stark.

Stereotypical male qualities come into play: violence and control, despite being negative behaviours, can be viewed more positively; for example, Silas uses these methods for the advancement of his people. However, mixed women are depicted as sexual, mentally unstable, depressed. More often than not they are seen as selfish, regardless of how sympathetic to their plight we may be.

Author and academic Dr Melissa J. Wagner, a mixed woman of Guyanese and British heritage, specializes in the exploration of mixed identity within literature. She spoke to us about this trope, which often appears in entertainment:

> There's this idea that she's evil, like the bad light-skinned person, but the evil concept also goes back to this whole, you know, theory of hybrid degeneration. And so there's this kind of biological essentialism, where you were on the one hand inherently evil, cruel and oppressive biologically, or you could be weak and pitiable. Or, particularly for women, you were sexually deviant. And all of us are unstable and biologically abnormal.
>
> And it's always, it's always the women again who are being accused, tricking these men into falling in love with them. And no one would ever use that language to talk about men. It's only women who are capable of that kind of deceit and duplicity. And it's just the intersection of patriarchy, misogyny and racism all wrapped up into a nice, neat package.
>
> Mixed Up *podcast, Season 2, Episode 7*

Despite there being real-life stories of 'passing' or being able to move out of a lower class because of having lighter skin, it's also important to examine the racism that did exist towards mixed people in Antebellum America. We dig deeper into this in Chapter 9, but as always throughout this book we want to stress the importance of looking back at the history which might otherwise be glossed over.

MIXED-RACE WOMEN AS TARGETS FOR ABUSE

In old laws and public statements regarding miscegenation and interracial relationships, the children of white and Black people are referred to as 'mulattos' or 'mongrels', words which have their roots in the context of animals and cross-breeding.

Dr David Pilgrim, a professor of sociology at Ferris State University, wrote extensively about the 'tragic mulatto myth' for the Jim Crow Museum of Racist Memorabilia in Michigan. He chronicles the reality of how mixed people were treated within and outside plantations as well as in the marketplace, saying that even the mixed grandchildren of the enslaver would be brutalized on the plantation and that 'mulatto women' were also targeted for sexual abuse.

According to the historian J. C. Furnas:

... in some slave markets, mulattoes and quadroons brought higher prices, because of their use as sexual objects. Some [enslavers] found dark skin vulgar and repulsive. The mulatto approximated the white ideal of female attractiveness but without need for restriction, respect or consent. All slave women (and men and children) were vulnerable to being raped, but the mulatto afforded the slave owner the opportunity to rape, with impunity, a woman who was physically white (or near-white) but legally Black and therefore his property.[1]

The greater likelihood of being raped is not the level of desirability or status that anyone actually aspires to. This is the root of the modern day 'pick me' stereotype that is put upon mixed women and gives far too much power to the idea that being chosen by a man is the pinnacle of success, especially given its historical connotations of enslavement, misogyny and the most vile degradation of human life.

Rosemary Adaser's experiences growing up in Ireland mirror the sexualization that we see in stereotypes about mixed-race women throughout history:

Thousands of Irish women moved over to the UK, but for the likes of people like me, you know, young girls with no family, no networks lacking in social skills, graces, functionally illiterate, I might add. By the time I left these institutions, life was incredibly, incredibly tough, especially as being a clever little minx, I was very well aware that I was seen as a sexual object and I spent my formative years, 17 to the time I left age 20, 21, I was fighting men off me, quite literally. So you can imagine going down your local street and everywhere you go, some man is exposing himself to you. Some man is making very lewd suggestions. Even going into changing rooms. In a shop to buy a top, for example, and the owner barges in and suggests that you become his prostitute. That he has a group of friends who would be more than happy to pay for someone as exotic as you. That's what it was like. And I only speak for my own personal experience here, but that's what it was like for me in Ireland. And that is because of the racism, the deeply structured racism of the Irish State and Church.

Mixed Up *podcast, Season 3, Episode 9*

A GLOBAL VIEW

The real myth seems to be that, globally, majority-white countries are some kind of racial melting pot in which we have all come together to live side by side in harmony. The historical reality was much more hostile and more violent than we are led to believe by the modern-day rhetoric around mixed people (children in particular) as some kind of banner for racial equality and the end of racial stereotyping. The ugly truth is that the intermixing of races was viewed as 'unnatural' and would be the downfall of America, given the industry of enslavement on which it so heavily relied.

It was the same sentiment in the UK with the 1930 Fletcher Report, written as a response to the increasing mixed population in Liverpool – a result of Black seamen having children with white British women. Muriel Fletcher at the time was hired to 'investigate' the homes of these women to observe their children and later described her findings as 'dysfunctional'. She wrote, 'there is little harmony between the parents, the coloured men in general despise the women with whom they consort, and the women have little affection for the men. They regret their union and stay with them for the sake of the children.'

The problem with a stereotype is that it *is* a stereotype – it oversimplifies the complex reality of what it is to be a mixed race, multicultural, multifaceted human being. It diminishes the truth of how race is perceived in America and in Western society. Because of this, very real problems of discrimination, violence and especially gender-based violence, poverty, mental health issues and abuse are ignored.

IS THE 'TRAGIC MULATTO' ALIVE AND WELL IN MODERN-DAY PORTRAYALS?

There has been an over-representation in media of mixed women within these stereotypes – promiscuous or hyper-sexualized, confused, depressed, abused – and the connection between being fetishized in the real world and disproportionately portrayed on screens in this way can't be overemphasized. Rosemary Adaser describes it as 'a historical sexual fetishism':

> My experience is through the lens of that fetishism, you know, which is almost like mixed race is 'the new acceptable Blackness', and that's all – it's actually wrong. It's warped to that young mixed-race girl who's on the receiving end of so much unwelcome attention. It is not a privilege. It is not a privilege. It is deeply harmful. It's deeply harmful to her spirit, which is yet to be developed.
>
> Mixed Up *podcast, Season 3, Episode 9*

The 'tragic mulatto' trope that originated in the nineteenth century is something that has permeated pop culture over time. It was a character we started to notice more and more frequently.

Charlotte Brontë's *Jane Eyre* was first published in 1847. In it, Bertha Mason is described as a beautiful Creole woman who is married to Edward Rochester, Jane's love interest. Before meeting Jane, Rochester falls in love with Bertha and marries her but describes her as 'violently insane'. He keeps her locked away in one of the rooms in his house with a nurse who is meant to keep her restrained. It's said that her beauty deteriorates the longer she is kept locked away and she becomes more and more 'savage'. Bertha is not only used as an example of the result of being 'racially impure'; she is often described as animalistic, beastly and demonic – ultimately, not of this world.

Spike Lee's *School Daze* hit cinemas in 1988 and was based on Lee's experiences as a student at Morehouse (a historically Black college in Atlanta, Georgia) in the 1970s. In it, Giancarlo Esposito plays Julian, who is the leader of a fraternity. He tells one of his pledges, Half-Pint (played by Spike Lee), that he won't allow virgins to rush in his fraternity. Julian offers up his girlfriend Jane Toussaint, a mixed woman played by Tisha Campbell, to sleep with him. She agrees out of her love for Julian and her obligations in fraternity-sorority life, ultimately being rejected by Julian for sleeping with his friend. She is degraded and used by the men who have her at their disposal, and ultimately sees the death of her social reputation among her own friendship group.

In Nicôle Lecky's *Mood* (2022) we see a mixed Black woman, Sasha, struggle to make something of her dream to become a singer. Growing up in East London as the sole mixed child of her white mother, with her stepfather and a younger sibling who is fully white, she has to navigate making it in the music industry despite the fetishization and racialization she experiences throughout the programme. After she's thrown out of her family home she gets sucked into the world of online sex work in order to make money and simultaneously fund her dream of releasing an album.

These characters are constrained by constantly having 'to choose'; or alternatively, because of a clash with a parent they are portrayed as anxious and depressed, often self-medicating with drugs and promiscuity. They are frequently used sexually and then rejected by the men in their lives and their stories rarely have a 'happy ending'.

There have been many moments in producing the podcast and writing this book when we have stumbled across references that are inextricably linked to this stereotype, not only in pop culture but in modern history. While there are prime examples of the trope that play out in cinemas and on TV screens, in literature and art, there is also the real-world example of Meghan Markle, who has had to endure it via the media.

She was first seen as a mixed Black woman who for the most part could 'pass' as white; then there was a shift in perception when her Blackness was emphasized and recognized by society at large. She was subsequently subjected to anger from the press and public figures for daring to take a position in the Royal Family as a Black woman, and a vocal one at that. She has been very open about her depression and the suicidal thoughts that arose from attempts to silence her through negative and inaccurate reporting.

Real-world examples of violence against Black and mixed-race women continue to be harrowing, and their treatment by society and its institutions – the Church, as we read in Chapter 4, and the Metropolitan Police over recent years – has garnered media attention.

In June 2020, two sisters, Nicole Smallman and Bibaa Henry, were found murdered in North London. Nicole was mixed Black and Bibaa was monoracial Black. Their mother, Mina Smallman, reported that the police hadn't taken the fact that they were missing seriously enough, so their bodies were found by Nicole's boyfriend, who had independently decided to find them himself. It was all the more shocking to learn that the police officers who were involved in the murder investigation took selfies next to their bodies and shared them in a WhatsApp group with colleagues.[2]

The following year, the kidnap and murder of Sarah Everard by Metropolitan Police officer Wayne Couzens was a bombshell case that sparked fear and rage in women in London and across the globe. This tragic and unnecessary loss of life reopened conversations around misogyny, rape culture, women's public safety and further investigation into the widespread abuse within the Metropolitan Police. We later found out through an article in the *Daily Mail* that Sarah was of mixed heritage as her grandmother is Jamaican.[3]

There was the case in 2020 of an 18-year-old mixed-race woman being attacked by a group of white men in Wisconsin. Alethea Bernstein claims she was stopped at a traffic light and heard someone shout a racial slur through her rolled-down window before being doused with lighter fluid and set on fire. This case did go to court but it was thrown out by the judge.[4]

In 2023, the Independent Office for Police Conduct began to investigate four Metropolitan Police officers over the strip-search of a young mixed-race girl. This investigation followed the scandal of misconduct against Child Q, a 15-year-old Black girl who was strip-searched by officers while on her period after being wrongfully accused of possessing cannabis at school. Another case followed: a 15-year-old girl of mixed white and Black ethnicity who is autistic was so traumatized after being handcuffed and strip-searched by Metropolitan Police officers in front of other male officers while she was on her period that her mother reported that she tried to kill herself.[5]

These cases serve as real-life examples of the impact of racial stereotypes and how promiscuity tropes create a society that places no value on the lives of mixed women thus characterized. Such tropes are often used by perpetrators to identify targets who are not protected by society and its institutions, and who are therefore seen as having no value. Often going unchecked, the stereotypes can adversely influence individuals and allow them – even those in positions of power – to enact violence, sexual or otherwise, on mixed women.

It wasn't until we interviewed Alexis, the author and TV personality formerly known as Natalie Lee, on our podcast about her book *Feeling Myself*, that we discovered that over half a million women are estimated to be raped or sexually assaulted in England and Wales each year. Mixed-race women are the most over-represented group within that statistic, according to the government's 'Tackling Violence Against Women and Girls Strategy' report in 2021.[6]

We bring up these specific cases of police officers abusing their power because, given the statistics, we can only assume that the police force, an extension of the Home Office, has not been given a directive to address the disproportionate representation of mixed women and girls in rape cases – and, worse than that, perpetrators within the force are being enabled.

The government, and therefore the police, is aware of these statistics, so why have no measures been put in place to even raise awareness of the issue? What does this say about how much the government, and by extension society, truly cares about what happens to Black and mixed-race women and girls?

The implication is that we won't be missed. We can be abused because there is a lack of protection around women and girls who are considered 'ambiguous' or can't be 'placed' and there isn't any value in women who cannot be identified as belonging to any one group.

Given the history laid out in this chapter and the modern examples described, we feel it's hard to ignore how racial fetishization and this tragic mulatto stereotype impact the real-world mixed-race community, and mixed-race women in particular.

8.

RACISM TOWARDS MIXED PEOPLE IN MODERN DAY

NICOLE

When we first decided to start the *Mixed Up* podcast, it was because we struggled to find much open conversation about mixed-race identity, especially the negative rhetoric and insensitive feeling affecting mixed people in modern discourse and recent history.

Uncomfortable topics and a lot of emotion come into talking about our identities, especially regarding race. The conversations online become so charged so quickly that we often stifle ourselves for fear of saying the wrong thing or asking the wrong question of the wrong person. We've discovered that it's important to hone in on this in order for us to understand where the animosity is rooted and progress collectively.

Once we started recording our podcast and interviewing our incredibly forthcoming guests – be they public figures, celebrities or listeners in our community – we couldn't ignore the hurt they felt from the racism, prejudice and pre-judgment that so many of us have faced.

We wanted to dig deeper into the racism that is directed at mixed-race people, examples of which exist in their most overt forms and are easily recognized throughout modern history, but also in instances that people may be more inclined to label as microaggressions. It's our feeling that it is easy enough to pick up on the 'capital-R' examples of racism when they occur, but we feel strongly that it is important to recognize that racial microaggressions, which usually begin when we are children or in our younger years, when our sense of self and identity is becoming formed, impact us in adulthood as well.

Having spoken to mixed-race people at length for the podcast, the common thread is that there are moments of 'othering', whether through subtle or casual racism, that leave them feeling lost, untethered, disoriented and ultimately rejected.

In an episode of our podcast, we spoke to Dr Melissa J. Wagner, who explained:

> We were seen as some kind of contamination of the white race … so many mixed-race kids ended up in care. We as mixed-race children were the arguments politicians used against immigration into this country. There's a very narrow definition of who's entitled to say they've experienced racism. People still today experience racism whether they're mixed race or monoracial.
>
> Mixed Up *podcast, Season 2*

In 1968, Enoch Powell, the Shadow Defence Secretary, was highly critical of the rates of immigration into the UK, particularly from what was known as the New Commonwealth – comprising of countries in the British Commonwealth that became independent after the Second World War – and delivered his infamous 'Rivers of Blood' speech at the West Midlands Area Conservative Political Centre. He quite literally predicted a race war and opposed the anti-discrimination Race Relations Bill legislation. He was supported by groups like the National Front, who wanted to ban all non-white immigration into the country.

He shared an anecdote from a white man in his constituency who said, 'I have three children, all of them been through grammar school and two of them married now, with family. I shan't be satisfied till I have seen them all settled overseas. In this country in fifteen or twenty years' time the Black man will have the whip hand over the white man.' Powell feared that the Race Relations Bill offered non-white people everything they needed to 'flourish' and would:

> [show] that the immigrant communities can organize to consolidate their members, to agitate and campaign against their fellow citizens, and to overawe and dominate the rest with the legal weapons which the ignorant and the ill-informed have provided. As I look ahead, I am filled with foreboding; like the Roman, I seem to see the River Tiber foaming with much blood.

Ultimately he predicted immigration and 'race-mixing' to be 'an act of suicide' for the country. He was criticized by party members and in the press, which resulted in him being removed from his position.

In our conversation on the podcast, Melissa spoke to us about the misconceptions of eugenics theory and its impact on her life growing up and on her own family dynamic:

> I still think we are in it, but I just think that it's been – that there's a certain amount of sub-diffusion about it in terms of Eurocentric racial theories that really began in the seventeenth century. So it's a long history. It goes back a long time before I was born. But you know, that kind of rhetoric about hybrid degeneracy was very, very prevalent. Like we were seen as abnormal, as freaks, as some sort of contamination of the white race. And that was how so many mixed-race kids ended up in care. I mean, my mother, she refused to marry my father.

Because she already had a son who was white ... When I was older she told me that she didn't marry my father because she didn't feel it was fair for my white half-brother to have a Black father. So this was my family dynamic.

Melissa talked about how scientific racism, and the way in which it was used in the context of racial mixing in her generation, had a trickle-down effect:

You know, there was this view in terms of European racial theory that there were different species and that mixed-race people were spoken about in the same way that you might talk in botany about a hybrid plant ... we still do get called mongrels ... and these words became applied to people of so-called 'mixed race'. You know, it was always a term to really just to dehumanize us.

Mixed Up podcast, *Season 2*

MIXED-RACE CHILDREN IN IRISH MOTHER AND BABY INSTITUTIONS

In 2021, the monstrous nature of Ireland's Church-run, State-funded Mother and Baby Homes became a global story after reports that children had been buried in a sewage system in the town of Tuam in western Ireland compelled the Irish government to open a full-scale investigation into these religious institutions. It was here that unmarried women and girls who became pregnant were sent to live, away from their friends and family, and as a result generations of mixed-race children and their mothers were hidden away.

An article in the *New York Times* entitled 'In Ireland, Lifting a Veil of Prejudice Against Mixed-Race Children' explained that women who were sent to these institutions spoke about the 'reject wards' which were so named for children considered to be unadoptable.[1] The criteria? Mixed race, disabled or Irish Travellers deemed unworthy of parents. Mixed-race children were less likely to be adopted and more likely to be transferred from institution to institution.

A government advisory group of survivors called the Mother and Baby Home Collaborative Forum joined together as a collective because of the horrific findings in these institutions, which included high infant mortality rates, 'reject rooms' where mixed and disabled babies were kept, forced adoptions and vaccine trials. Identities were erased, children were denied knowledge about their heritage, many were funnelled into industrial schools – prime subjects for medical abuse.

APARTHEID IN SOUTH AFRICA – A HIERARCHY WITH BLACK AT THE BOTTOM

Apartheid was a system of segregation based on discrimination on the grounds of race in South Africa and Namibia.

Under apartheid law, interracial relationships or marriages became illegal when the Prohibition of Mixed Marriages Act was passed in 1949. Although mixed-race relationships had occurred in South Africa among the Dutch colonizers and Indigenous South African women as far back as 1600s, interracial relationships were prohibited due to the National Party's rise in the early 1940s. They implemented a number of racial laws including the Population Registration Act and Immorality Act of 1950, which required every person in South Africa to register as one of four officially defined racial groups: white, Indian, 'Coloured' or Black.* They also prohibited sexual relationships between 'white' and

* The terminology used here reflects classifications borne out of the Apartheid project but that have become associated with a culture and the people that belong to it. See *Coloured: How Classification Became Culture* by Tessa Dooms and Lynsey Ebony Chutel.

'non-white' people. Unsurprisingly, relationships between those classified as 'non-white' were not criminalized.

From the late 1940s until the end of apartheid in the 1990s, the 'Coloured' group included people who were regarded as being of mixed heritage, not just Black and white. This applied to Bantu, Khosian and Malay ancestry as well as Indian, Sri Lankan and Chinese. Within this were the Cape Coloureds, who were the predominant population in the Western Cape despite being a minority group within South Africa itself. They were specifically known for their ability to code-switch because they were fluent in Afrikaans and English and so created a patois of the two.

The societal discourse around Black, Indian, Asian and mixed heritage people in South Africa shifted towards a focus on proximity to whiteness and the benefits and privileges some were afforded by the government in relation to white people, due to the racial hierarchy that the government themselves created. Apartheid was a system of racial hierarchy and segregation with white people at the top and Black people at the bottom.

There are parallels to the systems employed in the United States: the end of the Civil War saw the abolition of slavery, but a similarly vicious racial and social hierarchy remained as the Jim Crow laws were put into place. Between the 1870s and until the 1960s, these discriminatory measures denied Black people their basic human rights and subjected them to further marginalization, humiliation and degradation which had literally been codified into law.

Racism concerning racial mixing is a large part of our mixed people's history. For decades governments have prioritized keeping the white race 'pure' and separate from other races and as a result we have to deal with the impact of discrimination and rejection.

BARACK OBAMA: OUR MODERN-DAY MIXED PARAGON

President Barack Obama is the most prominent mixed-race figure in the world in recent history. He was elected to the 'highest office in the free world' as the United States' first Black president. Those two statements sit together in harmony for us – Barack Obama is mixed race, and he is also a Black man. It's significant not only because of who he is but what he represents culturally and historically.

It's important to acknowledge that, yes, being a biracial, highly educated Harvard graduate made it possible for Barack Obama to ascend to the presidency. But was it an easy process, with open doors and open arms from everyone who encountered him, even while he served? No. Because he is still a Black man.

In Samuel Sinyangwe's 'The Significance of Mixed Race: Public Perceptions of Barack Obama's Race and the Effect of Obama's Race on Favorability', people interviewed about Obama were more likely to perceive him as Black, even if they were 'race-conscious' and regardless of their own race, or if they could point out instances of 'anti-Black discrimination' in society:

> These race-conscious individuals perceive the force that continues to define many Black-white biracials as Black: being subjected to anti-Black discrimination in society. Even Barack Obama himself attributes his decision to identify as Black to his experience of being treated as a Black man in America. Without understanding this important component of Obama's 'Black' experience, it may be more intuitive to identify Obama as mixed race.[2]

Just as much as it matters how you yourself choose to be perceived, your identity is also shaped by how others perceive you.

Barack Obama was born in Hawaii, to a Kenyan father (who was largely absent from his life) and a white mother from Kansas, and grew up there. He also spent his formative years in Indonesia before studying in cities including Los Angeles, New York and Cambridge, Massachusetts before settling down in Chicago. It's easy to see how both his biological and his cultural make-up must have shaped his identity.

He even said in an interview with *60 Minutes* early in his candidacy, 'I am rooted in the African American community but I am not defined by it. I am comfortable in my racial identity, but that's not all I am,' stating from the start how he perceives himself and what he is comfortable with. When asked about growing up in a white household, the interviewer tells him, 'At some point, you decided you were Black', to which he responds, 'Well, I'm not sure I decided it. I think if you look African American in this society, you're treated as an African American. And when you're a child, in particular, that is how you begin to identify yourself.'[3]

Still, questions about how 'Black' he actually was ran the gamut of political discourse because his ancestry was not rooted in the enslaved Africans of the United States.

It's an interesting dichotomy, being the symbol of hope in 2009, a Black man elected to the presidency, but having your racial legitimacy questioned at the same time. It's clear that he could be whoever anyone wanted him to be – he represented whatever anyone wanted him to represent for themselves.

In *Obama: In Pursuit of a More Perfect Union* (2021), a documentary series for HBO, author and academic Jelani Cobb said:

Obama had this kind of kaleidoscope effect where people could look at him and see all sorts of different things. A person from the south side of Chicago could look at him and see another Black person like themselves. A person from an Ivy League school could look at him and see someone like themselves.[4]

In contrast, there's the overwhelming racism that he faced throughout his presidency and political career: from being compared to Osama Bin Laden because of their similar-sounding names, to being portrayed as a monkey in cartoons, to the 'birther' conspiracy perpetuated by Donald Trump, who touted the lie that Obama wasn't actually born in the United States. Trump and his fellow conspiracists tried to de-legitimize Obama by foisting on him their perception of his identity; this is how many mixed people experience society when they dare to state openly their identity or, worse still, their unshakeable belief in who they are.

You can ascend to arguably one of the highest political offices in the world and still have to field questions about your identity, argue for the legitimacy of your work and of where you were born. Regardless of how 'mixed' Obama is, his long list of credentials and education or his proximity to whiteness through his white parent – he is still 'other'. He is still subject to the everyday racism directed towards people of mixed heritage. Prejudices which informed 'water-cooler' conversations and microaggressions in offices across America were being played out in news cycles. Obama would – one assumes – have been familiar with the nature of these conversations, but would he have expected to need to engage with them given the office he held?

COLOURISM AND IDENTITY POLITICS

Colourism (a term first coined in 1982 by Alice Walker) is defined as prejudicial or preferential treatment based solely on skin colour. Closely linked with racism, essentially it means favouring people with lighter complexions over those with darker ones. It's a topic that has been spoken about widely, particularly in the South Asian, East Asian and Black communities.

Although discussions around colourism aren't new in these communities, the resurgence of the Black Lives Matter movement after the murder of George Floyd, as well as the Stop Asian Hate movement that grew after the Covid-19 lockdown and the attacks on the Asian community became more frequent, resulted in a feeling of hierarchical importance when it came to discussing issues of race – colourism being the measure by which it's decided who has the right to speak on them.

Throughout this book, it's our hope that readers are able to hold space for the idea that not only can two things be true at the same time, but multiple things can too. That is the beauty of nuance. It's the beauty of humanity, really. Nothing is ever binary.

There is no denying the existence of colourism and its effects. It is also true that a clear look at the history of mixed-race people throughout the globe shows that, regardless of how light or dark your skin tone may be, the effects of racism and being 'othered' by people can be long-lasting.

Mixed Black people have always been racialized as being of Blackness, not separate from it. Mixed Asian people are racialized as being of Asian heritage, regardless of their physical features and identifiers.

Jenni Rudolph, whom we met in Chapter 6, shared with us how the core of her identity struggles came from feeling that, despite being mixed Cantonese and Ashkenazi Jewish, she was always seen as a fully Chinese girl:

Growing up there [Huntington Beach, California], I grew up burying ... well, I didn't really have a connection to being Asian aside from appearing Asian and denying it when people would ask me, or like, not like pretending I wasn't Asian, but just kind of not wanting to be Asian and trying to shut down people's assumptions.

Some of them were really blatant, you know, like one person actually said to me, like, I bet you love doing homework. Um. And then a lot of comments about my appearance, like, oh, you could be pretty if you dyed your hair, lightened your skin, got plastic surgery ... a lot of mean comments growing up. Meanwhile, my classmates also did not like me being Jewish, because it's also a very heavily Christian area.

Mixed Up *podcast, Season 4, Episode 3*

Jenni spoke a lot about how she viewed herself growing up and how she struggled with internalized racism and a feeling of resentment towards her Asian mother for 'making her a minority':

But I also think that even if my mom had been better equipped to handle these kinds of conversations, I don't think I was at the place where anything she would say would really cut through and be meaningful to me because I was so entrenched in internalized racism and bitterness and resentment towards her for being Asian and for making me this minority, and I think, with however much love she could have approached these kinds of topics, I feel like as a kid, as a teen, I would have brushed it off.

She would tell me I was beautiful, and I didn't believe it because she's my mom. Of course she would think I was beautiful. Of course she would say that. It's very sad, but I didn't believe I was beautiful until white people told me I was beautiful.

And that wasn't until I started to look more ethnically ambiguous – and it's messed up and I wish it wasn't that way – but I don't think that child Jenni was in the place where she could have embraced that conversation and really listened and accepted that love in the same way that I'm in a better place nowadays.

Mixed Up *podcast, Season 4, Episode 3*

Jenni's story reinforces the idea that while she is mixed, there is never going to be an occasion where she is seen as white.

As People of Colour, these physical markers and identifiers – ultimately how we look and how people treat us on the back of it – contribute to the shaping of our identities and how we perceive ourselves. This is especially true in the adolescent stages of our lives, when the development of our sense of self is uniquely tied to our aesthetics, our skin, hair and facial features.

And, as much as the concept of race is a construct, we could argue the same of Blackness itself. We are in agreement that Blackness isn't a monolith, however it can be seen as a cultural categorisation that has been accepted as a collective response to racism and racial classification. This can be what makes it harder for mixed Black people when they feel rejected or excluded from the Black community, because ultimately there is a community. We should be able to voice our individual experiences of acceptance – or lack thereof – within our groups in wider society.

There is debate over whether mixed-race people (particularly those with Black heritage) are actually Black and whether or not they experience racism as Black people do. Or at all. It's jarring to see how people have maintained this line of thinking without realizing how ahistorical it is. As explained earlier in this chapter, apartheid in South Africa only ended in the early 1990s and its society and power structures still include mixed people within the category of 'other'.

In an article titled '"You Think You're Black?" Exploring Black Mixed-Race Experiences of Black Rejection',[5] Karis Campion did a survey of mixed white and Caribbean people who self-identified as mixed in order to understand the more nuanced conceptualizations of the Black identity and when these first feelings of rejection come into play. She wrote about how older Black mixed-race people in Britain who grew up and came of age during the 1960s to 1980s, a time when they were already racialized as Black, were often encouraged to identify as Black in the census, but also when 'mixed race' was not the stand-alone category that it is today. Fast-forward to younger Black mixed-race people growing up in the 1990s to 2000s: 'fluidity' of identity is a new concept that emerges towards the tail end of the 'identity politics era', a term that was coined in the United States in the 1970s but has had a resurgence during the 2000s.

Originally, the term 'identity politics' was used by Jewish women, women of colour and lesbians who criticized the blanket usage of a 'woman's experience', which didn't take into account differences in race, ethnicity, class and sexuality. It was a time when conversations around the intersections of class and race, specifically with regard to feminism, were thrust to the fore.

In her study Campion noted that mixed-race people began to be more open about how the binary discourse of race did not chime with how they identified and were socialized, but were then met with what she called 'horizontal hostility' from Black people. 'Horizontal hostility' is used here to describe the experience of Black mixed people facing Black rejection and how that impacts their perception of self and their expressed ethnic identities.

Overall, the article concludes that while we're all familiar with the way in which white society's 'cultural norms' reject us, the concept of rejection by our own oppressed ethnic group is still something we're not used to recognizing or calling out:

[It] can prompt Black mixed-race people to feel (ostensibly and momentarily) inferior but most importantly, position them as inauthentic Black people. Unlike everyday experiences of white racism which many participants were able to comprehend, horizontal hostility emerges as a phenomenon that is not as easily described or knowable. It tended to be articulated as epiphanies in their lives, unlike white structural racism which most were able to recognize and go on to find methods to negotiate relatively early on. However, many participants lacked the ability to make sense of and reconcile Black rejection.

Mixed people have come to expect rejection from wider white society – we are taught about microaggressions and what those look like alongside overt racism – but how do you come to terms with the idea that you can have your own identity ignored, overlooked or dismissed outright by the very people you know understand the struggle, people from that marginalized side of your heritage? If we are being honest, would this same rhetoric and rejection not also be considered microaggression, regardless of what group it is coming from?

In an interview we did with Claire Yurika Davis – you'll remember her from Chapter 6 – we spoke to her about her experience on the Netflix reality show *Next in Fashion*. She was open about being misidentified and experiencing this horizontal hostility among the contestants and on set from both sides of her heritage as a Jamaican Japanese woman. In the episode she shares with us how she was rejected by the other Black contestants, while simultaneously not being grouped in with the other Asians. This left her feeling totally shut out by everyone:

I don't mind if you don't like me, but don't say that you support all Black people and then look over me and not count me as Black.

Like, just tell me I'm shit. That's fine, but don't be like, I support all Black people and not support me. I actually didn't really realize how weird the dynamic is between Black Americans and anybody else that's Black. Because [someone] didn't think that I was Black. I was like, uh, am I in the fucking twilight zone? Am I invisible? ... It's really hard when people are like, 'You literally aren't in the club' and you're like, 'But I am. I'm literally right here and I am. So I dunno why you're excluding me. Like does that make you feel better?' It's pretty depressing, to be honest. It made me feel quite upset.

Mixed Up *podcast, Season 1, Episode 3*

Such experiences raise difficult but important questions about identity. For example, what does it mean to be Black? What does it mean to be Asian? How do we define these categories? Who has ownership over them? How do we take into account our very different lived experiences?

We spoke to actor and content creator Ryan Alexander Holmes about his experience of anti-Blackness in the Asian community as an African American Chinese man. At the height of the Stop Asian Hate and Black Lives Matter resurgence online, he shared a post that went viral:

I love my Asian community. I love my Asian family ... but it was a very accusatory post. So I'm just like, listen, like, I see so much anti-Blackness in the Asian community. I grew up in it. And like, for you guys to say that it doesn't exist is so false because I experienced it first-hand and I'm Asian. I just happen to be Black too, and if you have a problem with this and if you have a problem with me saying this, then you are racist too. Because an Asian man is talking to you right now, right? [That post] really changed my whole perspective of, like, years and years and years of holding on to these grudges and the animosity that I experienced growing up, you know, in LA after the riots, which [at the time felt like there was] tension between the two communities because a lot of that was manufactured by the media and their spin on the riots. And how it was, like, Black people against Asian people and then sort of adding fuel to that fire. But that wasn't necessarily real. They made it real.

Mixed Up *podcast, Season 4, Episode 1*

We often hear the expression 'Black is not a monolith', but we have to acknowledge that people across all races and ethnicities try to conceptualize 'Blackness' without taking into account the vast array and ever-growing diversity of the Black experience. The disparity between the Black experience globally and conversations around Blackness in the West is stark.

Interrogating or mulling over the minutiae of who is Black or African or not, and why not, are simply not ones my Ghanaian family have ever had with me. Growing up, my dad never felt the need to clarify this with me because he is Black, therefore I am, and that was simply enough for him.

After reading Campion's article I quickly realized that it was one of the first places I've read that shared anything about mixed people who were honest about some of their encounters with monoracial Black people, these feelings of rejection from the wider Black community and the acknowledgement of gatekeeping that takes place.

In an episode of *Mixed Up* called 'The Rise of the Mixed-race Dialogue' a number of our guests expressed that feeling of rejection or feeling othered. Eboni Dixon, a London-based actor of mixed Jamaican and white heritage, said:

In terms of feeling like an outsider, I have felt rejection from both my Black and white communities growing up. Like, I get comments like, why do you act so white? Why do you act posh? If you straighten your hair, you could pass as white. Not feeling like, Black enough to be Black and not white enough to be white.

Mixed Up *podcast, Season 1, Episode 5*

This sentiment comes up a lot; when we talked to mixed-race people in general, this was the recurring refrain.

Not long after the Black Lives Matter resurgence we spoke to Lenora Crichlow, whom we met in Chapter 6, actress and daughter of Frank Crichlow. Witnessing the activism work in her own household, as well as the online and grassroots activism that flowed following Black Lives Matter, has only made her feel more rooted in who she is. She spoke to us about the privilege of growing up in an activist household, as well as one that was rooted in love of family and community, which empowered her in dealing with other people's reactions in predominantly white settings:

I feel more Black, more British, more mixed race, more female than I ever have because those things about my identity don't feel like they come with being silenced any more … For me personally, I've found it incredibly comforting and empowering. And I think that the lack of isolation I feel in that, in those struggles now, is a game changer. I am blown away by the activism I've seen in recent years. Um, but I also recognize I'm in a bubble. Within a bubble.

Early on in Lenora's acting career she was working on an audition with an acquaintance who told her that she didn't think of her as Black:

> We were talking about the role. And I said something like, 'Well you know, being Black, being a Black actress is just ...' something like that. I was just talking about my experience. And she said, 'Don't say that.' And I said, 'What?' She said, 'Don't say that you're a Black actress.' And I was like, 'What do you mean?' She was like, 'You're not, you know, I don't, I never think of you like that.' And I was like, 'Oh my God, what is that even supposed to mean?'
>
> And what I realized after this very awkward exchange rolled out was that she somehow saw that – and I'm, I also can touch on the fact that my British accent affords me something here too – that she didn't think of me as a Black person. I can see how my lightness, my Britishness, and where I'm coming from has sort of made me this non-offensive person [to her]. And I've heard many very, very problematic, ignorant things. I say ignorant because I don't know how much of it comes from a conscious place of malice, but it's, it's jarring.
>
> Mixed Up *podcast, Season 2, Episode 24*

When we spoke to footballer Anton Ferdinand, best known for his time at West Ham United and Queens Park Rangers, for season 3 of *Mixed Up*, he admitted to his encounters of racism from his white family members, growing up mixed Irish and St Lucian:

> I encountered racism, not just from, uh, white people, but from Black people too. Mm-hmm, and one of them was my family. I remember things ... I remember things from when I was a kid ... but it's only when you sit down and actually think about the scenarios and things that have happened that you, actually you're

able to comprehend and understand what it is actually is that, that was happening to you at the time. And it's only as I grow older and I'm in this space and I'm in this – talking about this, which to me is not uncomfortable, but to many it's an uncomfortable conversation, right? I feel that, as a mixed-race person, it is needed for people to understand that mixed-race people do receive racism from both sides of their heritage, not just one.

Mixed Up *podcast, Season 3, Episode 1*

We've spoken privately and publicly on the podcast about self-censorship, and it was something that we both personally struggled with – not wanting to admit these feelings of rejection or horizontal hostility because it feels as though you're letting the side down.

Now, if you are mixed and you are experiencing this horizontal hostility from your POC community as well as racism from white family members or the wider world, this can weigh heavily on the psyche: feelings of displacement, confusion and anxiety about how you are perceived are painful.

MIXED FEELINGS ON MEGHAN MARKLE

Meghan Markle is a light-skinned Black woman. She has identified as biracial, which for some reason constitutes a rejection of Blackness to some people in the community. When she revealed in the Netflix docu-mentary *Harry & Meghan* that for part of her life she wasn't 'treated like a Black woman', her honesty was met with a lot of anger in online spaces. In our view, she was acknowledging her privilege with the frank-ness that she was being treated differently for a while. There was a time when she grew up 'not knowing' what that kind of treatment was like, but then she was faced with the fact that her Blackness has always been there, and there will be moments when people feel compelled to point it out, especially now that she is on the world's stage.

In reading her stories throughout the years, even before she married Prince Harry and joined the Royal Family, she has been forthcoming about the racism that she had experienced growing up as well as throughout her career as an actress. In an April 2017 interview with *Allure* magazine, she remarked:

> It was only outside the comforts of home that the world began to challenge those ideals. I took an African American studies class at Northwestern where we explored colourism; it was the first time I could put a name to feeling too light in the Black community, too mixed in the white community. For castings, I was labelled 'ethnically ambiguous'. Was I Latina? Sephardic? 'Exotic Caucasian'?[6]

This ambiguity and the erasure of her Black identity by Hollywood while she was starring in *Suits* is so contradictory to the way the media covered her once she and Harry stepped out together. After Meghan and Harry first came out publicly that they were dating in 2016, the coverage in the UK media and beyond was a constant barrage of racism – microaggressions and macroaggressions, overt and covert. It was clear to every media outlet that Meghan was a Black woman marrying into the Royal Family, and the relentless abuse hasn't stopped since. The vitriol spewed at Meghan by the press and the public was so vile that she was driven to consider taking her own life – she felt isolated and persecuted for just existing.

If this isn't a telling enough example of the level of racism aimed at a mixed Black woman or of the severity of the racism mixed people face, what is? What will it take for us to talk about it without caveating privilege in the process, and therefore diluting its obvious existence?

It's that nuance that we've been highlighting since the start of the book – and Meghan notes it herself – this feeling of being 'too light' but 'too dark'. We're sure that most mixed people who have experienced that dilemma have found themselves nodding along – how can you be both too much and not enough of something? It's the eternal dilemma. Even as a light-skinned woman, Meghan will have to continue to listen to the vitriolic racism spouted by the likes of Piers Morgan about her and her mixed children.

GRAPPLING WITH RACISM IN THE PUBLIC EYE

There are commonalities among mixed people in the public eye who suffer under the heavy weight of racist abuse levied against them and who share the impact of that constant vitriol on their mental health. We've seen it with Meghan Markle in her public interviews, and we heard about it first-hand when we interviewed Anton Ferdinand.

He told us that his first experience of hearing a racial slur was at a football game – the sport he started playing at age 9. He became the centre of attention in 2011 because of a racist incident with John Terry. He has been open about the impact of that moment on his mental health and his family at the time:

> I count myself lucky. I used the word lucky, and I'm lucky to be here if I'm really honest with you. And that's not me saying that I thought about doing anything, 'cause I didn't, but I'm lucky to be here because I now understand mental health. I understand that I was ignorant towards it. I was one of them people that didn't understand it. I was ignorant. 'How can you have mental health issues? What is there to be, was there to be sad about, was there to be done about it?' I was that guy, but now I've

experienced it myself. And I used the word lucky, because I'm lucky to be here, because I now understand and know that you don't actually realize the depth that you are in, how deep you are in it, until you come out of it. And a lot of people don't get out of it. So it took me [coming] out of a depressive state to understand that I was actually in something … I'm lucky to have the family and friends that I have, the group of people around me who was able to help me … And I didn't know there was a problem … I thought I was actually OK. Yeah. I thought I was fine because anything that's ever happened to me, I've always used football to deal with it. Always. And football has always dealt with it. So because I was still playing football, I just felt like I was OK. But then my manager's telling me … my manager at the time, Neil Warnock, he's saying to me, you wasn't the same person. You wasn't the same player.

Mixed Up podcast, Season 3, Episode 1

It's clear that it doesn't matter how well your career may be going, how much you are liked as a celebrity or an athlete, or whether you marry into the Royal Family … racist abuse seems to be an inescapable part of the job.

Colin Kaepernick's entire NFL career came to a screeching halt the moment he took the knee during the national anthem at the start of NFL games on 1 September 2016 in protest against police brutality and racial inequality in the United States. In what seems like a strange coincidence, this played out in the same timeline as Meghan Markle and Prince Harry's relationship debut to the public. Meghan and Harry's relationship was under extreme scrutiny in the British press and the coverage of both Meghan and Colin was heavily racialized – the two of them impacted the fabric of both American and British society just by existing.

Today mixed people are projected to be the fastest-growing demographic and at the same time are used to highlight the fact that we are moving towards a post-racial society (as was written in *National Geographic* as early as 2013[7]), while in reality celebrities and public figures, despite their privileged status, face struggles on the world's stage. Kaepernick explained his action by saying:

> I am not going to stand up to show pride in a flag for a country that oppresses Black people and People of Colour. To me, this is bigger than football, and it would be selfish on my part to look the other way. There are bodies in the street and people [police] getting paid leave and getting away with murder.[8]

He decided to kneel out of respect from then on. The action and its meaning became extremely polarizing throughout the US as well as the UK and grew to be a globally recognized symbol. In November 2017 he filed a grievance against the NFL and its owners, accusing them of colluding to keep him out of the league. He then withdrew it in February 2019 after reaching a confidential settlement.

During the height of his protests, the likes of Donald Trump verbally abused him in interviews on platforms provided by mainstream US media. But just as jarring was commentary from pundits such as former NFL defensive back Rodney Harrison, who in an interview with *SportsTalk 790* said: 'I tell you this, I'm a Black man. And Colin Kaepernick – he's not Black. He cannot understand what I face and what other young Black men and Black people face, or People of Colour face, on a daily basis.'

While Kaepernick's actions could be categorized as 'too Black' for the NFL and for Trump it was clear that, meanwhile, some members of the Black community were ready to dismiss Colin's protest and his Blackness out of hand because he is mixed. So in spite of being subjected to the racism which other Black people suffer, he was alienated both by those who stood to benefit from the protest and also those who could be considered 'kin'.

We should note that prior to the agreement coming into place the NFL had already effectively 'blackballed' him, thereby taking his living, his passion, his sport, his social status and any affinity he may have had with his peer group and stripping him of things which are ideologically representative of his African American identity. It could be said that, like that of a 'tragic mulatto' character, Colin's status within society met a metaphorical death that was facilitated by protagonists on both sides.

Despite their power and privilege, celebrities and public figures are still human. And we can't ignore the role the media continue to play in perpetuating racism and divisive identity politics for mixed people.

Naomi Osaka, a four-times Grand Slam singles tennis champion, who was born in Japan to a Japanese mother and Haitian father, was the final torchbearer for the 2020 Summer Olympic Games in Japan. Much has been written about her with regard to her heritage, and after she appeared before the world as a Japanese woman who is also Haitian, an op-ed ran in *The Australian* with the headline 'How Japanese is Naomi Osaka?' The question alone feels like an attack. Many of us who are mixed have been asked these questions before, and we never feel like we have the right answer, or at least the answer that the person asking us would want to hear. The author of the op-ed, Will Swanton, wrote:

I don't sense a deep connection to her from the Japanese public. She's a multicultural, multiracial, Japanese-Haitian-American woman with a wonderful mix of bloodlines in her veins.

I thought Osaka's igniting of the flame was the only flat spot of the opening ceremony ...

Something about it just felt wrong. She hadn't come from the mean streets of a Japanese town to conquer the world. If her life story has a message to any young tennis player, it might be this: get to America, get down to Florida. Osaka flew the coop twenty years ago, and she's stayed there.

At the risk of sounding crude, the truth is that she's a bit of a blow-in. She flew here, from Florida, to compete. Far better candidates grew up here.[9]

In not so many words, the headline affirms most of our fears as mixed people. It's not enough that she has a Japanese mother: she lives in America and is therefore not Japanese. Never mind that she's been competing under the Japanese flag since she was 14 years old. Although the language is meant to be celebratory around her multiple heritages, it feels like a slight because it signals it's inappropriate for Osaka to be lighting the opening ceremony flame in Japan.

In Osaka's Netflix documentary there are moments of musing on whether or not she is enough of one or the other, and you can tell how this weighs heavily on her mind.

She says:

I should probably try to speak Japanese more. I speak Japanese to my mom and my sister. They won't say anything about the way that I talk because I have broken grammar. But now I'm in this spotlight, I'm thinking, maybe I'm doing something wrong by not representing the half-Black, half-Japanese kids well.

Opening up about her decision to play for Japan during the 2020 Olympics, she says:

So I don't choose America and suddenly people are like, 'Your Black card is revoked.' And it's like, African American isn't the only Black, you know? And I feel like people really don't know the difference between nationality and race, 'cause there's a lot of Black people in Brazil, but they're Brazilian.[10]

When it comes to discussions about race and identity, there is a fundamental disconnect for so many – there is a difference between nationality (your country of birth), your race and your ethnicity. And when you are mixed race, this becomes even more complex when you talk about your identity; it adds to others' confusion, which you then feel compelled to clarify. Or called on to clarify, in Naomi's case.

What we've always appreciated about Naomi Osaka is that she is someone who doesn't seem afraid to be honest in her vulnerabilities. We feel as if there has been a lot of that sentiment in the mixed community of late – feeling vulnerable, not entirely knowing what to say, not entirely knowing what to feel but still taking on the responsibility of owning up to that uncertainty, because it's human.

This documentary really brought home to us that as mixed-race people we may not always have the answers. In fact, we are often on a journey of discovery into our own identity, which makes it difficult to be certain in our conviction; but although our personal, private journey often becomes very public, we deserve the latitude to be open and honest about trying to figure it out.

Rui Hachimura, another mixed Black Japanese athlete who plays basketball for the Los Angeles Lakers, has spoken about the difficulties he faced growing up as a mixed Black boy in Japan. In an interview with Olympics.com he said:

As a mixed-race kid growing up in Japan it was very hard you know, especially, you know, as Japan is one race. When I was a kid there wasn't many, you know … Especially in my hometown, it's small, in the countryside and I think we were the only Black family in the town. It was really hard as a kid, I had a hard experience.[11]

MODERN-DAY DISCRIMINATORY PRACTICES TOWARDS MIXED-RACE PEOPLE

The mixed-race identity isn't solely something that is questioned or invalidated by the different parts of your community; your bloodline can invalidate you from your home and your property by the government.

As gentrification has taken hold in Hawaii, living there has become less and less affordable and it is now one of the most expensive places to live in the US. The government has employed a scheme to prioritize *kānaka* – Indigenous Hawaiians – to their ancestral land, the islands that are their birthright. After years of colonization and displacement, thousands of Indigenous *kānaka* now have a claim to this land, but in order to keep it they must pass a 'blood quantum' that was set out in the Hawaiian Homes Commission Act in 1921 to prove they are at least 50 per cent Hawaiian by blood.

In fact the scheme is somewhat insidious, in that over time it has become near-impossible to keep families intact and for mixed Hawaiian children and grandchildren to inherit land that has been in their families for generations. Ultimately this is an exclusion of mixed-race people that has been codified into law, and in Hawaii, where Indigenous homelessness and unemployment rates are at a high, the stability of the culture and the community is jeopardized by a law that is meant to be protecting it.

In a news report, Carol Lee Kamekona explains that there are many multi-generational *kānaka maoli* homes in Maui and that often up to four generations might live together in order to survive and meet costs because housing is so unaffordable. She goes on to explain that she has seven children, none of whom can apply for the 'Hawaiian homelands' scheme: 'My kids will never get an opportunity to live here because once I die, once my mum dies, there is no 50 per cent blood quantum for my family. It's genocide. It's a way to get rid of the people.'[12] You get the sense that what is most upsetting for Carol is the fact that she will not be able to pass this important part of her ancestry on to her children. *Kamaʻāina* is a native word that means 'child or person of the land'; it's extremely sad that whether or not you can share in this important cultural aspect of your heritage boils down to the exact blood quantum you have.

PRIVILEGE DOESN'T ALWAYS PREVENT RACISM

In writing this book we felt it was important to draw attention to the fact that light-skinned privilege isn't the same as white privilege, and that any privilege which mixed-race people do have exists on a spectrum and in context.

We have seen that there are very specific ways in which mixed-race people have been discriminated against: historically through miscegenation and apartheid, and today in cases where your mixed bloodline can deny you your home and your property.

Many people believe that because colourism clearly does affect darker-skinned people negatively, racism towards mixed-race people (who are often assumed to be lighter in skin tone) cannot simultaneously be true. That if mixed people do face racism, it can't be something that is experienced as viscerally as by someone who is monoracial.

But, as is often the case when it comes to issues of race, it's just not that simple.

As Dr Melissa J. Wagner put it to us, you can be dismissed from your own community because you are mixed, and your feelings and experiences invalidated; it often feels like there are 'levels' of racism that you have to experience in order for your identity to be recognized:

> There was a very interesting conversation going on around Kamala Harris prior to the Biden administration getting in within the Black community. There was a lot of really, you know, virulent stuff about her belonging to the enemy, Indian people are the enemy. And she's not really Black and she's not Black enough and everything … I mean, she identifies as a Black woman … she went to Howard … Now she's the first Black vice-president. I'm like, OK, that's interesting. But you can be kicked out. I mean, I've been kicked out because … I was in the Black community, but now I'm on the wrong side of this Fenty 300 and I definitely cry 'too many beige tears' and all of this.
>
> Mixed Up *podcast, Season 2*

For our part, we want to acknowledge and give space for the very real racism that the mixed people we have spoken to have experienced, and for the stories they have shared with us. We also want to make sure that recent historical and modern-day racism is seen for what it is.

9.

WHY WE NEED TO RE-EXAMINE THE PHRASE 'WHITE PASSING'

Colour, for anyone who uses it, or is used by it, is a most complex, calculated, and dangerous phenomenon.

James Baldwin, The Price of the Ticket *(1985)*

EMMA

You can pass an exam, you can pass a note, you can pass over an opportunity or be passing through town. But there is something quite unsettling about the idea that you can label someone else as 'passing' for something.

When people are growing bolder in exercising their agency to assert and own their lived identities, it would seem at odds that simultaneously society is wedded to upholding the idea of labelling some with old-fashioned identifiers such as 'white passing'. Today it's much more commonplace to see individuals taking time to understand and craft their identities and, going further, to share the way they would like to be received by the world. It's not something that merely happens through an internal dialogue and a personal journey of growth: but now, more often than not, there is also an external declaration that accompanies that internal affirmation.

In the last few years we have seen a real push for people to be free to express their felt identity. We've witnessed a call for educational guide parametres to be put in place to see the uninitiated schooled in how they can and should respect the way people feel their personal identities, as opposed to forcing the identities we assume for them on to them and consequently labelling them with these. Often this labelling is out of a need to categorize, classify and designate people into groups – to assign stereotypical ideas in a bid to organize and make sense of the world. But in most instances this process is based on little more than appearance.

We're now seeing more extensive use of gender pronouns, which is a good example of the move to self-identify and to push back on society's mishandling of labels and mistaken ideas around external agency over personal identities. In 2020, a study by the Trevor Project found that 25 per cent of LGBTQ+ and youth use gender pronouns, and that a quarter of queer youth between the ages of 13 and 24 identify outside of the gender binary. The report notes that 'Respecting pronouns is part of creating a supportive and accepting environment, which impacts well-being […] the best way to confirm a person's pronouns is by asking or by introducing yourself with your pronouns, to give the person an opportunity to share theirs.'[1]

While many reading this may now be familiar with the term 'passing' in the context of gender identity, it has been our anecdotal observation that there is not much common knowledge of how the concept has historically affected and continues to affect people's lived experience when it comes to 'race'.

It is true that the use of the term 'passing' within and of the trans community has been questioned, as people argue that there is no one way gender should look. Indeed: how might one 'pass' for one gender or another if this is true?

Speaking to Travis Alabanza, author of *None of the Above: Reflections on Life Beyond the Binary*, if the idea of recognizing that gender doesn't have to look a certain way in order to be legitimate: breaking down the gender binary in this way – then should the idea of 'passing' be redundant already?

It's interesting. I love that you've brought it up in regards to white passing ... because race and gender get these, like, complicated comparisons. But I do think both of them are conditional, right? Both racial passing and trans passing are always conditional. It's never as stable as people think. People go, someone's white passing or someone's cis-passing, but then you place them in another environment and suddenly they're not, and so I think I always at first say it's conditional. It is always dependent on the people in power deciding who you are, and they can take that away from you. And I think what is frustrating about the passing conversation is we focus so much on whether or not someone passes or not. That we don't focus on challenging the structures that are in power that control whether someone is passing or not, or on what 'passing' is telling us about society. I think it's sometimes useful because in order to look at white passing or cis-passing, we have to admit that to pass is to be safer. And so that makes us ask questions about society and power, about what exists that makes racialized people [seem] more dangerous or visibly gender non-conforming people, more dangerous [to those in power].

Mixed Up *podcast, Season 3, Episode 4*

It could also be argued that the use of the term among those who are trans implies deception. Scrapping the label pushes back against this implication of trickery and duplicity that exists both in the trans community and in relation to race and mixed-race people – specifically those who present as white.

For a mixed-race person, the phrase 'white passing' implies an accomplishment merely in looking 'white enough' and, as discussed in Chapter 7, The 'Tragic Mulatto' Myth – this has its roots in Antebellum America. It was used to describe a mixed-race person, then usually known as a 'mulatto', a term which is thought to derive from the Latin word *mula*, meaning 'mule', the offspring of a donkey and a horse. These are now outdated terms that, happily, are widely agreed to be offensive.

People who were able to assimilate into the white majority without being recognized as having Black heritage were known as 'white passing'.

Antebellum America was characterized by the enslavement of Black people and an oppressive, violent and divided culture. During this period 'passing' as white was used as a means of escaping slavery, a way of obtaining freedom – because to be white was to be free and to be Black was to be someone else's property. Post-slavery, 'passing' was later used by some Black Americans to elude segregation, to obtain work or to travel more easily.

There is something particularly insidious about the phrase 'passing' being used as a category descriptor of someone's racial make-up today because it implies the active as opposed to the passive: it implies that someone is active in attempting to 'pass'. 'Passing' implies that this is something calculated that you deliberately do as a mixed person, when in reality, in its modern-day context, it tends to be something that is assumed based on how you look and how other people may perceive you. The person making the assumption is the active party whereas you who are merely existing in a modern day context are, in fact, the passive party. But still we hear the phrase 'white passing' being used as though we are living in a 1800s context where someone desires to 'pass' for survival or to lead a more privileged or indeed less dangerous life. We recognize, of course, that today there are advantages in existing within a white body, but it is irresponsible to imagine the two scenarios as equal in meaning and gravitas. One in its historical context – quite literally being based on survival and merely living – and the other being about a different degree of privilege, but also a categorization and ideological separation from one of their communities, that we ought to understand may not necessarily be desired by the person in question.

We have to consider the possibility that inclusion within, and acceptance amongst the family and community they live with might be their most longed-for existence. They may wish above all to really be seen as part of the group they belong to.

We spoke to Collette Hughes, who is mixed Indian and white British, for a *Mixed Up* episode on this very topic. She said:

> People say … 'You're really lucky because you don't look Indian, but you tan really well so you'd never know.' But I want to look Indian! I want to look the same as my family and I want to celebrate that side of me. When I was in school I had people saying, 'That can't be your mum', 'That can't be your nan', 'You don't look at all the same.' 'How are they brown and how are you white?'

This is a prime example of why the label 'white passing' can feel so disruptive and alienating – by the implication that you are distancing yourself from your heritage and are being wilfully dishonest to those around you. It perpetuates the idea that we have to 'pass' at race to be accepted. The implication of 'white passing' here is that you've made it. Somehow, you've crossed the finish line. But then – spoiler alert – you can't claim whiteness as your prize because you are not white, and as Travis points out in their earlier quote, it is all conditional. Nothing is fixed.

The important thing to note is that language evolves and changes. Terms that were acceptable in the 1800s are, thank goodness, not ones we use now. There may come a time when the phrases 'mixed' or 'mixed race' are phased out. Even now, although we agree we feel at home with them at present, and whilst many of our generation may seem to concur, the descriptor 'mixed race' is definitely being interrogated – because, of course, 'race' itself is a social construct, but also because people are beginning to wonder whether the idea of being a 'mix' rather than 'whole' feels reductive.

As mixed people it can often feel as though we are battling against how other people perceive us, and how this might differ from how we perceive and know ourselves. It can be incredibly draining on the psyche. Parallels can be drawn here with the way in which Travis describes how they feel about the pressure to express our identities in a way that fits with society's perception of them.

> I do think that where we're at in the trans community, I'm really
> bored of us turning our identity or trying to turn our identity
> into something that is clean and makes sense. It feels like we've
> responded to the pressure of oppression by going, 'Let's make
> ourselves really neat and understandable.' And so that looks like
> we're focusing on things like pronoun badges and drag queens
> reading stories to people.

Travis is speaking explicitly about the trans community; however this feels pertinent for people who are perceived as white because it is very difficult for them to make themselves neat, and as Travis says – there is no need to strive for this. In an episode of the *Mixed Up* podcast I said to Nicole that I have felt first-hand the challenges in not wanting to centre whiteness in the conversation around my identity, but also a pressure somehow to declare this part of my heritage to ensure there can be no accusation of deception, no charge against me later down the line with regard to not acknowledging the access that this background affords you. Whilst I don't begrudge this dynamic in any way – It *is* sometimes stifling, even in this context, and so I can well imagine how being mixed and presenting as white, and therefore being labelled as someone who 'passes' (especially when your family is not white), could be extremely alienating and isolating.

PERSONAL EXPERIENCES

The singer Halsey has been open and honest about her struggles with her identity as a biracial woman who is perceived to be white. In 2017 she did an interview with *Playboy*: 'I look like a white girl, but I don't feel like one. I'm a Black woman,' the singer explained. 'So it's been weird navigating that. When I was growing up I didn't know if I was supposed to love TLC or Britney.'[2] Halsey, who has a white mother and a Black father, calls herself 'white passing':

> A lot of people try to write off a lot of my experiences because I present white … No matter how many tears I've shed because I'm not connecting with my family or my culture in a way that I would like to, or because the waitress thinks I'm the babysitter when I go out with my family, none of that would compare to the tears that I would shed for presenting phenotypically Black and the disadvantages and the violence that I would face because of that.

Has she ever benefited from being white presenting?

> Oh, yeah, for sure. My family has a lot of guilt about [that], but I think this is really common for mixed families. You want your kids to have an advantage in life. That unfortunately puts them in a position of denying their heritage. Then you get older, you get woke, and you go to a liberal arts college and you go, 'Oh, my God,' and you start having flashbacks of all the micro-aggressions you faced through your life.[3]

In our first season of *Mixed Up*, we recorded the episode: 'The Rise of the Mixed-race Dialogue' and we had the opportunity to speak to people in the mixed community who would be considered by the wider world as 'white passing'. What struck us most about this concept of 'passing' was how they felt about it, mostly centred around guilt and shame linked to privilege, sadness about not looking like members of their family and also anger about not wanting to be left out, or left behind by their communities.

We spoke to actor/writer/director Gabriel Bisset-Smith about his experience of 'passing'. Gabriel wrote the play 'Whitewash' based on his life, growing up with a mixed Jamaican and Scottish mother. On the podcast he shared that when he was younger his mother would call him 'The Talented Mr Ripley'. She was speaking to how he could navigate most, if not all, communities, races and different types of people because of how he looked.

If you have never read the book nor seen the film *The Talented Mr Ripley*, the main thing to know is that deception is at the core of the main character, Tom Ripley and – spoiler alert! – he assumes another character's identity. His wily ways and murderous deeds allow him to obtain the ill-gotten gains and lavish lifestyle he has coveted. His ability to blend in seamlessly and take on a new identity is pitched ultimately, as a deplorable character flaw rather than a positive attribute.

That Gabriel was called (affectionately or otherwise) 'The Talented Mr Ripley', with all that label carries, is something that feels quite specific to mixed people (and, you can imagine, to anyone mixed who is perceived to be white in wider society). We've already mentioned the idea that some people have – that mixed people are deceptive by nature – so we can only imagine how there is an added layer of complication to navigating this for someone who isn't white but who looks it, and is assumed to be so by everyone else. Gabriel told us:

> I think from the day I was born, pretty much, I experienced white privilege from the fact that, you know, people thought my mother kidnapped me. Or when me and my mother went on holiday she would be stopped at customs and I would just walk through. And you feel a lot of guilt because sometimes when you get ahead in life you feel like a lot of that is to do with being accepted into white spaces and you're sort of gaming the system in that way.
>
> Mixed Up *podcast, Season 1, Episode 5*

And here's the thing: there isn't anything inherently wrong with being 'a chameleon' or being able to straddle multiple identities. It just becomes part of your day-to-day life. It's not inauthentic, it's just how you have learned to move through the world when you have to live as part of at least two different cultures and multiple perspectives. If anything, should it not be viewed as a valuable and beautiful thing?

Another contributor in this episode, Charlie (whose heritage is mixed Black Jamaican and white) says that she's always resented the term 'white passing' because she never saw 'getting away with being white' as a positive thing as it diminished the Black side of her. 'I'm so keen to not be a white ally, because I'm not white.' Charlie is describing something that is being decided for her; her position on the board of life with regard to the politics and the experience of race and activism are completely outside of her control.

When you consider Farzana Nayani's assertion (as discussed in Chapter 2) that racial delegitimization can be a damaging and stressful experience, it must then be so very hurtful to be positioned as a white ally, a side character to your own trauma. And all this when you're not in fact white, when you know yourself to be mixed Black. Gabriel spoke to us of the guilt and conflict these experiences brought up: 'It's polarizing because you don't want to be on the white side but your skin is white and you have to acknowledge your part in that system and you have to confront the way the world treats you.'

This feels like a lot to take on as a child or as a young adult. You're not in a position to be in control of how you look, how you were born, or how the outside world perceives you.

NOT A PERSONALITY TYPE

One thing we should be clear on is that 'passing' or presenting as white is not a personality type. It does not define a person. It isn't something that makes you who you are, but sometimes the way it is applied as a descriptor to people by others might have you believe that this is the case – that it supersedes any other label that might otherwise be applied. It's almost as though this categorization is seen to be the most important marker. And one might well ask – is this white supremacy at work again, tricking us into overstating the importance of whiteness?

While 'passing' is certainly not a 'personality type', there are some interesting ways in which people respond to being labelled in this way that become coping strategies or helpful shields that could perpetuate the misunderstanding that there's something inherently linked to personality here. Does Gabriel cloak himself in the character of 'The Talented Mr Ripley', taking it on in a jovial way before anyone else can get to it, almost in an attempt to vanquish the elephant in the room? Are we as mixed people sometimes so uncomfortable in our own skins that we feel the need to call ourselves out before others do? Maybe if we can embody the characters we've been assigned, just maybe, we won't be relentlessly questioned.

* * *

Why did *Love Island*'s Jack Fowler (whom we also interviewed on the podcast) self-identifying as a 'white man' out loud make me personally feel so uncomfortable? I'd be fibbing if I didn't admit I felt an urge to scream – 'No, don't say that – people won't understand that you are acknowledging being racialized as a white man, that you feel maybe you can't call yourself a Black man even though your dad and family members are Black, but that it wouldn't feel right not to recognize that people see you as white, and that as a result you haven't felt the level of oppression a man racialized as Black might. That you understand this and sympathize.' In the moment I understood where he was coming from, but somehow I felt uncomfortable at his articulation.

> I've always, um, kind of identified as just white Caucasian. Um, I'm never, it's – I'm just, I'm in a really awkward kind of bracket, But like, yeah. It's just, it's – there's no tickbox for certain things. And when I put out there that my dad is a man of colour, people were like, 'So what are you then?' And I'm like, 'Well, I don't really know.'
>
> *Jack Fowler on Being Mixed But Perceived as White,*
> *Race Dynamics in Love Island and Racism in Football,*
> Mixed Up *podcast, Season 2*

Why (if I'm honest) did it make me flinch ever so slightly, when in fact that's not fair of me and I have no business being perturbed by how Jack chooses to identify? Although I had no right to, I felt protective over his delicate truth and how outsiders might understand it, maybe because I'm older and slightly more jaded.

And is it because Besma intuits that her most Arab identifier is her name that she feels she can't loudly claim her Muslim Arab heritage? She recalls the conflict she felt in not being recognized as belonging to, and having cultural understanding of a group of people who are consistently marginalized in society when she was trying to advocate for them in predominantly white sustainability spaces that have a tendency to stumble into white-saviour role play.

Perhaps Rebecca Hall, the director of the cinematic interpretation of the book *Passing* (1929) by Nella Larsen said it best in describing both Clare (who is the central character) as well as the atmosphere of the film itself as 'destabilizing'.

An accurate word, because the whole notion of passing in a way destabilizes everything – the hierarchy built by white supremacy, along with the idea that you can't hold multiple realities and identities at the same time. Perhaps we can go further and say that the concept of mixed identity, or indeed any identity that we can't immediately recognize as an established, well-known category, might well be destabilizing for society in general …

Passing is about two mixed-race women who grew up childhood friends and who reunite in adulthood to find that one of them is passing as a white woman. It's significant in its historical context because it was written during the Great Migration, when Black people in the US began to leave the rural south and moved to northern and Midwestern cities to escape poor economic conditions, racial segregation and the discrimination that was still prevalent in the southern states.

During that time there was already moral panic not just about Black people moving into predominantly white areas or creating communities of their own nearby, but also that the blending of races would mean an indelible shift in the racial make-up, and therefore hierarchy, of a society that had been carefully set up and manipulated by white Americans to ensure that they maintained superior power structures.

Hall – who herself presents as white but who has African American heritage – also shared that her mother was quite obviously Black to her, but that she never described herself like that: 'because my grandfather was "passing", it wasn't in her lexicon. She wasn't given that gift of the label to identify with.' In a way, this is the crux of both the film and the question of identity and belonging – the question of who gives you licence to belong in certain places or to certain groups and whether in reality people have a choice.

'Passing', belonging, safety and performativity

While we are on the subject of who gets to decide on the admission criteria for any given group and the gatekeeping of membership to said groups, let's discuss the idea of performativity.

Performativity as a concept snuggles up rather uncomfortably close against the notion of 'passing'. They are cousins. The two are interlinked in that often those who are labelled as passing are more or less always simultaneously charged with performativity. As an exercise, let's carefully consider the validity of the accusation of performativity when it is put into context with some examples that speak to one version of the mixed experience.

I myself am mixed white and Black, but I am almost certain after over thirty turns around the sun that people in the main 'see' me as a Black woman first. And if that wasn't enough psychological drama, as you'll know by now if you've been paying attention – my family are white. All of the family I grew up with are white. My late mum was white, my dad is white and Northern, my not so little any more brothers are white. Both had long blond ringlety hair for much of their youth, and my mum was blonde and slight with azure-blue eyes that were mischievous, but piercingly scary in the switch of a moment. I describe them not to indulge in nostalgia, but to give you a vision of how I might have looked sat among them all in a row with our Cornish pasties on a beach, in a Harvester or at our local Chinese restaurant or alone – big sis waiting to pick up my littlest brother in the school playground.

So does my having a white family make me white? No.

Does it mean that I perform whiteness in the presence of my family when we go out for waffles and I am the only Black person at the breakfast table? No.

Does it mean I perform Blackness when I am meeting up with Black friends, when I have my hair done in cornrow or braid styles, or indeed while I'm backing jollof rice and stew with my Nene and my family-in-law? No – it most certainly does not a-beg.

You see, I am Black *and* I am mixed.

To look at me, any white person might label me as Black. But does that mean that I pass for Black in the Black community? I'm not sure – you'd have to ask around … At any rate, for me the most important thing here is that I am allowed to belong in both groups, and as my whole self – not labelled as 'other' or as an 'unknown quantity' that can't be trusted. This is not a science experiment, people, and I cannot behave like oil or water when I am neither. I am both.

Georgina Lawton sums this up in her book *Raceless: In Search of Family, Identity and the Truth About Where I Belong* when she suggests that 'belonging is everything'.

If this is true, we can begin to understand the natural compulsion to flex into the parts of your identity that most closely align with the group you're with – not as a performance, but as a compassionate understanding of said group that is borne out in the expression of who we are and whom we present ourselves as. It's not sneaky or deceptive, as it is often characterized, but instead it is a level of emotional work that aims not only to save you from the discomfort or awkwardness of feeling like a foreign body, but often this flexing and this way of fluidly fitting with the expected norm is intuitively done to ensure that the group (your group) is comfortable and feels safe.

I can definitely relate to this, and would go so far to say it is natural and maybe even respectful. After all, in many cultures it is seen as a sign of respect to understand and ingratiate yourself with the way of doing things.

Thandiwe Newton once said that she doesn't talk about her white family because she wants other Black women to know she is an ally – 'because I want Black people to feel they can trust me and feel safe with me – that I'm not a representative of this Establishment that degrades People of Colour'. It's about saying, 'You can trust me – I'm one of you. I belong here.' And it's most probably done on a subconscious level.

We have often noted mixed people in the public eye who pointedly align themselves with the side of their racial heritage that is not white. This is most obvious with mixed Black individuals; could it be due to the level of oppression Black people have suffered and how far they have been distanced from other races through these tools of oppression and white supremacy? There is something in the criteria of being part of this group that somehow feels more rigorous; perhaps mixed Black people feel they have the most to prove and that their position in the group is fragile.

We get the impression that some personalities in the public eye feel that they must overtly present 'allyship' and 'unequivocal Blackness' at all times as the first thing that enters the room ahead of them in order to reassure and maintain group membership. They are often active in social justice and speak out on Black issues. A need to prove that they deserve to be part of the community and earn their place is palpable in every move. They don't want anything to come up that might remind the community that they are 'mixed' and endanger their place within it. There can be no misstep, nothing that might be misconstrued as aligning with their 'other' side.

This assessment might initially come across as sounding cynical, but we've thought about it a lot, and believe that we should understand this approach as a truly valid and honest way of communicating identity and belonging to a group. If we come from a beautiful heritage and ancestry, why wouldn't we be joyful about exploring and claiming those parts of ourselves that lean into that, rather than lambast each other and argue over the bits we feel belong to us and us alone as People of Colour?

In *Raceless* Georgina writes of performativity:

> These existential struggles can be applied to anyone from
> multiple-heritage backgrounds or households: lacking racial
> representation, or an understanding of how to navigate racialised
> experiences, can produce near-comical scenarios when you come
> into contact with others who expect you to be in possession of a
> different identity, or worse, accuse you of performing an identity
> which to you is perfectly normal and leave you to assert yourself
> around others who look like you.[4]

Bringing this thought back to people who have Black or brown heritage but who physically present as white, we can begin to see how accusations of performativity and passing might meet at a damning intersection, and also how it might be impossible not to fall foul of them while navigating 'racialized experiences' in which others have no visual identifier of your complex and true identity.

Another of our guests on the podcast who spoke to her experience of this was Caitlin Bellah, an artist and photographer whose ancestry is

Seminole Freedman. This tribe was formed when the Spanish attempted to hang on to lands that they were finding difficult to defend due to the fact that they decimated the native population they relied on as militia with the introduction of Eurasian disease, colonist conflict, religious domination and cruelty. The Spanish in Florida needed to grow the population, so they invited enslaved Black people and Native Americans from the south to Florida to protect the land and live in freedom, and this is how a mixed tribe formed the Seminole Freedmen.

Caitlin described a scenario where she was working on a photography project about her ancestry, and in particular her grandmother, who was Black Seminole Freedman, and her mentor at her agency discovered her heritage. She went from being in what she had perceived to be a relatively safe environment to an extremely unsafe one in moments:

So what happened is I got this opportunity, I'd been living in Barcelona for years and I really, you know, admired an artist and, um, got the opportunity to work closely with their team. So I moved to Madrid. I had already had this idea to do this project, um, about Oklahoma or about Black history in general. And I'd presented it to this person that I would be working with. And I had mentioned, you know, my grandmother was from Oklahoma, which is where one of these stories takes place that I was presenting. And he looked at me and he said, 'Your grandmother, huh? So you're Black?'

Essentially, every single time from then on, they would sabotage opportunities that I would have to get the project going. Finally, one day we were having lunch with a group of people and he was talking about Kanye West and he asked me, 'Oh, so Kanye West voted for Trump?' And I said, 'Yeah ... I don't know much about Kanye West.' And he stood up and he said, 'I don't know how that [N-Word] would ever consider voting for someone like

Donald Trump.' And we were in a group of people who were all fluent in English, people who worked in the fashion industry, who worked for, you know, big brands. And I thought, you know, you sit there and when you hear something like that and no one said anything. And I timidly said, 'I don't think that you should say that.' And he was just laughing like a crazy person.

I think that, you know, and this – I wanna say this 'cause I think it's important – um, that I think, obviously light-skin privilege exists. I don't wanna diminish that, but at the same time I feel like sometimes when you're mixed, it just sometimes puts you closer to white people who would be abusive because they're in your family, or they're maybe in your community; if you're raised like I was away from your Black family, then maybe you were growing up in a white community. And that's been my experience, cuz this happened and it was shocking and it happened in my adulthood. But I just wanna say it's not the first time that something like this has happened to me or to my siblings either. And I've heard it from other mixed people too that are a little lighter, that they've experienced aggression and racism but they feel like they can't talk about it or they feel like people aren't going to empathize, because 'Oh, you're white.' And it's like, no. If you are a Person of Colour, if you don't have two white parents, you know, you don't have access to whiteness completely. You will always be 'other' if people know, unless you are completely silent about it and you never talk about yourself at all, and you act like half a person, You will always be a little bit in danger … I don't wanna apologize for my existence.

Mixed Up *podcast, Season 4, Episode 5*

Caitlin, along with other guests, highlights a really important point here: that people who are perceived as white are not safe from racism. There can be a compulsion to minimize racist trauma experienced by mixed people, especially light-skinned mixed people or those who can be at times perceived as white. As Caitlin's quote demonstrates, the discovery that someone is not white by an individual who is racist can create an extremely volatile scenario where that racist will exhibit all of the responses of someone who feels they have been somehow 'duped' and then doubles down on punishing the person they feel they have been tricked by.

'Reverse Passing'

The study 'Passing as Black: Racial Identity Work among Biracial Americans' presupposes that 'biracial people have considerable agency in asserting their identities and argues that 'biracial people use strategies to conceal (i.e. pass) cover, and/or accent aspects of their racial ancestries'.[5] Referring to the interview data, the authors decide that their 'biracial respondents ... most often identify as biracial, but in some contexts, they pass as monoracial'. We agreed that we found the suggestion that these biracial respondents were engaging in a sort of 'reverse passing' offensive. In some ways this line of thought feels like the face of the enemy of progress. The research paper does note that some scholars argue that passing may be a relic of the past, but the authors assert that the phenomenon of passing still occurs today and that, in stark contrast to 'passing' in the Jim Crow era, which involved passing as white, respondents are more likely to report 'passing as Black' today.

Neither of the authors are of Black/white mixed heritage, and that leaves us wondering whether they are best positioned to come to a truly compassionate understanding of the lived experience which the biracial respondents communicate. Is this a case of the authors misreading people's assertion of group membership, and their commitment to the business of belonging, unnecessarily shrouding it in negative connotation?

When we understand that race is a social construct, and that we as mixed people do what we can to feel and communicate a sense of belonging to the groups with which we associate our identity, can we accept that it's normal for this to be a fluid state for us? Is it time to sit with the idea of understanding ourselves as both, not one – even perhaps more of one thing on one day than on another – and as contextual to whom we are talking to in a given moment as something that is truthful and real, and lived?

If we really deep all of this – negative assessments of mixed-race individuals who present as white, or who perhaps don't present, for example, as South or East Asian – despite the fact that they have an Asian parent and where this is the only family they know – feels, at worst, extremely ungenerous, and at best maybe a little churlish. Another way of seeing it, as Georgina points out in *Raceless*, is that 'Mixed individuals … align themselves with the part of their racial heritage that so often demarcates their lived experience, the part the world can see. Also, it isn't "performative" to identify with your socially constructed racial category.'[6]

The idea that mixed people are utilizing whichever part of their identity that suits them, or that it's sneaky in some way, is simply people doing too much. Why is it so hard to believe that someone can have a fluid and multi-layered identity? Is performativity with regard to being mixed race or 'passing' something we should just throw out as a discussion point? Is it a non-starter?

'The moment we are active operators in a capitalist system that has us here as "avatars of ourselves"', to quote Ayishat Akanbi, the topic of performativity is potentially a non-starter. Unfortunately while mixed people are not a monolith, there is a universality to the identity labelling that is often dictated by others as opposed to mixed people themselves, and when it comes to the use of the label 'white passing', the most famous example is probably that of the one in which the first modern day member of the British Royal family to be Black was told she ain't Black, by Sharon Osbourne (a white woman) saying of Meghan Markle, 'She ain't Black.' When challenged, Osbourne followed up with, 'But yeah, she doesn't look Black … to anybody.' Later, Candace Owens waded into the debate: 'You would not be able to discern just by look-ing at Meghan Markle that she's Black.' The irony is that Meghan Markle simultaneously had to contend with vile racial abuse in the media and people speculating about how dark her child might be when born.

At the time, even Meghan's identity as a mixed-race woman seemed to be up for debate and dissection by just about everyone. Was she really Black enough to be suffering racism? Should she recognize her many levels of mixed-race privilege before daring to request that she not be harassed, debased and abused by the media and the people of the UK?

We remember vividly when she wrote an article for *ELLE* confirming that she identified as a mixed-race woman, probably to stem the inces-sant questioning. Was she ambiguous, was the racism she faced really all that bad given that she is light-skinned, and indeed if she herself doesn't identify *only* as 'Black'?[7]

No level of privilege can protect a Black woman (mixed or otherwise) from the brutal misogynoir dished out to us on the daily. And how interesting it is that we mixed-race Black women are rarely ever asked to speak about our own experiences and the issues that are literally 'us' – the ones we ought to be asked to comment on – while we are consistently (often justifiably) told that other issues of Blackness or race are not ours to front.

Meghan said that the onslaught of racist violence she'd experienced as a woman many define as 'white passing' made her feel like she didn't want to exist. This is the dichotomy of being visible but invisible. Of being privileged but also unsafe. For Jeremy Clarkson, with his sickening article in *The Sun*, for Piers Morgan et al., Meghan seems to be desirable but simultaneously easy to loathe – and this is not just about the woman herself but also the recognition that they are fascinated by a Black woman who has managed to 'pass' into the upper echelons of white society. A place where they do not believe she belongs. They are incensed that she exists in these spaces, let alone speak out about her discomfort. How dare she? And somehow this makes their distaste and anger even more palpable:

> Meghan, though, is a different story. I hate her. Not like I hate Nicola Sturgeon or Rose West. I hate her on a cellular level, [...] At night I am unable to sleep as I lie there grinding my teeth and dreaming of the day when she is made to parade naked through the streets of every town in Britain while the crowds chant 'shame!' and throw lumps of excrement at her.[8]

And perhaps on a 'cellular level', rather than a conscious one, even more irritation comes from the idea that she does not desire them. They consider her to be beneath them because she is ultimately of Black heritage. It is visceral. Piers Morgan commented: '[we] ... got ghosted. We all got frozen out. She had reached a loftier place and there was no room for people like us.'[9]

Morgan has often spoken of how he perceives Meghan to be 'fame-hungry', arrogant and above her station. To quote him directly, he recently described her as 'a smirking cynical cat who got the commercial lottery-life-win cream'.[10]

Ultimately, this chapter's discussion takes us right back to where we started in Chapter 2, where we argue that it is problematic to question how Black a mixed person is, how Chinese they are, how Indian they are based on our own stereotypical and often shallow notions of what that looks like.

There is no pro-forma way to be 'Black' as a mixed-race Black person. It is damaging to dictate mixed people's identity in a way that gatekeeps part of their heritage from them or denies them being both and not one or the other. Denying them the fluidity that is real life to them is damaging and only perpetuates some of the negative consequences of abhorrent structures that have served only to oppress.

10.
EVERYBODY HAS
A HAIR STORY

NICOLE

Don't touch my hair

I first relaxed my hair at the age of 10. I was in a perpetual war against it and I was determined to win.

I can't remember who first introduced my mom to gold tongs and a flat iron comb, which were the tools I loved to hate. I used to constantly pick at the scabs they left behind on my forehead and the tops of my ears – but it was worth it every time. My hair was straight. And that was what mattered.

It was all we knew back then about what 'pretty hair' looked like. It was constantly being fed to us on TV, in movies and in magazines. Especially magazines. I was an avid magazine reader in those days; I was always spending my money on the likes of *ELLE Girl*, *Teen Vogue*, *Cosmo Girl*, *J-14*, *Seventeen* … it was a different time for media back then, let me tell you. Long, flowing, straight hair – always glossy, never frizzy. Easy to maintain.

There was so much about my hair in its natural state that I didn't know, and at that time positive messaging about looking different was non-existent. Turning on the TV or sitting down to watch a movie, there was only one type of hair back then. But today, any generic shampoo or conditioner ad campaign over the last few years is shown on every hair type they can get their hands on to demonstrate the universal nature of its magic.

My mom, unlike me, has a short bob, which to me is the universal haircut of Filipino moms of a certain age, but of course when she was younger she had very long, sleek, pin-straight hair. More than anything I just wanted my hair to be easy to style – like hers. It was obvious that she struggled with not knowing what to do with mine and had to ask her colleagues at the Jamaican Embassy for advice. Naturally they told her to take me to the Black hair salon, because there they could do a relaxer.

Filipinos, more often than not, have very thick, wavy hair. In fact it's often now used in hair extensions, due to its strength and cuticle shaft, but when I was growing up it was all too easy to lump Asian (specifically East Asian) hair types together – the assumption being that if you were any type of 'Asian' your hair could grow very long, sleek and straight. No one ever took into account that Filipinos have very different hair types and textures to other Asians as well.

I distinctly remember being told that I had 'the perfect hair for a relaxer' by my hairdresser, and at 10 years old I was immediately proud of myself! I had no idea what that meant, but I was happy that life would somehow be made easier – only very swiftly to be overcome by the burning sensation and chemical smell. I didn't cry that day, although I wanted to. Mom knew that it *really burned* but she held my hand, mainly to stop me from scratching my scalp as I sat there. And that was that! I began a decade-long journey into straightening my hair, one that my mother and I embarked on together.

Talking to her about it now, as adults, both of us can see what a waste of time, money and energy it all was. Looking back at her then, I can completely understand and empathize with her thought process. She saw that I was unhappy with how I looked, she heard me agonizing constantly about how much I wanted straight hair, how I wished my hair could look like this or that. She wanted to make me happy.

Unfortunately, at that time we never had the opportunity to get to the root of the issue. I had been made to feel as though the hair texture I was born with not only wasn't good or beautiful enough, but that it was difficult and hard to maintain, and that it must be changed and manipulated to make my life easier. And I internalized that message from a young age.

It was one of the first things that I noticed about being 'different', actually. It was the thing that I knew I could immediately change about myself to become more like the vision of beauty that was sold to us through all those TV ads I mentioned. At that time I felt like there wasn't a lot of me being reflected back to me, so the best I could do was try to mould myself into what I thought other people (and myself at that time) thought was pretty, was fashionable, was cool. When you're that age you're just trying out things to make you look good, and for me changing my hair was the first thing that came to mind.

As a young Black girl, it felt like this was just part of the deal. Something you just have to get on with. You just deal with it. Part of the process of doing your hair is the pain that you just have to endure.

How our hair is so intrinsically linked to our identities and our emotional state of being has a deep history. Emma Dabiri writes in *Don't Touch My Hair*:

Hair-straightening for people of African descent emerges from a traumatic history. Since the advent of the slave trade – the centuries-long trans-Atlantic trade in Black flesh – our humanity has not been something straightforwardly assumed. While most of the world's population is melanated (is that a word? It should be!), there are few populations beyond those of African descent (and some Polynesians, Micronesians and Melanesians) who have Afro hair. Our hair is the physical marker that distinguishes us from all other racial groups.[1]

From the beginning, my dad never wanted me to relax my hair and was extremely vocal about how he preferred my hair natural. 'Why don't you leave your hair alone? Your hair is beautiful as it is, why would you ever want to change the hair that you were given?' He was never heavy-handed about his disapproval, and I know he does believe that my hair is beautiful as it is. But whether it was short or long, whether it was styled or not, he also understood the significance of the relaxer. The relaxer was a symbol of assimilation. It was a way to chemically manipulate my curly hair into straight hair and he simply couldn't support that.

He is an African man, he is a Ghanaian man – and he knows the significance that our hair carries. He grew up in Ghana but he always told me he was only made aware of his Blackness when he moved to the United Kingdom, and then again when he ultimately settled in the United States. He knew that my getting a relaxer every few months meant a slow, painful process of stripping away a physical marker of my Blackness, and that this might later come back to haunt me in terms of my identity.

It's easy to look back now and understand where he was coming from as an adult, as the dad of a young girl. The choices we all made then didn't just come to us on a whim but were deeply ingrained in us as products of a Western, colonized society.

EMMA

A pilgrimage

One of the first people I was drawn to during Freshers' Week at university was Leanne.

She was a mirror to me in some ways. Leanne is also mixed and from London. She was lively and she always seemed to have a squib full of wisecrack balled up under her tongue inside her cheek. She has blue eyes, her hair is golden, coiled and perfectly formed, and her voice is deeper than mine – a little husky. In this way, and also in her mannerisms and when she spoke, she came across as far older than her years. I learned later that this might also have been due to her being one of many siblings. Her voice and her confident demeanour engendered trust in me quickly, and I remember that when she laughed her raucous East London guffaw made me feel a little safer, a little more at home in this new place that was alien to me.

One of the first things we discussed was our hair and hair products. Leanne declared that she would be making a pilgrimage to somewhere she had looked up on the map called Fishponds. She had done her research and apparently this was where all the Afro hair products lived in Bristol. This was where we would find all the things we needed to tame and beautify our curls, which we both agreed scathingly had become unacceptably dry and lacklustre since we had arrived in Bristol, not having had access to the Black hair products we needed in the town centre.

So we made the journey, chatting all the way. Leanne was also Jamaican, but unlike me she was very close to her Jamaican family. It seemed from our conversations that she had access not just to the Black side of her heritage but to all of the information and confidence that could bring when it came to styling her hair and caring for it – even when trying new things like dyeing it almost bleached blonde (which she told me she had done recently), hence why it was 'bone-dry', as she described it, and in desperate need of a deep-heat treatment.

I may not have realized it at the time, but I yearned for the gentle ease Leanne represented to me, not just in the way she carried herself but in how self-assured she was in her independence, how comfortable she was in who she was and the things she intended to do.

Back home in the suburbs of London, I had always had to seek out my friends' older sisters or friends of friends to do my hair if I wanted it canerowed or braided when I was growing up, and it wasn't just about achieving a hairstyle that would present me to the world as unmistakably Black, as part of the culture: it was more than that. Catching the train down to Willesden or Stonebridge in the evenings, I wanted to experience the sort of bonding moment with my culture that only takes place in someone's living room. Where you sit gripped for the first, or maybe even tenth time between a relative stranger's knees as they pull and twist and contort your hair into a style you've requested, or sometimes, perhaps – quite often – a style that, if you squint, maybe kinda resembles the style you requested, but is mostly whatever they wanted to give you.

That gift of time.

The patience and careful hand it takes to braid your hair is like an exchange of love somehow. And when it's done and you inspect your tight, fresh-to-death style in the mirror with the soft hum of the TV in the background, and you glance back at the woman who gave you this gift, this superfly symbol of who you are – they are no longer a stranger.

Every woman has a hair journey

I won't try to speak too much about the hair stories of non-mixed individuals, but one thing I have learned with regard to mixed people is that every head of hair is very, very different, and that most people have no doubt been on a hair journey. It *is* necessary, however, to set out some historical and social context for many of the personal experiences we will explore in this chapter – to speak specifically to the relationship Black women have with their hair.

I have a relationship with my hair that is both beautiful and complex, and I am sure this can be said for many women. In the survey 'Black British Women and Their Hair' conducted by Zainab Kwaw-Swanzy, the author of *A Quick Ting On: The Black Girl Afro* (2022), almost 33 per cent of respondents report that they have had a difficult journey with their hair and that they are still in the process of learning to love it, while 46 per cent say that they previously had some issues, but that they have learned to overcome them and now love their hair.[2]

With the resurgence of the natural hair movement in the 2000s, many Black women have been moved to embrace and nurture their natural hair textures. Stripping back to zero and growing out the creamy crack years has been in many cases inextricably linked to pushing back against the Eurocentric beauty standards that have been so damaging to the self-esteem, individuality and love of the authentic Black cultural identity.

Kwaw-Swanzy's survey documents that half of the women spoken to *agree or strongly agree* that 'Black women's hair is a political statement no matter how they wear it.' Kwaw-Swanzy surmises that most of those asked agreed that Black women's hair was indeed a political statement that directly correlates to who they are and and how they have been treated, and that they are not afforded the luxury to style their hair however they wish without assumptions being made about them. One respondent even mused: 'In my opinion it's rarely the intention of Black women to be political with their hair but it's viewed by others as being a statement.'

Looking back, the way I wore my hair was never a political comment. It wasn't something I did as a conscious statement or political act of protest. I wasn't cognisant of pushing back against societal norms or of raising a proverbial fist in unison with a Black Power movement when I started wearing my hair in its fullest expression of Afro. I believed … I still believe I was simply existing.

But now that I am grown, I can reflect with much more maturity and see that my decision (although at first – my mother's decision) was one that was a signal. It was a white flag, a marker of belonging, a membership card to a group I had not always felt I could exist within without question.

I remember being approached in the street or in the shopping centre as a clueless teen by mostly middle-aged white men and women who would raise a fist at me and sometimes pointedly mouth or enunciate the words 'Black Power'. At the time I didn't really understand why they would make the assumption that solidarity with the Black Power movement was my specific and intended message and I certainly didn't feel I had a particular affinity with the political revolution for which they seemed to believe I was a local representative. As far as I saw it, I simply wanted to be.

But now, having done a lot of exploration and unpacking through the podcast and other conversations, I understand that the way I wore my hair *was* an affirmation I chose to make time and time again. An affirmation about my in-group and where I believed I belonged. A choice to appear Black and, quite frankly, as Black as possible. I chose my Black-affirming features because I wanted to be claimed by the community. This is not to say that I wanted to reject my white heritage, it is simply that I also craved access to the Black side of it.

For a long time I had no Black community to be enveloped into at the hair shop, or at Auntie's house on a Sunday. No cousin or elder or sister friend to braid my hair … and while my white mother learned to canerow, I had long stopped giving her licence to practise and perfect this skill, and in turn she had long stopped trying to force me to let her. This is something about which I hold a heart-wrenching regret for to this day.

I was recently talking to Nicole after recording the episode of the podcast called 'An Honest Exploration into the Experiences of White Mums Bringing up Mixed-race Children'. We had listened to a number of accounts of white mums who had taken the time to learn to canerow and plait their children's hair. Many of them spoke of their pride in being able to do their child's hair and they often marvelled at the joy of this bonding experience. I suddenly got choked up when we reflected on how emotional it was hearing from the mothers. I remembered how unkind and thoughtless I had been in response to my own mother's efforts as teenagerdom surged through my veins and I became self-absorbed and unable to muster compassion for anyone's emotions but my own. I recall a time when, Dax tub and hairpick in hand, she had wanted to canerow my hair again and it had been quite a while since the last time, so she was out of practice. I remember being suitably ill-tempered about the whole thing. On reflection, it was one of those instances where she couldn't win because as soon as I sat on the carpet between her legs, I am pretty sure I had decided she wasn't skilled enough to deliver what my teen-perfection-obsessed brain wanted. Only a very slick, very tight style would do and I was already resolute in my assumption that she couldn't deliver.

We sat for hours, as is normal when braiding hair, and it pains me to recall that when she was finished I took one look in the mirror, declared that it didn't look right and insisted it was unpicked and taken out not long after. Brutal.

My heart breaks a little for my mum every time I think of it, and I don't know if I forgive myself for this unkindness.

I am of a fairly light-skinned complexion, yet my hair texture is very curly, thick and dense when brushed out. I almost always wear it as a full Afro, and people often compare my hair to that of Angela Davis and her 60s styles, or the renaissance woman that was Marsha Hunt with her fro. I do agree that, even if subconsciously, for many who see my hair, there certainly is an implicit political meaning in it for them – and so I can relate to the aforementioned survey respondents' assertion in Kwaw-Swanzy's research, as well as acknowledge an affirmation of my Blackness in my choice to wear my hair in a fro. I am Black and white mixed, and my lighter skin tone perhaps cues up the fact that I am 'mixed' in people's minds, but my hair? My hair makes me unmistakably Black. Its texture is such that it stands and can be combed out into a perfectly formed round. I would pass the pencil test without issue. But maybe most pertinent is the way in which my hair, without much manipulation at all, does naturally resemble what became a symbol of Black resistance, power and pride in the 1960s and 70s. Although globally popularized by American figures of the civil rights and resistance movements and then by the fashion of the time, it was and I think still is seen in its simplest expression as an expression of proudly putting your Blackness on show.

When I was younger, I remember my mum was adamant about how powerful and glorious my hair was. She told me it was beautiful, often. She hated it when I would scrape and force it back into what in hindsight she may have viewed as the most ridiculous of white girl hairstyles – flattening it and gelling its volume into tiny incomprehensible spaces and shapes it was not meant for, knowing full well it would be doing its damnedest to escape: little springs and coils that were wiring their way out of a chokehold before the day was out.

In my early teenage years the mission was to be as inconspicuous as possible. I just wanted to fit in. I recall moulding my hair into a middle part and bun with strong-hold gel before creating the two downward antennae that were supposed to fall as slim strands either side of my forehead to frame the face. For me, though, they were curly and would spring upwards to present more like little caterpillars that stopped just before they reached my eyebrows.

What is my hair type?

Even in my thirties I am still figuring this out.

I'll level with you: when people tell me definitively that they themselves have type 4c hair but their child has type 3a, and then begin to extrapolate what this means for their hair-care routines, I'll often nod and smile, trying to avoid being caught out for not having much of a clue as to how my hair type would be categorized.

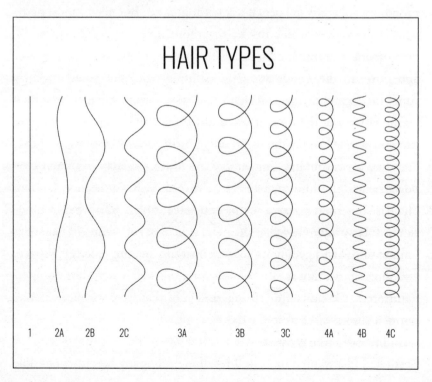

HAIR TYPES

| 1 | 2A | 2B | 2C | 3A | 3B | 3C | 4A | 4B | 4C |

I know what they are talking about, of course. I've seen and heard of the chart to which they refer. I mean, I've not been living under a rock, and a quick Google will bring up any number of diagram representations of the hair texture classifications they are describing. It's true. But, having studied them closely searching for a reliable conclusion, time and time again I have had to settle for the idea that perhaps I have as many as three different curl patterns growing out of my head. Or alternatively that my curl pattern sits between two of those listed on the chart. Or maybe, at the very least, my curl pattern depends heavily on what day it is, whether I have washed my hair recently, whether I've brushed it out or not in the shower before letting it dry, or even what humidity of weather it's been experiencing ... I still haven't been able to figure it out on my own. So do I subscribe to the categorization and how it might help me care for my hair? I'm not sure. I'm not wholly convinced ...

I do believe that anything that represents more open sharing of information about how to care for our non-Caucasian hair types is great news. Yet sometimes I can't help but wonder if this texture chart and system is yet another way to categorize the uncategorizable, another way to divide us and to sow division, or set us apart. Maybe it is another tool that will encourage us to spend our days talking about how we are more different than we are the same, to batter hierarchies deeper into the subconscious as we discuss how Becky with the good hair is somehow better and more desirable, or at least more palatable than Oluwatoyin and her 4c coils. It seems to me that this is what much of the toxic yet popular rhetoric that has sprung from the introduction of this chart's labelling system into the mainstream vernacular reinforces. Of course, texturism existed long before the chart did, but now it seems we have a new way to add specificity and finality to not having drawn the most desirable or the best hair type in the lottery of genetics.

For me it is also somewhat of an oversimplification of the business of hair politics. If you are mixed Black, like me, it may be useful to speak to many different Black men and women about how they style and work with their hair, to glean information – the chart initially gave me the false impression that if you sit in one category there may be little point discussing your hair with a woman/or man whose hair is apparently in another. However, I can speak only for myself but I have learned over time that this is not the case.

Historically, features that could be easily identified or labelled as distinct to a person's 'race' were used to justify the enslavement of Black and mixed people in Europe and the Americas. As we've already touched on, hair was one of the features that were used to separate 'Black' from 'white' – those who could be enslaved and destined for indentured servitude from those who should be free. Categorisation via hair was part of the project to dehumanize Black people in order to vindicate the business of slavery. For some slave masters, this distinction was insisted upon, particularly where the appearance of their slaves' hair differed little from their own. One account, from Shane White and Graham White's *Slave Hair And African American Culture in the Eighteenth and Nineteenth Centuries*, tells us: 'Mistress Uster ask me what that was I had on my head and I would tell her, "Hair," and she said, "No, that ain't hair, that's wool." [But] I had straight hair and my mistress would say, "Don't say hair, say wool."'

Native Americans or First Nations people often had their long hair forcibly cut, and long hair become outlawed in some places by the colonizers because it was known that hair held very important meaning for the First Nations tribes and the intention was to 'kill the Indian and save the man':

From birth to death, hair is respected as an intimate extension of the self as well as a connection to the world. Of course, the specific powers of hair vary from tribe to tribe – for the Navajo Nation, hair is traditionally only cut in circumstances of mourning, while the Apache peoples hold hair cutting ceremonies each spring to ensure health and success. That's your connection to the land.

Hair is your strength; it's the teaching that's been passed down from generation to generation. It's who you are. It's your spirit. The longer your hair is, the more connected you are to the land … Every nation has different teachings but long hair means the same to all. Spirit. Strength. Connection. Identity.

(Nlaka'pamux elder Ernie Michell, Goldrush Trail, CA)

The historical tracing of how hair has been used to separate, subjugate and classify us (and by us I mean People of Colour and Indigenous peoples) as more or less savage and uncivilized supports the idea that the curl scale is in some ways problematic: it can be yet another thing that entrenches these ideas of striving for whiteness, the notions of colourism wrapped up in the way we describe, grade and view our own hair as better or worse, easier, or more or less Eurocentric and closer to white beauty standards.

Texturism has become the sister wife of colourism and their internalization can push you towards trying to legitimize your Blackness or reaffirming that your hair does not fit the looser, more European curl pattern that has become synonymous with desirable 'curly girl' hair and 'good hair'. The tool wasn't made for this, but has it become something to bash people over the head with?

NICOLE

It's not just hair

Reading Emma Dabiri's *Don't Touch My Hair* was the first time I had ever come across anyone identifying hair as a feature of racialization, not just skin tone. While it wasn't the first time this idea had been presented to me, it was something I'd never seen laid out so plainly before. The revelation came quickly that for us as Black women, our hair is as much, if not more than, a distinct physical mark of our race as our skin colour. It always comes back to hair.

Just as the paper bag rule (if you are darker than a paper bag, then you are Black) exists as a remnant of slavery, so does the pencil rule. For mixed Black people, it's hair texture – straight away, no matter how light you are – that acts as a determinant for people to perceive you as Black or not.

The discourse around our hair types and textures should merely be one that marvels at how incredibly different they can all be. Our hair will look and feel different to different people and we should be able to wear it however we choose: natural, relaxed, loc'd, braided. It's just hair, after all, but the judgement from others around what we do with it can often make it feel like a political statement that holds much more weight. Like it's everything.

What I find so important and so powerful about Dabiri's book is that it really breaks down the stereotypes around mixed people, in particular light-skinned mixed people who have some Black African heritage, and the expectation for them to have loose curls or 'good hair'. The two are not mutually exclusive. Just as mixed people have many different skin tones, their hair textures are also just as varied. Not only that, but it looks at what hair was like or how people felt about their hair before there was any stigma attached to it.

THE NATURAL HAIR MOVEMENT

The movement to protect our hair has now shifted from learning how to care for it and what products to use to exercising our right to live healthy lives without fear and discrimination within wider society.

When it comes to Black hair and traditionally protective styles, you can be excluded from school for wearing your natural hair, you can be discriminated against in the workplace and with regard to housing, and you can even be criminalized for it because of the persistent idea, stemming from years of systematic and historical dehumanization, that Black hair is unruly, untidy and unprofessional.

In 2020, The Halo Code, an anti-discrimination campaign, was signed by one of the UK's biggest employers, Unilever, in order to protect workers with Afros, dreadlocks and protective styles. In the US, the Crown Act was first introduced and signed into law in California in 2019, expanding the definition of race in the Fair Employment and Housing Act and State Education Code to protect those in workplaces and schools against hair discrimination. The Crown Act has since been signed into law in twenty-four other states.

It's important to point out that this doesn't just apply to Black hair but to Indigenous hair and its styles as well: the American Civil Liberties Union of New Mexico sued the state's largest school district after a (now former) teacher allegedly cut a Navajo student's braid during class. Incidents have been reported of Indigenous children being sent home for having long hair. In Arizona, referees officiating a high-school basketball game prohibited the girls from wearing their hair in a *tsiiyéél*, a traditional Navajo hairstyle. A California school board also pushed back against a Native student wearing a traditional eagle feather in his hair for his graduation ceremony.

It's plain to see that hair has never just solely been a Black issue. Change is slow, but it's coming, and we certainly have the natural hair movement to thank for that. As social media brings us ever closer together, stories of hair discrimination and violence spread like wildfire. But at the same time, it has allowed traditional and cultural practices to be adopted by the West.

Historically, the Global Majority altered their hair to assimilate themselves to white society, but now we are seeing a renewed interest in ancient practices and traditions. We believe this is an important exploration for the mixed community in order to find connection within their heritage groups.

SOUTH ASIAN TRADITIONS

The importance of hair in Sikh tradition and spirituality

In the Indian religion of Sikhism, allowing one's hair to grow naturally shows respect for the perfection of God's creation and is viewed as a symbol of purity and strength. This is called *kesh* and is the practice of one of the Five Kakaars. Traditionally, men's hair is combed twice a day with a *kanga* and tied into a knot, held in place by the *kanga* and covered by a turban. Sikhs believe that this a symbol of their faith and devotion to God; since their persecution during the Mughal Empire, they have been unwilling to cut their hair in order to disguise themselves and would rather face death. In the twenty-first century, in the aftermath of 9/11, there was an increase in hate crimes towards all perceived as Muslims. Sikhs wearing turbans, mistaken for Muslims, were also targeted.

The Indian practice of hair-oiling

Much like braiding in the African traditions, hair-oiling in India is something that is passed down generationally, primarily through mothers telling stories while oiling their daughters' hair. There, long, sleek hair is the beauty standard among women and this practice is also meant to encourage hair health. In the Ayurvedic system, the act of caring for the hair and scalp is akin to caring for the mind and soul.

The act became a pop culture moment in season 2 of the Netflix series *Bridgerton*, where elder sister Kate is shown oiling her younger sister Edwina's hair. She warms the oil and massages it through her sister's hair in a moment of tenderness and familial bonding. The Sanskrit word *sneha* means both 'to oil' and also 'to love' or 'affection', indicating a connection between these acts.

These traditions are meant not only as symbols of love of God (or gods, depending on the religion) but symbols of love for oneself or one another. Akash Mehta, hair-oiling expert and founder of the hair wellness brand Fable & Mane, gave us his take on the rituals and how they keep him connected to his heritage:

Indian beauty rituals can connect the mind, body and soul, a moment of bonding with yourself and loved ones, and the oil head massage is an example of this. Our ancestral place is India, and the ingredients that are often found in an Indian kitchen, such as turmeric, coconut oil and mangoes, are now used as our core ingredients in the Fable & Mane products we make for others to enjoy. My grandma would visit from India and give us loving head massages with her handmade blend of Ayurvedic oils. She'd read stories to us while doing this and it became a core formative memory that's so peaceful and heartful. It was bonding in its purest form. When you're a child, story time is so powerful, so with the added element of a head massage it creates this unique experience that we will cherish forever, and surely pass down to our own families. Childhood memories are something that everyone can relate to, but the powerful ones shape who you are and what you do. They are something everyone can connect to and find solace in, especially when they are linked to your culture and heritage.

The best way to oil hair is to take a few drops of your hair oil, rub your palms together to warm the oil and massage into the roots, starting on your crown – this *marma* point (the Sahasrara or Crown Chakra) helps to calm your whole body and is a really important part of the hair-oiling ritual. Then, run the remaining oil through your strands to hydrate the ends. After massaging, wrap your hair in a braid or bun and leave in overnight for the best results.

(Authors' interview with Akash Mehta)

Hair rituals from East Asia

In China, before the Qing dynasty (1644–1911), long hair was highly valued and not cutting it was viewed as a symbol of self-respect. Confucius taught that the act of not touching the hair or skin was also a sign of respect for the ancestors, *xiao*. Meaning was attached to hair in other ways too, including marriage status, class, ethnicity and political alignment. During this time, young girls and unmarried women wore their hair long and down, or in a singular braid. Only after they were married were they then able to coil their hair up as a marker of their marital status. Women who were widowed would cut their hair or shave it off entirely, signifying a death.

The Tang dynasty (618–907) is a notable time in Chinese history and is viewed as a golden age – cultural advancements, reform and prosperity meant that hairstyles also evolved and became more intricate in design and used ornaments like chopsticks and pins made out of jade, gold and pearl.

During the Qing dynasty, Chinese men traditionally wore their hair tonsured (shaved at the front and long at the back or in a single braid) after the Manchus came to power. The Manchus passed a Queue Order which required this hairstyle for men by law, on pain of death.

It was only after the Communist revolution that Chinese men began to cut their hair short all over, primarily in accordance with Western standards. From that point the tonsured hairstyle and queue braid was viewed as a threat to the Communist regime, indicating one's loyalty to the Qing dynasty.

Looking back over history, we were surprised to find that hair has never stopped being a political statement or indicating an alignment. Considering how far back these traditions go, it's no wonder it carries such significance in our day-to-day lives. Ultimately, how we present ourselves has meaning, and we don't have to shy away from that.

In Japan, the Heian period (794–1185) was a key period in the country's history, when Japanese culture is meant to have truly emerged and evolved, deliberately rejecting influences from Korea and China. It was a time when long black hair, sleek and straight, was also seen as the standard of beauty, particularly among noblewomen; the average length of a woman's hair was one metre. Noblewomen, written about in stories and poetry of the time, often grew their hair to seven or eight metres. During the Edo period (1603–1868) hairdressing flourished and gave rise to the traditional Japanese hairstyles we know today which are still worn by brides and were heavily influenced by geishas. For men, the *chonmage* was popular during this time and is commonly viewed as the traditional samurai hairstyle and, more recently, the hairstyle worn by sumo wrestlers. It was cut and styled specifically in such a way so as to keep a helmet on and ensure that the head did not overheat.

The Meiji period (1868–1912) was a time of major Western influence and meant an outright rejection of the *chonmage*. The government required men and women to cut their hair short by law. Pamphlets were distributed to Japanese women to promote a new way of tying their hair while also keeping it short, telling them how traditional Japanese hairstyles were 'inconvenient', 'unhygienic' and 'uneconomical'. What came next was an assimilation of Japanese people into Western norms of the time and, as in many cases throughout history, what feels like a watering-down of traditions in order to conform with modern (i.e. Western) trends.

Reading this was a reminder of how the erasure of traditions and cultural practices – be it a lack of knowledge around language or how to prepare certain foods or awareness of lineage or cultural tradition – is often what leaves mixed-race people feeling displaced.

Indigenous/First Nations culture and traditions

Although there are many different Indigenous tribes throughout North America, in general long hair is seen as a symbol of spiritual strength and power among First Nations people. Hair is viewed as a direct link to the land and a connection to nature, a physical manifestation of one's spirit and life force.

The varying hairstyles and braids in themselves helped to define individuals, nations and societies within the nations of North America during and after colonial times. The act of combing, braiding and caring for a family or tribe member's hair still carries an important significance and intimacy. Allowing a non-family member or someone outside the tribe to touch one's hair is usually seen as a sign of bad luck. First Nations traditions also chime with those of the South Asian community, where storytelling or singing is part of the ritual.

Ornamentation varies from family to family and tribe to tribe, but is used as a signifier depending on the tribe's distinction, the ceremony, or during times of war. For example, some tribes wear one, two or three braids. Some will paint their hair, or include beadwork. Some wear headwraps with fur, wool or feathers for dance and other ceremonies. As in some other cultures, when there is a death often braids will be cut in mourning.

During the 1800s in Canada, the residential school system was effectively a network of boarding schools for Indigenous children in order to isolate them from their families and traditions and assimilate them into Canadian Christian culture. In the United States they were called industrial schools. One of the first acts of violence that took place was often the forcible cutting of the hair; even to this day, survivors often speak of the humiliation and degradation they felt. Even now there are still schools that require boys to have haircuts 'above the collar'.

There is still much that people outside the tribes don't know about traditional hairstyles because they have meanings that are sacred and remain solely in the community and within families.

African traditions

I thought that I knew a lot, if not enough, about African hair as it is something that took up the majority of my thoughts as a young person. But ultimately that came from the Western school of thought primarily focused on trying to tame it, to manipulate it in a way that I felt would be at least palatable, if not beautiful. I knew it more from a postmodern perspective, the cultural significance of having relaxed hair versus an Afro and what people would perceive about you from those styles. It wasn't until reading *Don't Touch My Hair* that I understood not only the history but also the maths and the science.

With what I understand from other cultures across the globe, it's clear that braiding is a beautiful, shared connection that holds a lot of significance. What is fascinating, as Dabiri rightly points out in her book, is that African hairstyling is 'a place where maths is unconsciously applied in each step of the process'. And from studies on Black hairstyling and braiding, it is clear that it could not exist without these calculations and formulas. Algebra and geometry live in our hair and the way in which it is meticulously styled.

The practices we are familiar with today, like box braids and cornrows, are the ones that have survived the Middle Passage, and through them we stay directly connected to our ancestors.

In the fifteenth century in West Africa, hair, and specifically braided styles, were a signifier of age, marital status, social status and tribal group. When West Africans were captured and then brought en masse to other parts of the world, their hair was deliberately shaved off because of claims that African hair was viewed as 'unhygienic', which seems to be an obvious link to the reason why most people today think that African hair cannot grow long. Much of the imagery we see in American textbooks, for example, shows Black people with cropped Afros in the early days of slavery. In reality, our hair was something that had been taken from African people at that time and has since had a major influence on how we view Black hair today.

As we now understand it, the taking or removal of our hair contributes to both the ideological as well as the physical removal of our history. The knowledge that was passed down through maps that were drawn in canerow, the maths described above, and even the knowledge of how to care for our natural hair passed between us would have been developed, if not lost over time, as those who were enslaved were not able to practise in it. This equates to generational suffering and trauma – you might say the literal severing of the roots of our heritage.

When we met Winnie Awa, Nigerian-born founder of the Carra app, we wanted to obtain more insight into why she felt it was the next step towards reclaiming a love for our natural hair. Carra app uses AI, combining the power of experts, data and community to provide relevant personalized routines, guidance and product recommendations for our textured hair needs. We have heard that lots of mums of mixed-race kids have used the app, which is said to be slowly changing the lexicon for textured hair:

I grew up in Nigeria in the 90s and my earliest memories around hair revolved around getting my hair braided or put into threaded styles by an auntie every Sunday. I really enjoyed choosing the styles from the vintage posters, and now that I look back I think it instilled in me this innate penchant for self-expression through my hair which has remained till today, but by the same token my hair was also straightened with a hot iron at a very young age. In fact, I do remember really looking forward to getting my hair chemically straightened because I associated that with being grown up. I wanted it to look like the girls on the pack of the relaxer (many of whom we now know never actually had their hair relaxed). I suppose that this was the beginning of desiring something outside of what my hair was like naturally.

Curl definition and dryness are some of the top concerns for mixed hair care [via Carra] … I think generally there is a [false] expectation that mixed hair is always loose, luscious curls – but the reality is that, like the tighter coil patterns, there is really no one size fits all. Some [curls] grow down and others grow out, some are full, while others are thinner. I think these misconceptions lead to an expectation that a one-size-fits-all approach is required to care for textured hair in general which is not strictly true.

(Authors' interview with Winnie Awa)

Steaming is a technique that has been around for many years and is often used in Afro hair care because it can be of particular benefit to low-porosity hair, which struggles to absorb moisture, colour-treated hair and hair that's previously been chemically treated. London-born and -based mother of two Judy Koloko is founder of The Steam Bar. She is Nigerian Black British.

Like many successful beauty brand concepts, The Steam Bar was born from Judy's personal experience, when she noticed a gap begging to be filled. A long-time user of steaming services to support her own hair health, she noticed a lack of premium products and places which women of colour could visit and have this experience:

> Many People of Colour, like me, for years have worn wigs, weaves and extensions, causing trauma and stress to the scalp. The art of steaming is a ritual that has been neglected over time, but through its propensity to increases softness and stimulate growth I believe it can be vital in helping us care for our scalp and hair.
>
> My steaming experience goes back to when I was a child at home. This would consist of a specific mask or treatment being massaged into my hair and scalp, with my head then being covered with a plastic bag or warm towel to help retain heat from the head, allowing the treatment to take effect.
>
> Over the years, and owing to issues with my own scalp, I looked to revisit this childhood ritual and sought out salons that offered the steaming treatments I once enjoyed; looking for a moment of calm and tranquillity. This is quite a spiritual moment for me, sitting under a device that resembles a hood hair dryer; feeling the pores opening on the scalp – a dedicated moment to honour and nurture my crown and reclaim my sense of self.

This ritual feels meditative, calming, like taking a pause from life and society, a world where we are always on the grind.

(Authors' interview with Judy Koloko)

EMMA

Crying in Hype Coiffure

There were many times, definitely as a child and then as an adult, when this happened to me. I have been in tears either in the salon, or just as soon as I had slipped out of the door and round the corner out of sight.

Hairdressers have told me they cannot do my hair. I have witnessed them hide in the back of the salon, not wanting to be tasked with what must have appeared to them to be an insurmountably difficult and arduous task of sheer volume. I have left both Black and white hair salons in tears at having my hair butchered, or because I have been made to sit for hour upon hour upon hour just waiting and watching as everyone else's hair was done (despite them arriving long after me).

As I got old enough to go to hair salons by myself, I began to feel that to do anything with my hair other than wear it out was more hassle than it was worth. By this time, it had been years since my mum would buy me Black hair magazines like *Hype*, *Black Hair* magazine and *Essence*. I still remember spending hours studying the little square images of all the sculptural slicked styles and short, neat bobs and texturized curls. I would search the pages for hours deciding which style I wanted most, asking my mum what would suit me. I remember I was obsessed with Moesha's [Brandy's] tiny braid style, but also so many other American styles at the time that were just unachievable for my hair. Sometimes, when I suggested certain styles my mum would cock her head and say 'Hmmmm – I'm not sure you'll be able to get that one.' And I wonder now if she knew that many of the styles were achieved with a relaxer, weaves or wigs.

Me now? I had no idea of course.

On one occasion, when I was maybe 10 or 11, my mum took me to a Black hair salon to get my hair braided. I remember how excited I was, having been studying my magazines. I'd picked out the perfect style. I don't remember too much about that day, but I do remember that the stylists took one look at my hair and insisted that I first needed to have it relaxed in order to then have it braided. My mum barely waited to hear them finish their proposal before she yanked me out of there. When I protested, she tried to explain that I should be mindful of people who might wilfully damage my hair.

At that age I knew damn well I had no chance of being allowed to straighten my hair. My mum's words and her adamance that no chemical would touch my head over time began to take hold to transform my relationship with my hair to the point where its conspicuity became my superpower. I knew I would be noticed if I walked into a room with my Afro because it made me stand out, it was different, so I began to embrace it. Somewhere along the way my mother's habitual reaffirmation of my hair's celestial beauty had been imbued and it became my 'thing', my crown, my safety. It was the one thing I had that was special that nobody else (at the time) had, and I carried that with me into every room.

Although I did eventually find power in my hair, it would be disingenuous to ignore the journey. I've lost count of the times I have had to hold back tears until after leaving the salon, having not had the confidence to insist on what I wanted, or after paying through the nose for a badly executed style, or hiding under a headscarf waiting for my then boyfriend to pick me up as I tried to make myself small behind a lamppost – humiliated that I had paid for the mess that now sat atop my head.

Whether it was simply not being able to articulate myself, intimidated by the assertive hustle and bustle of a Black hair salon or the upset of an over-zealous Caucasian hairdresser thinning out my hair and advising me on how to make it less 'frizzy', it certainly has been a journey.

Nowadays, things are very different both for me personally and for the world at large looking for information on how and even where to go to do their hair. There is an abundance of information on the internet, in magazines, among hairdressers and anecdotally that never existed when I was growing up, but despite all this I am still on the journey. I am still learning about my own hair, how to manipulate it, and about its relationship to my identity. I am not yet an expert in any of these things. I have learned over time that some Black hair products don't work for my hair texture, nor do the standardized Eurocentric ones you find in high-street and mainstream shops like Superdrug or Boots, but for me it's been a lifetime pilgrimage of trial and error that has brought me here to this point.

Just recently, when I was at airport security, as I loaded my things on to the conveyor belt a woman commented on my hair, which I was peacocking to its fullest extent at the time. It was giving Erykah Badu meets Foxy Brown. She was telling me how she loved my style. Chatting away as I gathered my belongings back into my case, she asked me what I did for work and we eventually ended up talking about the *Mixed Up* podcast. Head cocked, she immediately started in, commenting, 'The thing I don't understand is why the white mums never learn to do their kids' hair.' I felt the heat rise in my cheeks and under my collarbone, but I stifled my shame and my sadness down. I felt overexposed, and like my own late mother was being judged by this woman. I also felt personally disrespected. Without asking me whether my own mum was white, she had made this wayward comment that seemed to resign us all to unkempt or uncared for hair because our negligent mothers just couldn't be bothered to learn to plait. I can't lie – I took it personally for a moment, but I pushed down my embarrassment and just swallowed it. I said nothing … I guess I am well practised.

I suppose if I extrapolate why this felt so raw, it's a reflection of this sort of pilgrimage I've been on with my own hair and how inextricably linked knowing and learning my hair has been to the relationship I have with myself, with understanding myself, and also, crucially, the relationship I had with the parent who traversed some of that journey with me – my mother. I can relate to the idea of the struggle or challenge white and monoracial parents face in figuring out how to protect and care for their mixed-race children's hair – and all of this before even getting into mastering the ancient arts of braiding, oiling or steaming, for example.

He has a really big, beautiful Afro. It is curly, it is just beautiful and I'm very jealous of his hair, if I'm honest, but he goes to a school in an area that is quite middle-class, and he is the only mixed-race Black child in his nursery class. When he first started that nursery, I used to do his hair in a bun, plaits, braids, everything. I used to spend so much time on his hair because he loved it. He would get up in the morning and say, 'Mommy, please, can you do my hair today?' And I would sit on YouTube and I would follow Instagram accounts and I would try my hardest. I didn't wanna let him down. And I would sit up for hours and I would just try and make sure that I could do his hair. I even borrowed a doll head from my sister-in-law to try and learn how to canerow because I just wanted to make sure that I could do what he wanted me to do with his hair. Then we went to the park one day and he had his hair in a bun, and this little boy came over to him and he kept saying, 'I'm not playing with you because you're a girl,' and just kept saying it over and over and over again, and you could see my son's eyes. And he was looking at me, he was getting so upset ... About a month ago now he came to me and he said, 'Mommy, I really want a haircut.' I said, 'What?' He said, 'I really want a haircut, like my best friend.' And I said, 'But you're never gonna have hair like your best friend – your best friend is blond and he has hair like Mommy, and your hair's not gonna go like that.' But he just was like, 'Why, Mommy? I really want my hair like him.' And I said, 'But you're not going to – you're mixed race and he's white and our hair is different.' And he said, 'But Mommy, no one looks like me in my classroom. No one has the same hair as me. I don't see anyone with hair like me.'

It just hit me, like you are four years old and you've recognized in your middle-class school that you can't relate to anybody ... We got a fantastic book called *Hair Love*. We spoke about his hair and now he's going to a new school starting in September. And I mentioned that there are gonna be lots of new children that look like him – mixed-race boys. I've seen them, they've got big curly hair, and his eyes lit up.

He's like, What? Because he loves his hair, but he's getting forced by society not to love his hair. And when he's older, he's gonna – he's gonna appreciate that I never did that. I hope he does. Anyway, it turns out after we had that conversation, he doesn't wanna get his cut any more.

> Mixed Up *podcast, Season 2, 'An Honest Exploration into the Experiences of White Mums Bringing up Mixed-race Children'*

I have compassion for the fear and apprehension in not knowing, and also how it might feel daunting with the onslaught of opinions coming from all angles of the internet. Even with all this information it still feels difficult to find something specific to mixed hair, and it's easy to get sucked into the paralysis that comes from the idea of doing hair 'the right way' taking precedence over having a go at doing it at all. This notion feels prevalent when it comes to both the natural Afro hair movement and when it comes to braiding and appreciation for the benefits of the specific care associated.

There is also a kind of guilt, a shame in the idea that we mixed-race women are supposed to be the ones who won with the natural hair movement, the ones who are represented in it over again – the ones who 'hijacked it', as Jacqueline Laurean Yates writes in her 2017 Yahoo article 'The Big Debate: Have "Mixed Women" Hijacked the Natural Hair Movement?'[3] I wonder if sometimes those who to this day feel like they haven't reached a good place in their hair journey feel a little lost and without a way to voice that feeling.

BUILDING A HEALTHY, LOVING RELATIONSHIP WITH YOUR HAIR, NO MATTER YOUR HAIR TYPE

It feels as though we are in the midst of a cultural shift when it comes to hair. When we look back at history, we can pinpoint where Western influence reinforced its standards regarding hair and beauty. But what has become more prevalent in the modern day? The hairstyles, rituals and beauty traditions we mention have become seemingly more acceptable, to the point of being adopted by white people as trends in some instances.

When we started this chapter we imagined that it would be the tell-all on mixed hair – how to 'tackle it', how to 'manage it'. That it would have every answer we have all been waiting for our whole lives, the ones that would have seen us avoid painful salon interactions and countless bad hair days thanks to unnecessary thinning, burning and primping. But in the end this would never have been possible because, just as the mixed identity is not a monolith, we all have very varying hair textures.

And, more importantly, we recognize that the guidelines that spoke to our younger selves, desperate to tame and change our various crowns to fit beauty standards, only speak to the language of yesterday.

Instead, we want to empower you with access to the rituals of our ancestors. Hair can provide a window into our heritage, and maintaining rituals that hark back to that heritage can help build a healthy, loving relationship with ourselves and our hair.

11.

THE CONVERSATIONS I NEVER HAD WITH MY PARENTS

One of the recurring themes that seems to strike a very emotional chord with many of the people we've been privileged to speak to while recording *Mixed Up* and in writing this book has been the conversations many of us wish we'd had with our parents.

Some wish they had been able to explore the things they found challenging about being of mixed heritage when they were younger, and some are still grappling with questions that have gone unanswered for fear of upsetting a balance, distressing a parent or opening up a Pandora's box.

EMMA

I can relate to this myself. Only this morning I was on ancestry.com searching for answers to questions I never had the courage to really press my mum for with regard to my biological paternal family. She's gone now, so I can't ask her these questions.

I can't say that I feel regret, because I try not to live my life in that way, and because I know I am loved and I am content in that, but I'm coming at it with the simplicity of being all too familiar with the hole grief leaves you with. The feeling of being untethered and no longer grounded in some way.

I think maybe, given the chance again, I would ask those questions; I would foster those conversations no matter how difficult.

I have no children as yet, but as I've grown older, more and more as time has crept on, I've begun to really understand the need to have these answers, not just for yourself but for your own children if you do decide to have them.

*　*　*

The subject of this chapter is something we knew would come from mixed people, giving their child selves the room to tell their stories without any external input from parents or parent figures.

These kinds of letters are often written as a cathartic exercise, a form of journaling that enables you to process your emotions and ultimately release them from being bound up in your mind and body. We wanted to remove any barriers or inhibition and allow space for vulnerability. Most of us are familiar with holding ourselves back, with trying to ignore or push down how we feel or felt, especially as adolescents, so this is that release.

We asked some of our mixed-race community to tell us what conversations they would have had with their parents, the ones they wish they had already had before they were grown up and time and space had passed between them. These are some of the letters they have penned to their parents.

Dear Dad,
I once asked you why you never applied for a British passport, despite living in the UK for nearly fifty years. You couldn't understand why I was asking; you were Jamaican, not British, and you wouldn't be living here forever – so why would you need

a passport? You were right (which was rare, but only I could get away with saying that!), and you did live out your final years back home on the land where your ashes are now buried.

That land is still quite the mystery to me. It's taken a long time for me to feel Jamaican, and when you died I lost the physical proof that told people that's where I'm from. People don't believe me when I say I'm part Jamaican. They question how dark my skin is and the texture of my hair and my English accent. My son has even fairer skin, even finer hair and feels even more distanced from my heritage even though it runs through his blood.

How did you feel having a child who looked like me? Was it more important for you to tell me stories of St Elizabeth and show me photos of your beloved grandmother?

I'm desperate for your grandson to feel a connection with your home, and to proudly say his grandad was from Jamaica, but I feel defensive of him knowing that people will question him. How can he stay steadfast in his pride and not be shamed into hiding behind his whiteness? I know he holds the same fire in his personality as me and you, so I'll do my best to show him how to own his identity. You would adore him.

I love you,

Charlotte x

(Charlie Elliott, mixed Jamaican/white British)

Hey Mom and Dad,

How are you both? How's Nan? How are Granny and Grandad? I haven't called them in ages – I should definitely do that more.

I was talking about them today, actually, and the things that they've passed down to me. Nan encouraged me to read and she always made me feel special when I'd stay with her on the weekends or go on day trips. As for Granny and Grandad, they've supported me unconditionally, no matter what I wanted to do. They've taught me the importance of community and maintaining a sense of humour well into your eighties – plus how to cheat at board games.

They also gave me both of you. They formed you in ways that have now formed me – Dad, I've inherited my love of music from you, and my bottomless band T-shirt collection. Mom, you showed me how to get the most out of life. You also gave me two heritages, British and Indian, although two words aren't really enough to encompass all of what that means, we never actually spoke about what all of that means. I don't blame you – I don't think any of us had the language to have that conversation in the 90s and early 2000s.

Mom, you gave me India – but with an East African Punjabi twist. When I was younger, you took me to melas and family weddings. Visiting Granny and Grandad in Hounslow, we'd eat mogo and maraghe, but only in my twenties did I start to see the difference between the food we ate and what was popular for British Asians who didn't move over from Kenya, Tanzania or Uganda. As a teen, I thought I was getting the names of my favourite dishes wrong and felt embarrassed. Now I know I was just calling them by their Swahili-Punjabi names. This realization started to drop others into place – no wonder I always felt like I was trying to fight my way into the British Asian community from the outside: not only was I half white, I was coming at things from a completely different cultural experience. Fuck!

Dad, I'm going to say that you gave me Birmingham. I'm on the fence with Britishness (I don't drink tea but I do say 'sorry' a lot), but I'll proudly claim my home city and defend it to the death. I've never really felt like I had to fight to be British –

people mostly see me as white, thinking I'm Italian or Spanish, but Britishness isn't something I necessarily want. I have feelings about this country and what Britishness symbolizes, so I'm happy to sit out of that circle. Indian-ness though? I'm still prising the doors open for that one.

Maybe I'll never feel like I fully belong, always trying to get people to see me and my heritage. While I know that the cultural markers we use to signify belonging to a racial group are arbitrary, I'll keep wearing my jhumka earrings in the hopes that someone will see them and ask if I'm Punjabi. 'Yes!' I'll smile, thinking of you both, and how I'm so much greater than the sum of two parts.

All my love,

Izzy x

(Isabella Silvers, mixed Punjabi/white British)

Mum,

You, of all people, know I'm not inclined to be a big talker or openly share my feelings, and please, don't even think about giving me a cuddle, hahaha. That's probably why I'm so drawn to writing; it allows me to express my emotions without putting myself in the vulnerable position of having to say them aloud.

I've always hesitated to express my feelings to you out of fear of causing you unnecessary pain.

I haven't even shared my recent diagnoses of ADHD and autism with you because I worry you might blame yourself as a parent for not recognizing the signs when I was younger.

I recall phrases like 'We don't see colour' and 'You're just one of us' being expressed at home, always filled with love and the best intentions. I never doubt that. However, this narrative inadvertently led me to believe I shouldn't care about it either. I conditioned myself to embrace this narrative outwardly, but deep down my lack of knowledge about my background and heritage has been a source of so much self-doubt and mental struggles for as long as I can remember.

For forty years, I had no proper understanding of who I was. I wish more consideration had been taken, not just from you but also from the adoption services to make sure I was connected or learned about my heritage and culture. Today, I am incredibly proud of my Black heritage, but I still feel I am constantly playing catch up and learning new things.

Lizzy

(Lizzy Kirk)

Dear Parents,

You never talked to me when I was growing up about the consequences you faced being a mixed-race couple in the 70s. I never heard about the rejection you had from both sides – I only pieced things together from the (many) overheard arguments that would flare up in late-night rows while I 'was asleep'. (I never was, you were very loud.) Mum – You never spoke to me about how you grappled with your own challenges about your mixed-race identity – born in Africa of Indian and African descent, ostracized from both communities and, I think, ashamed of your own identity. I've pieced this understanding together over the last few years with conversations with a kind and wise auntie who I was estranged from during my childhood. You never told me the truth about your heritage, Mum. You told me you had Egyptian and Iranian heritage – perhaps because this was seen as a desirable 'exoticism' in the 70s and 80s, but I literally spent over thirty years thinking I was something that I am not (and I now have the DNA test to prove it). It is only later in life that I understood your real heritage and that that in itself was something you had hidden – I am still piecing together why, but I think you held deep traumas about your identity that you unwittingly passed on to me. You used to talk about how you hoped people would see me as 'Spanish' or 'Italian' because of my colouring and curls. They never did of course.

It is sad that you wanted people to.

Dad – you never warned me that while members of my white family would love me and cherish me, they chose 'not to see' by colour, which led to them making racist comments openly in front of me. I'll never forget how my beloved grandfather raged over Stephen Lawrence's murder – not because an innocent Black boy was killed by racist thugs but because the papers were making such a 'fuss' over the killing of a boy who was 'obviously a drug dealer'. You never warned me how much I would internalize messages like that – distressing on so many levels, but for me as a young girl struggling with my identity and desperate to please, while I knew that was a terrible and wrong thing to say I could never speak up about it and risk being ostracized by people who loved me.

You never gave me the gift of honesty and acceptance of my mix and the strategies I would need to exist confidently in a world with a mix which made me feel never enough to fit in in any communities – certainly not white, not Indian and not Black ones.

I found my own acceptance and strategies in later life, mainly through discovering a whole community of other mixed people who have generously shared their own stories of grappling with complex identities and societal expectations. Even at the age of forty-eight I am still discovering amazing things. Last year, a kind Black African colleague at work, upon hearing me say I had

African heritage, explained to me that African people usually choose to identify themselves through their tribe, which made me realize I had no idea what tribe my African-ness was from. Cue a call to aforementioned wise auntie, who explained to me we were from the Yao tribe while expressing surprise I had never been told that!? At least the puzzle still comes together. These discoveries – plus therapy – have been the gift I needed. But I wish those gifts had come from you both. I know now you both have been burdened by your own traumas and pain – and I think there are mental health issues that underlie a lot of the behaviours, but while I can forgive, I can never forget.

'C'

Dear Mother,
Your whiteness smothered me
Far from all-embracing
It killed our kinship
My navel a reminder
Something was missing
A breakdown facing your reality
The baby you craved
Different
From that which you imagined
You were ill-equipped to love me
Racism coloured your vision
And I am my father's daughter
Too alien from your white roots

My brown skin turned ashy
With no care
My flat feet bound in
Corrective shoes
My curls protested your brush
You balded me in your bid
To control the wildness you
Believed they held
I am shorn
Born into your lack of
Understanding
I am the stranger
In my own family's midst
The Black Sheep of which
I stand alone

Your arms held neither
Warmth nor sanctuary
From the wider world of hate
To build a sense of self
Your aquiline features were no mirror
To see me reflected
So I learned to deflect it
Your maternal bitterness
I was your problem child
So many pre-conceptions
Grew a wall between us

Melissa J. Wagner. (Abridged version of the poem)

FINAL LETTERS –
EMMA & NICOLE

Dear Mum,

Somewhere right at the back of my mind are the flowers I remember from when I was a baby. They are hazy, and more like bobbing colours that won't hold still long enough to form perfectly recognizable shapes, but if I really concentrate I can find them for you.

Sometimes it hurts to look for them.

And sometimes it brings me a tiny smile, because when I find them I find you and I am in your arms. I am small, and although it is back when you must have been so afraid – I am safe. You are keeping me safe.

It is your promise.

A different kind of promise between just us that you'd never make again. Not even when my brothers came along.

A bond so tight that sometimes when I grew older I thought it would choke us both, a comfort like memory foam that even from a tiny babe – instinctively I knew would always spring back to fit me.

I don't know if I really remember the flower boxes, or if my mind sketched them into the negative space where their absence is.

Anyway – the flowers …

They are what we see from the balcony of our second flat. The one after the bedsit where you could touch all of the walls if you stood in one spot. The one where we shared a toilet with many many people. The one you had to move out to after I came and Nana Tiggy had to come and help you clean without letting Grandad know.

From what you said – you couldn't stay at home, and I think Grandad worried what the neighbours would say about you having a brown baby with no father.

These bits of the story are definitely the ones you helped me draw in as I wouldn't have known these things when I was so small. They are the things I have scribbled over and tried to erase when I sketch out my memories.

Instead I prefer to draw in the magic squirrels and the wizards Grandad painted for me with his stories once he came round to the idea of me, and after we became thick as thieves.

Perhaps he couldn't make out the shape of things in his mind's eye either at first …

After a time, the flowers were not on that tiny balcony in their flower boxes any more, and instead they grew in my Nana Tiggy and my Grandad Ernie's garden. We planted so many flowers together.

The garden – it was perfectly manicured with so many bright colours bobbing and weaving together. I was older then, so I can recall the shape of love and the colour and variety of marigolds, and geraniums, and the blue of your favourite forget-me-nots is now paint splashed across the interior of my memory.

The perennials were always my favourites because I didn't like the idea of something beautiful dying so early. Instead I loved the idea that once you planted the seed – the earth, the patch of land you planted it in was changed forever, and there would be something beautiful where there was a patch of earth that wasn't so pretty before. It would bloom as long as you took care of what you had planted – as long as you nurtured it – it would continue to blossom every year.

Emma x

Dear Mom and Dad,

It's weird that we never talked about it. We talk about everything now. I often think back to my teenage self and wonder how such strong people raised such an insecure girl. You are both so self-assured. When I think back to my teenage self, all I can think of is how small I tried to make myself.

The embarrassment, the shame of wanting anything different from what I was given, what I love so much. Our family.

I have always been proud of you both and where we come from. If anything, it is my favourite thing to talk about because it's what made me. It's what made us an 'us'. But I know that now with thirty plus years of hindsight.

Looking back, even the whisper of questioning would make me wobble. I always felt like I wasn't doing a good enough job of being Ghanaian or Filipino.

I think back to a *Mixed Up* podcast interview we did with Jassa Ahluwalia, who I admire so fiercely, about language. I came away from the interview feeling jealous of the fact that he can speak fluent Punjabi. I wish I could speak Tagalog. I wish I could speak Twi, Fante, Ga … Language is what ties us together, it connects communities, it allows for stories to be told, so I feel like I'm letting the side down not being able to speak our languages.

But I am grateful that you taught me to never be silent. To be honest with myself and with others. Which is I'm sure what brings me to this point now, where I have connected with so many mixed people all over the world through the podcast and for this book.

When we went to the Philippines in 2022, it was the first time I had been back there since I was four years old. And it was the homecoming that I had always hoped for. Burying Tita Chel felt like an ending that I am still not ready for, but her death felt like my rebirth.

A new me since going through so much life and loss, constantly feeling like I had to show the world who I am and that it's valid – your lessons are finally sinking in. It took a while!

There's something to be said about us never talking about race in our house when I was younger, but I know you were focused on other things. Raising me with love, feeding me, clothing me, keeping me safe. Despite not having those conversations then, we have them now, and they are still so valuable to me.

I don't know about having children or what that feels like yet, I hope I do someday, but I can see how so much of us lives in each other. You made me who I am, and I am so happy to be here.

Love always,
Nicole

As soon as we started releasing our episodes of the *Mixed Up* podcast we were struck by the amount of emotional feedback that we received from listeners, some of whom have even contributed their words here in this chapter. It was a cathartic outpouring that has become a growing conversation for all of us who have found each other and taken solace in being open about our personal experiences in this way.

We have heard from listeners embarking on heritage journeys, we have had listeners who have taken courses on exploring expressions of their mixed identity, we have heard of people learning languages to bring them closer to their heritage.

Ryan Alexander Holmes explained how he came to learn Chinese, not out of a deficit and feeling inferior because he was mixed Black *and* Chinese and other people might expect him to prove himself as Chinese, but instead to get a grasp on a language 'that was already his'. We have heard stories of people digging into their ancestry and their DNA and working to learn things that they were not able to glean from their parents for whatever reason.

There has been so much work and considered action taken by the mixed people we are in community with to explore within themselves and feel empowered by their multiple heritages and cultures.

Hearing directly from mixed people has taken us on an incredible journey since we started the podcast and in writing this book. We have seen mixed people hold space for their past selves, we have seen them reflect on their younger selves and how they felt as they grew into adult-hood – all of which has been healing and something we feel honoured to have witnessed.

It's our hope that this is an opportunity to share more of ourselves with one another. And that this evolves into even more conversation and dialogue over time. We'd love to see a future where more parents are asking their children insightful questions about the things they may want to learn about with regard to race, ancestry, belonging, heritage and identity, and creating a space for their children to be vulnerable. We'd love to see future generations feeling comfortable to open up around these subjects – empowered to ask their parents the necessary questions and to initiate conversations themselves, knowing they have the right and the agency to explore.

And in the now, take these letters as just the start of bringing more mixed adults in community with one another, discovering the synergies and differences in the experiences they didn't have the courage to share, even with their parents while growing up.

Hopefully, reading between the lines of their letters will help you feel more empowered to do this exploration for yourselves – the way reading them did for us.

12.

HE WHO CHASES TWO RABBITS WILL CATCH NEITHER

I think it's the very essence and the foundation of everything that I do.

Because the first thing it forced me into doing was becoming something of a chameleon … when you're riding that tightrope and you turn it from a tightrope into a wave where you're not just teetering, you are kind of enjoying it. You find the ability to speak a number of languages, so to speak – to a number of different types of people … and … it was just a natural progression to be an entertainer, to entertain people and want to bring joy because it all comes from … that kind of needy early stage of being a mixed person. Or just like, 'Please just can I just fit in quietly here?' But if you can turn it into an empowering thing, it can also be quite positive because you start to get a sense of self and you build your own confidence. And then it stops being this desperate, needy thing and it becomes more like, 'No, I'm gonna use this to bring people together to celebrate my own ability.' Everything I've done, everything I've written has been based on duality in some sense.

Mixed Up *podcast, Ben Bailey Smith on the beauty of duality, British values and what happens when a teacher tells you to 'Just put white, it's easier.'*

EMMA

There is a Japanese proverb that one of our guests, Claire Yurika Davis, introduced us to when she joined us on *Mixed Up*: 'He who chases two rabbits will catch neither.' The saying means different things to different people, but in this instance we are going to apply our own translation.

As it relates to those of mixed race, this proverb could easily be interpreted as accepting that there are not two rabbits at all. In fact there is just one – one rabbit that encompasses all of the multi-layered character traits and attributes that come from your dual or multiple heritage. It's possible to be of dual heritage and be whole.

The word of warning in the proverb is that you should chase only the one rabbit and beware of splitting yourself in two by trying to pursue two rabbits – the two sides of yourself that are conceptually separate in your mind's eye (and that will likely run in different directions). If you can accept that there is just one rabbit, and that you are 'both' rather than 'half' of one thing and 'half' of another, then you'll be more likely to prosper. It is in this self-discovery that you'll find the magic.

So far, we have explored the challenges and the often knotty reality of being of mixed race. But there is a lot to be said for – a lot to say about – the magical way in which existing across two planes can unlock creative thought and nurture the imagination. When you let go of external forces, ignore people who insist that you decide which part of your heritage you ascribe to and allow the different facets of yourself to flow together naturally, it can be surprising what can be created. Not only that, but if you can view duality as a strength, then you might begin to notice things that can only come from your unique vantage point at an intersection of cultures.

Personally, I have often unwittingly been drawn to the work of artists and creatives who hold dual heritage or mixed ethnicity, perhaps because I am looking for some sort of learning that helps me gain understanding of myself and my experience through feeling bits of it reflected back at me. I'm looking for an education of the self, about the 'wholeness' or 'completeness' of oneself through the art I choose to invest in.

I have come to realize that this is not a serendipitous happenstance or coincidence, but that these artists see me and reflect my world back at me in some way that speaks to my soul. In a way that speaks to the idea that mixed heritage is complex and yet simple, composed of many layers and parts but also one cohesive way of being that doesn't require compartmentalizing in order to find artistic solace. We want to share some of our favourite artists and creatives – the ones that encapsulate that feeling of completeness and exploration at once through their work, as well as some of their thoughts on how their mixed identity influences their creativity and their inspirations and the why of it.

It's our hope that when you read this chapter you yourself will feel inspired – that you, like us, are proud of the incredible achievements of our community – and that you can flip back to these pages in those moments when you feel drained or creatively adrift. Hopefully the words of these incredible artists, performers and designers will give you encouragement and keep you moving forward.

For us this chapter is a perfect manifestation of so many of the elements and touchpoints that we encounter in the book. We really want you to be able to enjoy the art and hope that it will allow space for personal interpretation.

BETH SUZANNA

Beth Suzanna is a Bristol-based illustrator with a love of bold colour and shape. Her work takes the form of playful analogue collage and expressive pastel line work.

She is an advocate for diverse representation, while using striking composition to capture the atmosphere of spaces. Her playful style and

@bethsuzanna 'Hair is Care' [paper cut] 2022

use of bold colour and shape make complex political narratives and issues easy to digest.

I love the tactile nature of my process, whether it's collaging directly from life or sketching a little bit of vibrancy into the everyday. Creating work centering my mixed heritage has been my way of embracing and understanding parts of myself I previously couldn't articulate. Growing up in a predominantly white area, I think this work started as subconscious.

It became even more prevalent when I moved to Bristol to study illustration. The city's history is inextricably linked to race and racial conflict through its ties to the slave trade; being the site of famous resistance moments it sparked a wider interest in racial justice and how to communicate this in a visual way. I think being mixed race has in many ways given me an openness and empathy to perspectives outside my own lived experience. It's resulted in my desire to make my work accessible for anyone and everyone to engage with.

Fast-forward to June 2020, a few days after finishing my illustration degree, watching the Colston statue fall. It felt like a full-circle moment in the newly found understanding I now have of who I am and the work I want to make.

Making work celebrating the same Afro-Caribbean hair I was once teased for allowed me to shift my perspective. Nods to diverse representation and uplifting positivity are love letters to my younger self, only now it's conscious, confident and colourful.

(Beth Suzanna, June 2022)

CHARLOTTE EDEY

Charlotte Edey is an artist and illustrator. Her work is primarily concerned with contemporary issues of selfhood. Cultural signifiers and personal mythologies are shaped through a process of world-building. The lens of identity frames these worlds, exploring how the intersections of identities shape both interior and exterior landscapes.

My own background is mixed British, Bajan and Irish. My grandfather was a part of the Windrush Generation from St Michael, Barbados and my grandmother a transplant from Cork in the Republic of Ireland. Their union in Manchester to me is not only romantic but deeply symbolic of time and place. That

'Shell' by Charlotte Edey, 2017

one counterbalance of the xenophobic 'No Blacks, No Irish, No Dogs' policies of northern England in the 1960s was the birth of a generation of mixed-race Black and Irish children is a very English love story. A lived example that the personal has always been political.

A lot of my work is concerned with questions of identity, and embodiment as an extension. Identity largely relates to our inner landscapes: how our personal mythologies and lived experiences become the lens through which we see the world. By contrast, the bodies we exist in are shaped by the political structuring that we navigate externally, whether these are gendered, racial, sexual or economic power structures. Themes of fragility, contemplation, isolation, impossible spaces and balance, the exploration of selfhood and personal mythologies are recurring in my work. The politics of space are explored through the lens of identity; how the intersections of identities both shape our interior landscapes and define the structuring that we navigate externally … imagined realms are peppered with symbolist motifs that connote the body politic, magic, the erotic, biracialism and gender.

I feel that these tensions between interior and exterior drive my exploration of place. They explain how my characters or identifying elements not only populate these worlds but form it, shaping it in their own image. I feel strongly that my landscapes are anthropomorphic or figurative, speaking to an idea of interiority that is rooted in selfhood. The body is articulated if not literally then always symbolically: curvilinear landscapes mimic the contours of the figure, the use of organic archetypes like the moon, the shell and the sea connote an elemental femininity, fabric folds speak to a garmenting that is undeniably evocative of the body, and everywhere are curls. Hours or even days of my life have been spent dissecting our relative curls, kinks and waves. Natural hair as a political and cultural signifier is woven into my work through ribbons, plaits, clouds, flourishes, spirals and thread. The visual sensation nods to a magic realist sensibility, but to me the essence is deeply human.

(Charlotte Edey, November 2022)

LAXMI HUSSAIN

Laxmi Hussain is a London-born artist whose work exists somewhere between the abstract and the realistic. Having studied architecture, she enjoyed and excelled at the drawing and fluid art techniques within the course, and this became a basis from which to explore all aspects of drawing.

After becoming a mother Laxmi began drawing daily, finding artwork to be a valuable means of reclaiming her own identity amid the emotional blurrings of motherhood. These experiences of motherhood can be seen clearly within her work, which also explores themes surrounding the body, specifically looking to challenge negative associations and normalize representation of all types of bodies within art.

I am of mixed Indian and Filipina heritage, but very much grew up with all the influences of the Philippines due to my mother. I mostly identify with being Filipina. I think it's a quite common dynamic that one may lean into one or the other, and that is definitely us. My mum was very proud of her family, and Philippine culture is very family-orientated, and this was just an extension of who she was – she took us home to the Philippines every few years and although there is great geographical distance between us, myself and my siblings are so close to my mother's family. It is quite remarkable actually, especially when you think that on some occasions, due to how big our family is and not always being in the same place at the same time, some of us may not see each other for decades but talk on a regular basis. We connect through our heritage, the use of common identity and quirks in our mannerisms and characters which only our family and other Filipinos recognize. It's very special.

In stark contrast, I have very little Indian family. I've never visited India and, apart from my two half-siblings and their family, I have no other connections to this side of me. My father only shared food, which is also the common language of the Philippines, which my parents connected over and made central to our own blended family. Being London-born I am a Londoner through and through. I never leaned into this when I was younger, but as an adult I actually feel this is a big part of my identity and I don't dislike this like I did as a child trying to fit into either of my backgrounds.

My work is influenced by many of these things. My children are even more mixed, being the children of myself and my husband, who is mixed Somali and Iranian, was born and raised in Dubai, but his family then migrated from Somalia to Yemen and so speak Arabic. Then he migrated to London when he was eight (sorry, quite a mouthful). I think that being both of mixed heritage and then raising children who are doubly more mixed than us, it is not always possible to teach and share all of the elements of heritage which identify us. My husband and I have the issue that we have not been immersed in heritage at all in some instances due to close family members being estranged.

Art is the one thing that I identify as being me, it is something I can give to my children which allows me to share the feelings of home, which to me has had to be forged in how I interpret my heritage through intimate feelings. I think it is important that when we come from mixed heritage we are allowed to feel that we can interpret our identity through feelings within places which may not necessarily come from our heritage itself – in my specific instance, there is no immediate history (that I know of) of artists in my family. The places in which I am from are rich in art, architecture and craft, but I didn't see that growing up – I

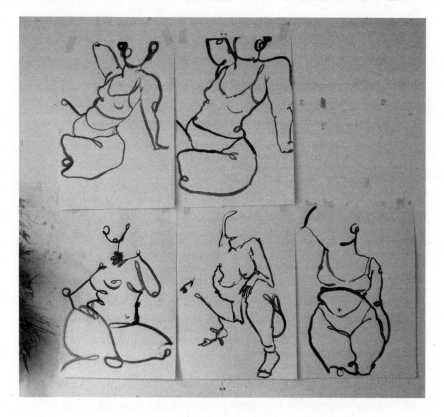

Paintings by Laxmi Hussain, 2022

wasn't taught in depth the nature of how creative all different people are, rather it was sort of glossed over mostly in favour of 'the greats' – mad that we still refer to them this way today.

People always ask me, where does this come from? Or who in your family was the artist? Almost as if this was something passed down specifically. In fact I think it was nurtured through the way my own heritage shows me what is possible thinking in an alternative way to the world in which I grew up. My mother expressed and demonstrated that her family didn't have a lot and they made things possible with very little, for example everyday home items were made by hand with bamboo, palm and various other things, a lot of which are native to my parents. These items are beautiful and an art in their own right – this feeds into the way I practise my art every day, a different way of creative thinking.

My mother's family leans into a matriarchal set-up, and this followed through in our family here – but in many ways, although she wasn't the oldest in her family, very often she was also quite a top figure for wisdom for her family in the Philippines as well just because of how forthright and determined she was in leaving home at 18 to come to England – not following in anyone's footsteps and just wanting a better life and to be able to support her family. She did all that and more, and although she worked so hard here she was always present as a mother, she instilled in us her determination and hard work ethic. I am my mother's daughter.

As a child of immigrants who came to this country for better opportunities and to be financially stable, pursuing art as a career is not something that they wanted for me. It isn't seen as a career that provides financial stability, but I am just as determined as my mother has always been. My mother openly shared her work, her feelings and even hard times with us as children, and this is what I carry forward with my work. This may not be something we ordinarily associate with heritage, but I feel that this is key – my mum's sister has this trait, as do many of her brothers, as did my grandparents. My children are also immersed in my life in all aspects and take part in almost all of those things, which is very much a reflection of the culture I see whenever I travel back home to the Philippines.

When my mother died, I completely immersed myself in my art, becoming more committed to it. I felt a huge loss of connection to her side of the family, not because I couldn't communicate with them but because any learning from her stopped that moment she was gone. A few days after she died I became distraught over the idea that I would never be able to ask her, 'How do you say so and so in Tagalog or Ilocano (her dialect)?'

Over the last few years since then I have channelled my work to sharing the closeness of home she instilled in me. All of it relates back to her in some way. So much of it is about reflecting her feelings so I can show my children everything she taught me, and I realized more and more since she died that everything about the way I feel about being comfortable and confident in who I am came from her. In the way I see my body particularly. I remember tender moments like my mum taking her long Sunday baths and asking me or one of my siblings to rub the dead skin off her back with a pumice stone, I remember her working out in the house (that Jane Fonda era) as a young child and us all jumping in with her. My children see me in my body for who I am, and not for all the judgment I might put it through because of societal norms, just as I did with my mum – through love and tenderness. I try to depict this in my work, I want it to be normal that we can all see ourselves in art, I want my idea of art to reflect the moments of motherhood which are real to me, to share my body as it is, not as the idea of a body I'm told I should have.

(Laxmi Hussain, November 2022)

SASHA HUBER

Sasha Huber is a Helsinki-based internationally recognized visual artist-researcher of Swiss/Haitian heritage. Huber's work is concerned with the politics of memory and belonging in relation to colonial resi-

Sasha Huber, *Tailoring Freedom – Renty and Delia*, 2021.
Metal staples on photograph on wood, 97 x 69 cm

due left in the environment. Connecting history and the present, she uses archival material within a layered creative practice that encompasses performance-based reparative interventions, video, photography and collaborations. She is best known for her artistic research contribution to the 'Demounting Louis Agassiz' campaign, whose goal was to unearth and redress the little-known history and cultural legacies of the contentious racist Swiss-born naturalist and glaciologist Louis Agassiz (1807–73), an influential proponent of scientific racism who advocated segregation and 'racial hygiene'.

In my art journey, the starting point was my Swiss/Haitian heritage. I found a way to tell my story from an expanded decolonial perspective, helping me to make sense of the complex world we live in. Working with the staple gun in particular represents for me the stitching of the colonial wound as a way of care and healing. When I discovered this method for myself it was like planting a seed from which gradually a tree has emerged that has branched out over time and which is growing deep roots which weave many stories into a continuous tapestry.

(Sasha Huber, January 2023)

BEN BAILEY SMITH

Ben Bailey Smith is a mixed Jamaican/white British comedian who told us he uses his dual heritage as a focal point in all of his work – as a musician, actor, comedian and children's book writer. He is known for his roles in *Andor, The Inbetweeners, Brief Encounters, David Brent: Life on the Road, Doctor Who* and *Law & Order.*

Sometimes it's very thinly veiled. Sometimes I'm talking about it explicitly like I did in my stand-up. Other times it's wrapped up in metaphor, you know? I might be talking about class – moving from being working-class to middle-class, or I might be talking about rich and poor; I might be talking about, you know, God and the devil, light in the dark, but it's all just a metaphor for what I see as the ultimate eye. The colour of my skin shouldn't mean anything because deep down I don't actually believe in race. It's just something that someone invented to make some money one time. I don't really believe in borders. Like, money, it's all just made up. Someone imagined it, right? But it's more like, I accept what it means to you.

To me, and to every mixed person I know, we're sort of beyond that, man. We've already elevated beyond conversations around Black and white because it never meant that for us. We never had that luxury of 'This is my team, this is my tribe.' And that's why I don't think it's a coincidence that Obama became the leader of the free world. I don't think it's a coincidence. I said this as well. It's no coincidence that Jimmy Hendrix became the greatest rock guitarist on the planet, or Slash. I don't think it's a coincidence that Drake is one of the biggest, if not the biggest-selling rapper of all time. It's not a coincidence that these people are mixed. It really isn't. No. They have a way of going, 'Fuck you, this is what I'm doing.' 'Yeah. This is what I'm doing. And I believe in the way I'm doing it, the language I'm using to do it speaks to you Mr White guy and you, Mrs Black Lady, you know?'

It begins in a personal place. And then as you grow with experience and intelligence and you build your empathy, you realize – wait a minute, I need to use this to do something really positive.

And that's why activism is a big thing, and art and creativity, because we feel like, wait a minute, I've got this message that's sort of running through my veins, you know? Absolutely. And then on top of that, I mean, on a lighter note, we're an oddity, right? And I still feel it to this day. I mean, when I was a kid – I'm a child of the 80s and I really virulently felt the oddity thing. Either it was just straight up aggressive racism, like people freaking out because of what you represented – the beginning of the end – the pollution of blood. You know? 'You're ruining everything.' Black Power guys, the white nationalists – you ruin everything for all of them in what you represent – the beginning of the end. Whereas we are walking around as little kids thinking, 'Oh, I thought I embodied equality.'

(Ben Bailey Smith)

CLAIRE YURIKA DAVIS

Claire Yurika Davis is the founder of cult London brand Hanger Inc., which pioneered cool-girl sustainable fashion by using innovative materials like latex. Many of her design storytelling is inspired by aspects of her dual heritage (Japanese/Jamaican). Collections like Sleepy Chan took their inspiration from Japanese tea ceremonies; Spring Demon referenced Japanese Bōsōzoku biker girl gangs. She starred as a contestant in the TV show *Next in Fashion* in 2020 and has since talked to the press about the impact of the show and what happens when your identity is reduced to suit other people's narrow understanding and inability to mentally digest the duality or fluidity of it. 'How can you be one thing if their perception of you visually along with the stereotypical notion of what that means for your character traits and personality don't match up?'

Identity is always a gradual process, isn't it? When I started my fashion brand Hanger I didn't really know anything. No branding or marketing or anything. I just knew how to make clothes, so I didn't really have those other bits unlocked at all. It was maybe around two years down the line that I think I came into putting my actual stamp into the whole of the brand, and that came after working with my heritage inspirations and things that really resonated with me, because when you're at fashion school, you're really taught to work with a lot of inspiration, but you're not really encouraged to work with your own identity. It's really about a lot of outsourcing and researching other things. So I actually didn't have that much practice in looking inside myself for what I already had. So I kind of had to break out of that way of working while running my brand. I was doing experiments working with Japanese motifs – looking at my family house: each

Design sketches by Claire Yurika Davis , Hanger Inc. Ltd, 2016

family house has its own symbols, so I was looking at graphics like that and things that inspired me that were from my Japanese side. Also in methods of working and ideals. And then I went into finding Japanese cinema as my inspiration, I developed a way of working that was more about storytelling. When I was a kid, my dad was a massive martial arts fan and so basically he got me, and we were very similar people, so he got me into everything that I like now.

With film, he was really, really into sci-fi. Sci-fi martial arts and anything that had fighting in it – kung fu, but especially Asian cinema. One of my previous collections is about a girl gang that ride around and beat people up, but only people that deserve it, you know, and it's just a fun way to explore. It's a way of exploring Japanese culture because I'm not there and I'm quite disconnected from it because I don't know the language and it's really exciting to investigate that side of my heritage.

When I think of myself, there are so many different elements to me that, you know, sometimes I'm in this mood, or sometimes that mood or whatever it is. So I kind of would design for myself, but in every different facet, and as such I was designing for, like, a group of people, you know, a gang or a collective, something that's representative of different facets of humans and how we can change and can be fluid and flexible. 'Cause I think that's really important. Instead of just going – here's my one muse and she's a sexy, powerful woman all the time. No one feels like that all the time. What about when you are tired? Or when you are hungry or, you know, when you are sad? You're not always this one person. And I really find that way of working quite limiting. So I really built up the brand identity, about a group identity and something that people can feel …
comfortable but also powerful in. That is the mood – people basking in their own identities and the fact that they are going to be fluid. It's more about emboldening people to be whoever they are, regardless of how they're feeling and who they are in that moment.

I'm always trying to encourage acceptance, and a lot of the time people look at me as an individual and think, you know, you are really strong and, you know, you've got so much creativity and power and all of this stuff, and that's part of me and part of how I act in the world, but also that's not necessarily who I am all the time; and there needs to be room for people to be all of these facets all of the time, even at the same time, to be strong and weak at the same time. To be timid and loud at the same time – these things can coexist, and I think it's really important for people to accept that in their own lives and identity, because I think there's just so much thinking, especially with this individualistic perception: everybody has to be one thing and they have to be like an arrowhead that's going in one direction all the time. But it's unrealistic because nobody is like that. And also it's not a fabulous goal either, because we all have so many different elements. It's a shame to ignore any of them.

You need to accept all of these things to be at peace. If you're at odds with any of the parts of your personality or how you act, if you don't accept them, then they become massive blockages within you and, you know, it's not really a healthy way to live your life.

(Claire Yurika Davis, 2020)

CAITLIN BELLAH CUDJO

Caitlin Bellah is a photographer, filmmaker and artist who is descended from the Black Seminole tribe. Caitlin's grandfather was the president of the African American San Diego Genealogical Society and he inspired her to use her art to tell stories and preserve their histories. Caitlin is very fair-skinned and might be described as presenting as white. Caitlin notes that her journey of learning continues as she develops her relationship with her people and so deepens the connection between her craft and her heritage, allowing the intertwined nature of the two to evolve and grow her as an artist.

I feel like in a way, if mixed people were able to be more open and speak freely, we could come from a point of view of seeing two sides or more of a particular culture, or even of seeing and feeling two cultures at once and perhaps be able to be translators, or even storytellers that can build a bridge between people. I feel like that could be our function in a way.

Because of the way I look I don't even post photos of myself and I don't always really feel that I have the right to explore or talk about these things. I've been meeting people from Oklahoma, but also from Africa, from all sorts of places. And they ask me, OK, so now tell me about yourself – It's an exchange of stories, and if you don't give something of yourself, you can't expect anything back. They want to see what you have in common and that you're not just trying to consume their story for your own gain. I think that's been happening a lot. And that's

Cousin Dominique photographed at Little River, 2022

how a lot of misinformation happens, so they need to hear first that you have an interest from a pure place. You know, like this is a part of you as well. So I've been having to learn how to do that and interview people ... It's been in transition since I got the idea from you to talk to my Seminole Freedman ancestor. I've been working on a project about the history of African Americans in Oklahoma, and now I've started to really focus on the five 'civilized' tribes in quotes, and the Seminoles in particular. I'm trying to make a book, an exhibition and a documentary, interviewing people about their ancestors and then taking certain stories from them and making them into art.

(Caitlin Bellah Cudjo, 2022)

Hopefully, having heard directly from these artists, you will have learned how being of mixed heritage can be a catalyst for creativity, and how this creativity can take many different forms. And while hearing from the artists directly is valuable, simultaneously art is personal and inherently open to interpretation. It's our hope that you have been able to draw your own inspiration and meaning.

The artists we were keen to highlight are here not solely because they are mixed creatives but because they are explorers of identity. And it is in moments of art that we often find ourselves reflected back. Sometimes we aren't even looking, but there we are in a painting or a play or a stand-up set.

Sometimes we unlock something new about ourselves we may never have thought about before. Or we are able to feel a particular emotion that has long been boxed up and buried. Sometimes we just revel in the beauty of the work and the talent that has been laid plain in front of us. All of it is valid and here to be enjoyed.

13.

MAGGI IN YOUR SHEPHERD'S PIE

EMMA

You may be wondering why we have dedicated an entire chapter to food. The truth is, food binds us. Not only is it a universal connector for us in our present, but it can keep us connected across an otherworldly space and time continuum. If we lose someone, we can almost feel them, perhaps even conjure them back for a minute if we create the right environment and nourish ourselves with the foods with which they used to feed our bodies and our souls.

When food becomes a bridge to home

Before I went away to university my mum taught me to cook our two easiest family favourites – spag bol (an adopted British favourite, although clearly Italian – but that's a different story/book altogether) and stuffed peppers, a dish my nan still cooked for me right up until she passed away earlier this year. Her recipe is a variation on gefüllte paprika – a German dish that consists of richly seasoned meat and rice stuffed into a pepper and then braised in tomato sauce, and later roasted in the oven. It is, for me, one of the most heart-warming mouthfuls of food I've tasted.

It reminds me of home, of feeling safe. It is both rich and sweet and as close to a consistency of mush as my idiosyncrasies around food textures will allow. Now that I am older and have sampled many countries' delicacies I notice that it is very similar in texture to the foods served to children or loved ones in other cultures when they are sick or need comfort. For Chinese people this might be congee (as I learned from one of my best friends when she recounted how her mum would care for her and her sisters when they were feeling poorly), a savoury mixture of rice and soup of a gelatinous consistency. In Jewish culture, Mrs Less, the lady who would look after me when my mum was at work, introduced me to chicken soup. For my Naija family it's probably pepper soup and eba, and I know now through my friendship with Nicole that in Filipino culture the equivalent would be rice soup.

Food is one of the greatest calling cards of home that we have.

It is only now, later, through investigating my nan's heritage a bit more after she died, that I realize that the dish she would always cook for us is a German one. So too were the circular gingery cake biscuits that looked like little full moons covered in snowy icing. She gifted my brothers and me them, never missing a year right up until our last Christmas together – Pfeffernüsse. When I was very young I thought Pfeffernüsse were a fact of Christmas, standard fare for everyone. This was until, of course, I asked another child if they had had their Pfeffernüsse yet, and somehow understood from their bemused look that they had no idea what I was talking about. You see, my nan was German Swiss, and unwittingly she passed on a little piece of this culture to my mum and my brothers and even my dad through this dish, through these foods that became so familiar to us.

Having these dishes cooked for me and being taught to cook them allows me to keep her with me in some way. I hope someday to cook this dish for my own children and give them pfeffernüsse at Christmas, every Christmas, and when I watch them eat her food she will live on in us.

We know from talking to the listeners of *Mixed Up* and the many mixed-heritage people we have met through our podcast that many have grown up without access to one of their parents, and therefore have little knowledge of one side of their heritage and in some cases no geographical connection to it either. Imagine, for example, a mixed Filipino/German who has been raised by their German mother. They are in their late thirties and still living in Germany, with no opportunity to visit the Philippines and no one to teach them how to cook the Filipino dishes they have heard about and long to try, but they may want to feel connected to their Filipino heritage. Or instead imagine someone who grew up with both their parents but one of them didn't cook, so they did not get to learn the traditional dishes of this parent's ancestral cuisines.

Food is not only a great point of entry, it's also a relatively low-risk and easy one. And this is not to diminish its importance, because of course it is food that connects cultures. Nicole has mentioned often that her mum and dad bonded over the similarities between their Ghanaian and Filipino cuisines; and we know that, despite the saga that is the jollof wars, I think that all of us across the West African diaspora and beyond can agree that jollof, whether Nigerian, Ghanaian or Sierra Leonean (etc. etc. – and no shade intended if I've not mentioned your own personal favourite), is the one of the greatest culinary feats to have ever made it out of a pot and on to our plates. Jollof is shared by all West Africans and all seventeen West African countries. Whether it's in banter, rivalry or a shared love, this food connects us and is an especially important reference point if you are in some way in danger of being estranged from your cultural heritage and or its various groups.

I would go so far as to say that the emotions and the attachments we develop around food are precious, transcendent almost.

As Michelle Zauner's memoir *Crying in H Mart* (2021) reminds us, it is sad to think that we might find ourselves quite literally crying between the aisles in a supermarket in a bid to find the comfort of the remnants of home – home being specifically the loss of a parent in Michelle's case. The first lines read:

> Ever since mom died, I cry in H-mart. H-mart is a supermarket
> chain that specializes in Asian food [...] H-mart is where
> parachute kids flock to find the brand of instant noodles that
> reminds them of home [...] you'll likely find me crying by the
> banchan refrigerators, remembering the taste of my mom's
> soy-sauce eggs and cold radish soup.[1]

She goes on to talk about how it is the only place in which you'll find a humongous vat of garlic, because it's the only place that grasps exactly how much garlic you'll need to cook the kind of food 'your people eat'. And while I relate to the sadness of searching for a lost loved one or a parent who has passed on in the food that they used to cook, or in the familiarity and nostalgia of the taste of a dish, it can also be a gateway to a moment with them, or indeed a connection back to the ancestry or culture you felt close to through them.

As Mexican chef and immigration activist Cristina Martinez once said, 'through food you find home'.[2] Building on this, through food we can trace stories of culture, generations past and migration. We can almost begin to deconstruct and exercise certain parts of our dual heritage that may have felt distant or unavailable to us in a geographical or familial sense.

When we interviewed Lydia Pang on the podcast, she explained how food had done just that for her in exploring the Chinese Hakka side of her mixed Chinese/Welsh identity. For her it was such a powerful way to soak up cultural meaning that she created a zine called *Eat Bitter* which contains recipes that reflect the way in which Hakka people's forced migration led them to become adept at foraging hard and sometimes seemingly barren lands. The term 'eat bitter' is about this historical story of finding sustenance in difficult circumstances, but it is also more generally about survival.

Food can be a powerful way in which to combine cultural flavours that we know are part of our story but may be more distant to us, with the tasting notes of the environments that are more familiar, even if those familiar places and their culinary flavours are inextricably tied to that displacement. When parents migrate, people may lose touch with bits of their cultural practice, but often, the food remains.

Perhaps food can truly help us make sense of belonging, and more specifically belonging in two places at once. It can be a tool for exploring parts of your mixed identity that you may feel you don't have direct access to.

When I was at university in Bristol, whenever a big night would come to an end, I would drag my friend to my favourite Caribbean takeaway. Right in the heart of St Paul's, which is home to a large Caribbean community, Tasties was open into the early hours, and at the end of an alcohol-fuelled student night out I always had a hankering for the brown stew chicken, dumpling and rice and pea perfection they served up. I almost always ordered the same thing. And part of the charm was that, after a few visits, I realized it was not me that was ordering but rather it was me accepting whatever I was told I was having, because that was what was available. But still we did the dance – I would pretend to choose my dish, the man behind the counter would tell me I would in fact be getting x and y, because, well, that was all there was … and I would agree that that was what I would have after all. Our server was always the same – a little terse, seemingly quite unbothered. And somehow it felt familiar and homely … addictive almost. Maybe, because I didn't have this kind of food back at home, it was an important ritual for me to maintain.

At the time, I didn't connect with the multiple levels of meaning this simple but regular restaurant date held, but when I first recounted it to my husband he noted that it was a little sad for me that this was (at the time) the table I could find to take myself to, to eat Jamaican food. The only table I could find, to sit at to fill up on so much of what I was lacking, was this relative stranger's table. This stranger, with his clipped kindness, and the reliably delicious food he plated up.

As I said, food binds us even in the most unlikely of circumstances. In the pages that follow, we are sharing recipes and stories from contributors. This chapter is for those who can see themselves in these recipes, or even in the stories accompanying them.

RECIPES

Melissa Hemsley's chicken tinola

There are 7,641 islands that make up the Philippines. My mum, Evangelina, is from a very big family from the province of Pampanga, just north of the capital city of Manila. She came to the UK forty-five years ago to do a Master's, met and married my British dad and had me, the younger of two daughters. Whenever *EastEnders* comes on the TV or there is any mention of it she will say, '*EastEnders* started the year you were born you know!' I understand now what a culture shock it must have been for her. Not least because she married a military man and brought us up in army barracks in the UK, Germany and then back again to the UK. My first food memory is her peeling me sweet little prawns that she dipped in salty vinegar and feeding me with her fingers along with little parcels of white rice. Heaven!

Because of the 7,641 islands, Filipino food is an incredibly diverse mix, and after centuries of trading with China and Indonesia and 400 years of Spanish rule you have dishes like adobo, braised chicken, pork or fish with vinegar, bay leaves and peppercorns and tons of garlic and pancit noodles (like a chow mein). My absolute favourite is this chicken tinola, which is a taste of my childhood and is full of ginger and brothy goodness and vegetables. Even now I can't smell ginger without thinking of my mum. She still just eats the vegetables, always making sure the kids (even though they are now grown up) get 'the best bits', the meat etc., to help us grow big brains and 'become a doctor!'

I've always thought of my mum as the best cook I know, but my *titas* (my aunties) love to tease her and say that she is the worst of all the siblings! They are very charmingly competitive. I grew up (once we settled after all the army house moving) in Kingston-upon-Thames, with Fridays and Sundays being the busiest times of the week. Sundays were based around going to the Catholic church, and helping out with reading and playing with the little kids at Sunday School. We'd say hello to all the other Filipinos – there's a huge Filipino community in the UK. I'm always a bit sad that my mum didn't teach me Tagalog, but she says she was too busy and I was too annoying to sit and teach!

Fridays were always the most social and most delicious day. All our *titas* (aunties, but in this case not relations, just older Filipino ladies) would come over bringing dishes and dishes and dishes piled with food that they'd finish off in our kitchen. They'd stop to pray together for an hour. Then we'd all eat. Then everyone would go home, laden with Tupperware and foil-covered plates of the (deliberately made) leftovers, everyone taking home a bit of everyone else's dishes so that all the food was shared and no one had to cook again for the weekend. I'd find it hard not to get a second wind and want to stay up eating everything cold out of the fridge before bed!

My mum, the queen of leftovers, inspires all my cooking, and as it's my job she's informed my career too! I learned all about being resourceful, frugal and thrifty from her. She can turn a few ingredients into the most flavourful, delicious, comforting meal. She is generous, kind and loving – just like I like my food! Hope you love her chicken tinola recipe below.

TAKES 1 HOUR AND FEEDS 6

INGREDIENTS
2 tbsp ghee or coconut oil
2 large onions, diced
8 garlic cloves, roughly chopped
Knob of ginger, about 7 cm long, finely chopped or grated
6 large chicken thighs, approx. 800g
6 large carrots, roughly sliced
4 medium potatoes (or peeled squash or a mix), roughly diced, around 600g
2 litres water, or enough to cover the chicken
500g green or white cabbage (I like the sweetness of sweetheart pointed cabbages)
1 tbsp fish sauce

FOR THE SIDE SAUCE
4 tbsp tamari or soy sauce
Juice of 1 lemon, about 3–4 tbsp
Good pinch of black pepper (or white pepper)

Serve with hot white rice.

HOW TO

- Heat the ghee or coconut oil in a large saucepan and gently fry the onion, garlic and ginger for about 10 minutes over a medium heat, stirring from time to time until soft and translucent.
- Add the chicken, carrots and potatoes to the pan, plus a good pinch of salt and pepper.
- Cook for a few minutes and then pour over the water, pop the lid on, bring slowly to the boil then immediately reduce the heat and simmer for 40 minutes or until the chicken is cooked through.
- Meanwhile, shred the cabbage finely and mix the ingredients for the side sauce in a small bowl and set them aside.
- Once the chicken is cooked, remove the thighs from the pan and set on a board. Add the cabbage to the pan to gently cook for a few more minutes. Check the potatoes and carrots are tender and turn off the heat. I like the cabbage to still have bite.
- Use a knife and fork to shred the chicken and return to the pan (keep the bones to make a broth another day).
- Season well by adding fish sauce, then taste to see if it needs more salt, then serve up each bowl and let everyone add the side sauce to taste. Add a big spoonful of cooked rice if you like.

Ana Da Costa's minchi

Let me tell you about my background. I was born in Macau, south-east China, which was a Portuguese colony until 1999; this will give you a little bit more clarity when I tell you that my mom is Chinese and my late dad was Portuguese. No, I am not 'exotic'. (Yes, I hate the word 'exotic', but it's the one most often used when I explain to people where I am from.)

My Portuguese name is Ana da Costa, but I was also given a Chinese name, 高安娜. Does it mean anything? No. It's literally the closest phonetic translation of my name.

Growing up, I never really knew my place. I am what they refer to as first-generation Macanese – Macanese refers to someone who is a native of Macau and of Portuguese and Chinese descent. I knew how to be Portuguese from my dad and I knew how to be Chinese from my mom, but Macanese meant nothing to me growing up.

Most of my best friends in school were Portuguese, so I identified as Portuguese, and would get slightly offended if people ever referred to me as Chinese or Macanese. Naturally, I wanted to belong and to be accepted by my peers. But, looking back, I don't think my friends cared; they loved me for me.

I moved to London at 18 for university, and for the first time I felt I could accept who I truly was with no shame or fear of being an outcast. I am a multicultural, trilingual half-Portuguese half-Chinese woman and I am proud of who I am.

I have tried my best to educate myself about what it really means to be Macanese. And as I am first-generation, there wasn't much to learn about my family tree; I didn't have a long line of proud Macanese ancestors, unlike some of my friends, whose families could be traced back to the 1700s.

The language, Patuá, is essentially dead. It's only spoken by a handful of people in Macau, so trying to learn a dead language from scratch and having no one close to me to practise or speak with was out of the question. The only other thing left was food.

When I was still in Macau living with my parents, we would have lunch and dinner together every day (OK, OK, every day is an exaggeration, but 90 per cent of the time we would). It was our family time, there's nothing special about it. My mom would always cook delicious food for us, Dad and I would almost always bicker about any subject. My mom would cook something we really liked. If we had a favourite dish, she would cook it for us until we got sick of it. This is my mom's love language. Perhaps, as with some other Chinese moms, there wasn't much physical affection or many 'I love yous'. Telling me I should lose weight while filling my plate up with her food was her way of showing love (there was, of course, a lot more she did to show love, but if I was to list all this you'd be bored). But being a Chinese immigrant in Macau, she only knew how to cook Chinese food. Portuguese food she later learned to cook via my late paternal grandma. So you see, Macanese dishes were never on the dining table as I grew up.

Macanese cuisine is essentially Cantonese Chinese food with Portuguese and Southeast Asian influences, and right now there are only a handful of restaurants that serve Macanese food in Macau. Truth be told, by the time I had left home I had only eaten three Macanese dishes.

Now, at 33 years old, I have sold out my own solo Macanese pop-up at The Hoxton. I am not saying I'm an expert in the cuisine, but I have made it my mission to learn as much as I can so I can champion it and show it to as many people as possible.

The recipe I have chosen to share with you is minchi. It is probably the most famous Macanese dish and the first one I have had and cooked. I am 99 per cent sure that the word minchi comes from the English 'mince'. It's a minced-meat hash dish that's usually served with a fried egg and steamed white rice.

FEEDS 4

INGREDIENTS
250g minced pork
250g minced beef
½ tsp baking soda
1 tbsp light soy sauce
1 tbsp dark soy sauce
1 tbsp sweet soy sauce
2 tbsp Worcestershire sauce
1 tsp brown sugar
1 tsp white pepper
1 tsp black pepper
1 tsp crushed red chillies
1 tbsp mild curry powder
200g potatoes, peeled and cubed
1L rapeseed oil (for frying)
1 shallot, finely chopped
2 garlic cloves, finely chopped
1 tsp cornstarch
1 spring onion, finely chopped

HOW TO

- Start off by putting your pork and beef mince in a big bowl, then add the baking soda, all of the soy sauces, Worcestershire sauce, brown sugar, black and white pepper, crushed chillies and curry powder. Mix well and refrigerate for at least 6 hours.
- Peel the potatoes and cut them into 1 cm cubes. Heat up approximately 4 cm of oil in a deep pan to 170°C. Add the cubed potatoes and fry them until golden, for roughly 10 minutes. Drain the fried potatoes and set them aside.
- For the minchi, heat up 2 tbsp of oil on a medium-high heat in a wok or large frying pan. Once the oil is hot, add the shallots and cook until they have softened and lightly browned, stirring occasionally to ensure they don't burn. Add the garlic and cook for a couple of minutes.
- Add the marinated meat and stir continuously, making sure the meat breaks up into little pieces. In the meantime, make a slurry in a cup with the cornstarch by adding 2 tablespoons of water and mixing well.
- Once the meat has browned and most of the liquid has evaporated, add the cornstarch slurry and keep cooking and stirring until the sauce has thickened. Garnish with the cubed potatoes and spring onions.

Naz Ramadan's Jamaica meets Cyprus breakfast of kings

My name is Nazli Ramadan. I am the co-creator of South London cult favourite Bando Belly, which aims to marry world cuisines in a way that never feels disrespectful to either culture. I was born to two first-generational parents from Southwark borough: my mum is Jamaican and my dad Turkish Cypriot. They made sure everyone would know I was mixed by giving me a very Turkish name, but I also had a big fluffy Afro!

I grew up with both my parents at home with my younger brother. My mum, although Jamaican, always made great efforts to embrace my father's culture. I was surrounded by a loving family, but my Nene (Dad's mum) was the most influential cook in my life! She would sing and cook, offering overloaded plates to anyone that crossed her door, from her neighbours to the window cleaner. Most people on my Nene's estate in Turnham, Brockley knew she was an amazing home cook, churning out pots and pots of delicious Cypriot food with songs, smiles and dancing. Her kitchen was warm and embracing and I spent countless hours there, even choosing to chill in the kitchen and watch TV in there rather than in the front room, where Turkish satellite TV would be blazing.

I always looked forward to one of the cousins bringing some fresh produce from Cyprus: the barrels of black olives, block of *helim* and endless links of *pasturma* – a spicy beef sausage which made my favourite breakfast of *pasturma*, scrambled eggs, buttery toast and lots of cucumber and tomato.

Everyone in my family would cook, taking a bit from the other's culture. My mum would make a great beef curry with Turkish-style rice with vermicelli in it – a recipe she learned from my Nene. My dad would make a mean ackee and saltfish, taking care not to smash up the delicate ackees in the process; or what can only be described as a big daddy breakfast where he'd make a fry-up with the addition of plantain and or ackee and saltfish.

I've always found that food has connected me to my cultures: understanding recipes and ingredients brings me closer to my heritage. On my family land in Northern Cyprus everything is grown locally and neighbours share homemade cheese, sausage and vegetables. My uncle grows everything, from okra to guava. Recipes in most families are passed down, and this gives us a non-severable and daily connection to our ancestors. Cooking these recipes helps us to reconnect to times past. Simple things like drying your own mint and using a pestle and mortar can re-establish these links to our heritage. Something I've found both of my cultures have in common is the love for outside cooking, especially grilling and BBQ, and using what is fresh and local.

The recipe I'm sharing today is a Jamaica meets Cyprus breakfast of kings. You can make it for one or multiply to feed a group.

INGREDIENTS
¼ Persian or Jamaican cucumber
¼ avocado or Jamaican pear
1 ripe tomato
1 tin beans
1 *pasturma* or *sujuk* sausage
1 plantain
2 slices hard dough bread
2–3 eggs

HOW TO

- Slice your cucumbers, avocado and tomato, lightly salt and set to the side.
- Season your beans to your taste. I like black pepper and onions, but you can add BBQ seasonings and paprika also. Heat them and set aside.
- *Pasturma* sausage comes with a skin you must peel off before slicing. Slice your sausage how you like; I like small cubes but larger slices are fine.
- Cook down your sausage until the oil comes out and the sausage is browning and a little bit crispy.
- Fry your plantain to your taste; I like my plantain just over-ripe and crispy. Set aside.
- Toast your bread and butter it.
- Drain any excess oil from your sausage pan, but keep a little as you're going to scramble your eggs in this pan. Scramble your eggs according to your preference.
- Assemble your breakfast: put the scramble egg and sausage on top of the toast and place all the veggies around it.

EMMA

I just got back from Jamaica. And as I very recently wrote, rather earnestly, in the Instagram caption accompanying my first photo video dump while I journeyed back to London, 'it felt like I had been waiting a long time to inhale and exhale like this …' I was headed home with a belly full of Jamaica, and I was content. If people found it twee, I really didn't care. I was high on gorging golden fresh ackee and saltfish in the sticky August Jamaica heat, and positively hedonistic from backing as many coconut jellies as I could get my hands on while the roadside breeze kicked up my shirt and cooled the trickle of sweat at my back. I am already craving the comfort foods that are coconut fried bammy, rough and ready mannish soup (a must during Jamaican Independence, I'm told) and sweet cakey, yet perfectly crispy on the outside, festivals … mmmmmm festivals.

People keep asking me to tell them what it was like to be in Jamaica. I have not yet found a way to articulate what it feels like to arrive 'home' in a place that you feel so deeply connected to and that you have never before visited. I still can't quite explain how important it was for me to spend time in the place my paternal ancestors hail from. I don't have words for the peace it brought me, both 'me' as a big woman and for 'child me', who has largely been estranged from this side of her familial heritage since a very young age.

My mind keeps bringing me back to food as a language to communicate all this. All of the textures and tastes will forever be associated with that first trip for me. And believe me – I wanted to taste it all.

It might at first sound flimsy to attach so much importance to food in this way, but I have always felt that there's an emotional attachment to food that is deeper than the simplicity of our love, like or dislike of certain dishes. And I have always, always been suspicious of people who attach only functional value to food. How can we possibly trust them?

There is, of course, so much more to say about this heritage trip of mine, but while I'm finding it too intense to articulate, what I can do is explain how good it felt to savour my national dish, ackee and saltfish, to get a taste of Jamaican culture and be taught to cook this dish with so much care … what a gift. It was a full-circle moment for me. You see, food is one of the biggest indicators of culture. Having this dish cooked for me and being taught to cook it allowed me to take it home with me. It allows me to take ownership and cook it for myself.

We may not be able to become 'proficient' in the spoken languages or the cultures of our mixed heritage; there is no badge we can apply for to become certified in them, and as crass as it sounds I believe that this is perhaps what some of us who are part of a diaspora and who have been displaced are sometimes striving for (in vain). But what we can do is become proficient in the language of our heritage foods. What we can do is practise the crafting of the dishes that feed our need to be close to home, to touch and taste it. We get to have this. If we choose to, we get to have this tangible thing.

* * *

Foods connect us back to family and heritage. They keep us rooted in where we came from, in what we have been taught by our elders, and they give us a sense of nostalgia, drawing us back like a tether that has been sketched out over space and time when we find ourselves far from the things and people that made us who we are.

For us, this chapter has always felt like something for us to gather round: while we can't take all of you for dinner and tell stories, this can be the place. A lot of chapters in this book may feel heavy with history and emotion, but here is where we felt some joyful and warm stories could come in.

Hopefully, reading these wonderful recipes and the commentaries of some of our contributors has illustrated how food really can connect us back to our identities.

14.
THE RISE OF THE
MIXED-RACE DIALOGUE

Beloved community is formed not by the eradication of
difference but by its affirmation, by each of us claiming the
identities and cultural legacies that shape who we are and
how we live in the world.

bell hooks, Killing Rage: Ending Racism *(1995)*

EMMA

What's in a name?

My name is an English one and derives from the old Germanic word
ermen, meaning 'whole' or 'universal', which feels kind of full circle as I
find myself writing this book for you all.

What I mean by this is that as we come to the close of this book and
the end of this particular journey in exploring identity, I realize that my
name is an aptronym of sorts. It is 'amusingly appropriate to my work' ...

It would appear that I have more in common with Usain Bolt than
perhaps even my misguided secondary-school sports teacher could have

imagined. We both have strangely fitting names, he being widely regarded as the fastest guy alive, a human lightning bolt of a man, and me finding that my work has brought me to a place where I stand in my conviction in telling you, and anyone who might dare to challenge this – that we mixed people are perfectly whole.

Being mixed race doesn't mean you are half of one thing and half of another. We *are* whole – no matter how tempting it is for people who have not yet understood us to try to do deconstructing, fractioning equations of our identities, attempting to squeeze them into the little boxes that make sense to them.

The theory of nominative determinism, purported by psychologist Carl Jung, suggests that people feel a magnetism towards professions or endeavours that fit their name. Jung pointed out Sigmund Freud, who devoted his life to studying pleasure, as the perfect example. His name means 'joy' in German.

The more I've got to know myself and my story in co-writing this book, the more I've learned about the decisions my mum made in parenting me and guiding me safely through childhood and adolescence, and about the experiences she went through and the transformation she found herself in the midst of when I arrived, the more I am convinced that my name is no accident.

When I was born my mum didn't know exactly what would await me, her little mixed baby, in the big wide world; but she knew that it would potentially build on the very real challenges of patriarchy and prejudice that she herself had already witnessed. She knew that I would be arriving as a combination of two starkly different worlds, political histories and power dynamics and that people might try to tear me apart. She was smart, my mum. So she gave me a name to remind me that, no matter how people might try to tug at the core of my being to dismantle my assurance in who I am, I will always be whole.

I am not the sum of my parts: I am all of them at once, I *feel* all of them deeply, at once – and that is what makes me someone that is often compelled to bring things and people together, to give what I can to make this place a better one for our collective futures and for our children. What I do may be a drop in the ocean, but if recognizing that I am who I was always meant to be makes just a few people feel more settled in themselves, then all the blood sweat and tears (yes, these pages are sealed in salt!) that we've poured into this labour of love will have been wisely spent.

I have found so much solace in hearing other mixed peoples stories, no matter how difficult and emotional some of them might be. If there's one thing I have learned it is that it feels good to finally be seen, and to make sure that the experiences of other people of mixed heritage are acknowledged across the broad spectrum of all their unique but also collective experiences. There is equity in community and understanding. And it's definitely therapeutic to talk.

This is something that we want to leave you with. Through all our conversations we have come across a recurring theme – one that may not be widely popular, but nevertheless keeps cropping up all the same. It seems to us that we mixed-race people have had a self-censorship problem. We are often busying ourselves with taking care of other people's feelings, being at once aware of opposing viewpoints and delicate emotional standpoints that we may not always share but that we can usually appreciate and understand, having in many cases a vantage point that enables us to consider both sides of a conversation.

And yet many of us have at some point likely found ourselves asking if we are enough of one or the other to be equipped to engage in certain conversations. And this, sadly, I believe, is often reinforced by wider society, unwittingly or otherwise. Nicole and I began the podcast during a time that felt extremely strained. It was the summer of 2020 and, as we mentioned at the beginning of this book, the Black Lives Matter resurgence was in force. George Floyd had recently been murdered by American cops and the world had watched the traumatic event online and in unison. Somehow it felt like there was a cultural zeitgeist afoot, and many were clamouring to find resources from which to learn more about Black history and context, about how to be a better ally, about how to support the cause for equality and safety. And yet many mixed-race people seemed to be searching for their place in it all, for their voice in it all. This appeared to be true not just of mixed Black people but of mixed people more broadly. And it was clear to us that amid their uncertainty and loneliness about where exactly to place their feeling of loss and in which community to turn to to hold their pain in all this, stood the vindictive and sharp rebuke of the internet, of Twitter voices that proclaimed them unqualified and unworthy to speak on George's murder and what it meant. I remember so distinctly talking to Charlie, one of our contributors. She is mixed Jamaican Black/white British, but to some she will present as white. She said quite simply with regard to the question of where exactly she 'fitted' in all this that she didn't 'want to be a white ally because she's not white' and this struck a chord with me. It hit home – the idea that she would even have to question that she would be forced into the 'white ally' camp because there was no space, no language for her anywhere else. The pain that conjures up is palpable.

I think that sometimes the politics of being of mixed race can feel stifling, especially when you feel a responsibility not just to yourself but to two or more distinct groups and their differing or even opposed agendas. It can be hard to raise your voice. It can be hard to assert your own desires, needs and indeed identity because there may not be the right words for it and because people may misunderstand you.

It is both the blessing and the curse of sitting in the in-between of it all. Being able to see but perhaps not always being able to be heard.

This is one of the reasons why for us it was so important to write this book and give voice to some of the things we have been entrusted with on the podcast, some of the language we have learned or crafted along the way to discuss being us.

Finally, as Eboni said in the episode 'The Rise of the Mixed-race Dialogue', the mixed experience is so nuanced and so individual to every person, but being a conduit for other cultures to communicate is a beautiful thing and there is strength and responsibility in that.

At the end of it all we are 'perhaps more similar than we are different'; and yet there is beauty in our difference.

NICOLE

You aren't 'half' or 'part' of anything. I used to get tied up in knots trying to describe myself. Caveating and stressing about how I was going to be perceived or received. I'd stumble over the words. Where should I begin?

Ultimately, the beauty in being mixed means that you have these incredible cultures, heritages, backgrounds and experiences to draw from. Those are the things that shape you to become exactly who you are supposed to be.

The anxiety comes from the slight cock of the head of a stranger trying to figure you out. It comes from the college application form forcing you to tick the right box. *If 'other' please specify.*

While our experiences may not be explicitly the same, there is a kinship in the common thread joining us together. Where we have been able to relate to moments of feeling othered, there has been an opportunity to look at solutions to these challenges through open and honest communication, building upon language and finding our voices.

In writing this book and in every interview we have done for the podcast, we have felt closer to our identities and our sense of selves than ever before. Even in stories that we don't personally relate to, there are those human moments of empathy when it becomes all the more clear how colourism and beauty standards – these concepts that feed off our insecurities and anxieties – are used as tools to divide us and distract us from taking down white supremacy.

But you have also read stories of community, of understanding, of growth and of joy.

The last few years for me have been an incredible education in finding the language – the language to speak about myself in particular. I have often felt guilty about not being proficient in my mother tongues; my Tagalog has always been poor, and my Twi, Fante and Gaa are practically non-existent. My lack of knowledge has been the stick I used to measure myself (and beat myself with) when it comes to being enough. When it comes to being a 'good' mixed person.

Something that has stuck with me from an interview we did with British actor Jassa Ahluwalia was that, when talking about his knowledge of Punjabi, he said 'language is a vessel'. It's how we share and communicate, so when you feel like you don't have the language you can't express yourself, you feel shut out, you feel disconnected.

That feeling of disconnect is something I am all too familiar with. While I have been to Ghana many times, I felt that because I couldn't speak to people, and even some of my own family members, in the way I was supposed to I was letting them down, and I would be letting my future family members down as well in the process.

But learning to forgive, having compassion for my younger self and all of the selves I have been before now has been a never-ending process. Anytime someone would ask me, 'Oh, why can't you speak?' I would say, 'My parents never taught me', which to some extent is true.

We spoke English in our house, and I'm sure when I was young I would dismiss their attempts to speak to me in Tagalog or in Twi. I can understand how much easier it would be for both of my parents to speak to each other in the language that they both know. It was simpler for me to blame them as a child because it simply wasn't my responsibility, I was not in control of what went on in our household. But now I'm here as an adult searching for language lessons online. I'm making a plan; even if I can learn a little bit then that's something. And even if I don't end up learning the languages my parents speak, then I'm comfortable with that.

I went back to the Philippines for the first time in thirty years in 2022. There were still remnants of Covid-19 restrictions in place, but it was a year since my aunt had passed away and she wished to be buried in the family plot next to my grandma and grandpa and my uncle, who had passed away several years before. I hadn't been back since I was about four years old, so there was a lot that I didn't remember and couldn't anticipate.

But the thing I could have never expected was how at home I felt being there. How at peace I felt in a place that I had barely spent any time in before. There are few places in the world that I truly feel at home and I can safely say that the Philippines is one of them.

Like I said, these last few years have been a real education but they have been such a shift for me. I was a very different person when we started this podcast and began writing this book. On top of the family bereavements and family breakdowns there was a significant time when I felt displaced. I was still trying to figure out how best to talk about myself as a mixed-race woman. If what I was saying was actually helpful, if people would understand where I am coming from. And while we all can have those insecurities and fears around not being understood, I know I had to have these moments of connection with our guests, with my own family, in order to really feel grounded.

When we recorded the episode 'The Rise of the Mixed-race Dialogue' it was one of the first episodes we recorded, and was shortly after the murder of George Floyd. With this resurgence of the Black Lives Matter movement, it was so clear then how much connection and community mixed people were craving after such a stark moment of violence while simultaneously feeling shut out of a conversation that directly impacted them.

And I think that all that is left now is compassion. Compassion for ourselves as people who are always growing and changing. There will never be one 'right' way to be mixed, so it is futile getting wrapped up in the projections or expectations of others. Our time is much better spent connecting with one another rather than berating ourselves.

It's also about having compassion for others who will, despite all odds, continue to box us in, try and tell us that we cannot be 'this or that' and attempt to silence us. We can only control what we can control, which is ourselves and our own reactions. That's not to diminish our own frustration and the pain we feel, but just having that understanding makes it a much lighter load.

Ultimately we have each other. You certainly have Emma and me. If you need us, hopefully you can go back to an old episode of the podcast and have a friendly voice in your ear. Together we are all building a future based on where we have come from and where we hope future generations will be.

ACKNOWLEDGEMENTS

Writing *The Half of It* and producing the *Mixed Up* podcast together has been the joy, and quite probably the most meaningful work of our lives to date.

A huge thank you to the communities we sought out for support, including Halu-Halo, Mixed Race Faces, Mixed Race Studies and The Halfie Project.

To all the incredible voices who contributed over the years to the podcast and to the book, we can't thank you enough for sharing your experiences with us. What an honour to share a space with you. We are deeply grateful to writers like Afua Hirsch, Akala, Emma Dabiri and Michelle Zauner, Farzana Nayani and Nikesh Shukla among others, whose words have sometimes been a mirror.

Thank you to Marcus – A-Team for true. Thank you for going above and beyond to do the most for us even when that meant hand delivering a mic to Big Zuu's Mumsie via bike.

Thank you to David Oyelowo for being the first to say yes. That was an important and generous gift that will not be forgotten.

Thank you to Mel L – for the support and the important intros.

Marianne – thank you for your incredible cover design. It speaks for itself. You are one talented illustrator and designer.

Thank you to Daniel, for coming onto our team, for offering your valuable time and your skill, for believing in our work, and for helping us level up.

Thank you to Hazel, who brought the flowers, and helped us to make things beautiful for our community. You saw the vision and understood the assignment.

Thank you to our editor Myles, for helping us make this the best book it could be, and to our agent James, who agreed to come into the fold when we most needed him and has supported us ever since.

To Eugene, James H, Bea and Martha who read early versions. And a huge thanks to Jess for supporting us with a culture read. You are a wonderful and brilliant soul, and we deeply appreciate you coming to our assistance when we needed you.

To Isabella Silvers, our fellow mixed-race journo! You have been endlessly generous in so many ways and we are forever grateful.

The biggest and most heartfelt thank you to you, the readers of this book and the listeners of *Mixed Up*. It has been an absolute joy to be in the community with you, to be in conversation with you, to have your contributions to this book and to the podcast over the years. This is something we will cherish in all our lifetimes to come.

The writing of this book has not come without significant challenge and compromise. We hope that as time goes on there will be more tangible support for first time Black, mixed race and brown authors, and authors from marginalized, diverse backgrounds across the intersections. Nova Reid speaks eloquently and honestly about navigating the publishing industry as a Black woman and we want to thank her for the phone calls with Emma, for the voice notes and for the care and guidance extended during this process.

ACKNOWLEDGEMENTS

Emma

To C, you are the constant and remain the only one who can help me go Super Saiyan. Thank you for everything. I know it's been a lot.

To my nana, you might be gone from this earth, but your legacy is right here in my words. Because I know how much you loved books, I can feel your pride beaming down on me right now.

To Nene – thank you for looking after me, for loving me as your own daughter, for teaching me to make Akara, and for always making stew and jollof with less pepe for me.

To my Northern grandparents, thank you for continuously showing me how proud you are of all the things I do.

Huge thanks to Zeena, EJP and PiP for sending candles, making picnics and assisting on shoots, for letting me cry on shoulders, in your caravan, and into my food during dinner dates. And for generally holding me together when I thought I might fall apart during the writing of this book.

Carter – thank you for being a mentor and for mumming me sometimes, but not always, and not in an overbearing way because you knew I wouldn't have liked it.

To Sophie, Elise, Lisa, Chantelle, Charmaine and Sam thanks for always listening and for blindly supporting me in each and every mad cap scheme, including this one.

To Audrey – for your friendship and the funny memes to lighten the mood.

To our community and contributors, thank you for so generously letting us care for your stories for a little while. Thank you for listening to us talk for hours over at *Mixed Up*.

To Nicole – WE did it! And not without difficulty, introspection, heartache and some loneliness inside our endeavour. But we had each other. Thank you for being my partner in this. Nuff said because all the rest has already been said over the last four years. X

Nicole

I am beyond grateful to Emma for being my friend, work wife, co-host and co-author. Having you throughout this process has been everything, I quite literally couldn't have done it without you. I am grateful to you for all the tears and all the laughter that got us through to this point. I am so thankful we have been able to get to do this together as a team.

Mom and Dad, you are my whole world. Thank you for your endless support and encouragement throughout my life. Despite everything you have always encouraged me to trust my gut, to follow my dreams and to chase joy – even when that leads me over 3000 miles away from you. Thank you for pouring love over me constantly. You made me the person I am today. Everything I do in this life, I do for you.

To Tita Chel and Moo-moo. I hate to think that when I started writing this you were here, and now you're not. I miss you both so much. Thank you for all your love and care, and for being proud of me all these years. They say that grief is love with nowhere to go, but I try to extend yours to others as much as I can. I am so grateful that you are my family, and I can't wait to see you again one day.

Michelle, despite being an only child, I am so happy that I found a sister in you. You are such a force of good in this world and I look up to you for that. You are the best sistahcousin I could've asked for. Thank you for wrapping me up in love and for being there for me always. Thank you for laughing with me, crying with me and rooting for me. You keep me going.

Sherell, you can't choose your family, but I am so glad we chose each other. I know we talk about not putting love on a pedestal, but ours is a love that can never compare. 'Best friend' is not strong enough to describe who you are to me, you are quite honestly, my family. Thank you for not only supporting me always (no matter what type of nonsense I be getting up to!) but for supporting my family when I am not there. It has been everything to me. You are everything to me.

Tom, simply put, I wouldn't be at this point without you. Our relationship may have changed, but it is something I will cherish always. Thank you for encouraging me and cheering me on from the beginning. I'm grateful to have grown in love with you.

Thank you to my family – I have always said I have the best family in the world and I'm sorry to say that the facts remain. Uncle Deane, Tita Fins, Tita Fanny, Tito Nic, Kuya Jopet, Ate Joanne – I love you all so much. I can't thank you enough for being in my life.

Auntie Tina, Auntie Sylvia, Uncle Charles, Auntie Ivy, Rudy, Deano, Adjoa, Nana Kofi, Jas, Brendan and Julian, who looked after me when I moved to London and continue to love and support me always. You have all contributed to my life in such an incredible way. I am eternally grateful for the family that I have been given.

To Izzy, thank you for being my best friend and neighbour, for constantly lifting me up, for offering counsel, for encouraging this conversation alongside us and for keeping it moving forward. You bring out the best in me.

My 'London family' who now live in many different parts of the world, but who I am forever grateful for their friendship – Tineka, Alex, Akshata, Megan, Rachel, Jeffrei, Laura, Kelly, Jess, Darryl. What an absolute privilege it is to have you in my life throughout these years.

ENDNOTES

Introduction

1. Muriel E. Fletcher, The 'Fletcher Report' or, *Report on an Investigation into the Colour Problem in Liverpool and other ports*, 1930
2. Aboriginal Protection Act 1869
3. Ann Phoenix and Barbara Tizard, *Black, White or Mixed Race?: Race and Racism in the Lives of Young People of Mixed Parentage*, Routledge, Oxford, 2001
4. Lori L. Tharps, 'The Case for Black with a capital B' *The New York Times*, 18 November 2014; https://www.nytimes.com/2014/11/19/opinion/the-case-for-black-with-a-capital-b.html

Chapter 1. All My Friends Are White

1. Akala, *Natives: Race & Class in the Ruins of Empire*, Two Roads, Hachette, London, 2019

Chapter 2. Childhood and Forming Identity

1. Farzana Nayani, *Raising Multiracial Children: Tools for Nurturing Identity in a Racialized World*, North Atlantic Books, 2020
2. J. Nicky Sullivan, Jennifer L. Eberhardt and Steven O. Roberts, 'Conversations about race in Black and White US families: Before and after George Floyd's death', 2021; https://www.pnas.org/doi/10.1073/pnas.2106366118
3. Farzana Nayani, *Raising Multiracial Children: Tools for Nurturing Identity in a Racialized World*, North Atlantic Books, California, 2020
4. *ibid.*

5. Barack Obama addressing the role race played in the US presidential campaign, 'A More Perfect Union' speech, National Constitution Center, Philadelphia, 18 March 2008

6. D, J. Kelly, P. C. Quinn, A. M. Slater, K. Lee, *et al.*, 'Three-month-olds, but not newborns, prefer own-race faces' Dev Sci. 2005 Nov; 8(6): F31-6. doi: 10.1111/j.1467-7687.2005.0434a.x. PMID: 16246233; PMCID: PMC2566511. https://www.ncbi.nlm.nih.gov/pmc/articles/PMC2566511/

7. Erin N. Winkler PhD, 'Children Are Not Colour Blind: How Young Children Learn Race', University of Wisconsin-Milwaukee, 2009; https://inclusions.org/wp-content/uploads/2017/11/Children-are-Not-Colorblind.pdf. See further reference section for more studies.

8. Aboud, F. E., 2008. See: https://www.researchgate.net/publication/287434559_Children's_Developing_Conceptions_of_Race

9. Dunham Y, Baron AS, Banaji MR, 'The development of implicit intergroup cognition', Trends in Cognitive Sciences, National Library of Medicine, 2008

10. Po Bronson and Ashley Merryman, *Nurture Shock: New Thinking About Children*, Ebury Press, London, 2010

11. Small 1988, Katz 1996. Small, J., 'Ethnic and Racial Identity in Adoption within the United Kingdom. Adoption & Fostering', 15(4), 1991

12. Ravinder Barn and Vicki Harman, 'A Contested Identity: An Exploration of the Competing Social and Political Discourse Concerning the Identification and Positioning of Young People of Inter-Racial Parentage', *The British Journal of Social Work*, Vol. 36, Issue 8, December 2006; https://doi.org/10.1093/bjsw/bch390

13. Mica Nava, *Visceral Cosmopolitanism: Gender, Culture and the Normalisation of Difference*, Berg, Oxford, 2007

14. Dinah Morley and Cathy Street, *Mixed Experiences: Growing Up Mixed Race – Mental Health and Wellbeing*, Jessica Kingsley Publishers, London, 2014

15. *ibid*.

16. UK Gov. 2021 Stats: https://www.ethnicity-facts-figures.service.gov.uk/education-skills-and-training/absence-and-exclusions/pupil-exclusions/latest/#by-ethnicity. Published February 2024.

17. Henri Tajfel and John Turner Social Theory. See: https://en.wikipedia.org/wiki/Social_identity_theory

18. Kamaldeep Bhui (ed.), *Racism & Mental Health: Prejudice and Suffering*, Jessica Kingsley Publishers, London, 2002

19. Stryker, 1980 / Stryker and Serpe 1982

20. V. N. Vivero and S. R. Jenkins cited in Dinah Morley and Cathy Street, *Mixed Experiences: Growing Up Mixed Race – Mental Health and Wellbeing*, Jessica Kingsley Publishers, London, 2014
21. Elaine Pinderhughes, 'Biracial identity – asset or handicap?' in H. W. Harris, H. C. Blue and E. E. H. Griffith (eds.), *Racial and Ethnic Identity: Psychological Development and Creative Expression*, Taylor & Frances/Routledge, Oxford, 1995
22. *ibid.*

Chapter 3. Interracial Dating and Relationships

1. Daniel Rosney and Roisin Hastie, 'Dating apps: Tinder, Chappy and Bumble "least preferred" way to meet people', Radio 1 Newsbeat Survey, 3 August 2018; https://www.bbc.co.uk/news/newsbeat-45007017
2. Business of Apps; https://www.businessofapps.com/
3. Christian Rudder, OKCupid Blog, 2014
4. bell hooks cited in Afua Hirsch, *Brit(ish): On Race, Identity and Belonging*, Jonathan Cape, London 2018
5. Georges Cuvier, Swiss Anatomist cited in Afua Hirsch, *Brit(ish): On Race, Identity and Belonging*, Jonathan Cape, London 2018
6. Tineka Smith, 'Love In The Time Of Black Lives Matter', *ELLE* UK, 12 February 2021; https://www.elle.com/uk/life-and-culture/a35486750/black-lives-matter-love-relationships/
7. Charles Carroll, *'The Negro A Beast' or, 'In the Image of God'* MO, American Book and Bible House, St. Louis, 1900
8. A. D. Grimshaw (ed.), *Racial violence in the United States*, Aldine Publishing Co., Chicago IL, 1969
9. Henry Yu, associate professor at UCLA's Asian American Studies Center, in David Pierson, 'Sex and the Asian man', *Los Angeles Times*, 12 May 2004; https://www.latimes.com/archives/la-xpm-2004-may-12-et-pierson12-story.html
10. Norman N. Nakamura, 'The Nature of G.I. Racism' Gidra, Vol. II, No. 6 (June/July 1970)
11. Karen L. Ishizuka, 'Looking Like the Enemy: Political Identity & the Vietnam War', Pacific Council on International Policy, 7 May 2019; https://www.pacificcouncil.org/newsroom/looking-enemy-political-identity-vietnam-war
12. OKCupid post; https://theconversation.com/asian-guys-stereotyped-and-excluded-in-online-dating-130855
13. *ibid.*

14. John Tierny, 'Single Female Seeking Same-Race Male', TiernyLab Blog, *The New York Times*, 13 April 2007; https://archive.nytimes.com/tierneylab. blogs.nytimes.com/2007/04/13/single-female-seeking-same-race-male/
15. OKCupid post; https://theconversation.com/asian-guys-stereotyped-and-excluded-in-online-dating-130855
16. Thien-bao Thuc Phi, 'Game over: Asian Americans and video game representation' *Transformative Works and Cultures*, Vol. 2 15 March 2019, DOI: https://doi.org/10.3983/twc.2009.084
17. *ibid.*
18. Ann Lee, 'The new heart-throbs: how Hollywood embraced east Asian actors, from Henry Golding to Simu Liu', *Guardian*, 10 November 2019; https://www.theguardian.com/film/2019/nov/10/the-new-heart-throbs-east-asian-actors-henry-golding-simu-liu
19. NBC News, NBC Asian American, 'Where Stereotypes About Asian-American Men Come From', 27 September 2016, YouTube: https://www.youtube.com/watch?v=5KF18Cqy53o
20. Facebook App 'Are You Interested?' 2013
21. Michele Norris, 'Visualising Race, Identity and Change' *National Geographic*, 17 September 2013; https://www.nationalgeographic.com/photography/article/visualizing-change

Chapter 4. Adoption, the Care System and Being Mixed

1. May and Cohen 1974, Rich 1986, Small 1991, Wilson 1992
2. Eugenics and Scientific Racism, National Human Genome Research Institute: https://www.genome.gov/about-genomics/fact-sheets/Eugenics-and-Scientific-Racism
3. Lauwers Delphine cited in Annette Ekin, 'The Children Colonial Belgium Stole from African Mothers' Aljazeera, 3 February 2021; https://www.aljazeera.com/features/2021/2/3/the-children-colonial-belgium-stole-from-africa
4. Emma Dabiri, *Don't Touch My Hair*, Penguin, London 2020
5. Australian Bureau, Year Book Australia, 1994; https://www.abs.gov.au/AUSSTATS/abs@.nsf/DetailsPage/1301.01994?OpenDocument
6. Dr Cecil Cook, 'The History: Northern Territory' (PDF). Sydney, Australia: Human Rights and Equal Opportunity Commission. December 2007. Archived from the original (PDF) on 26 February 2008
7. Lucy Bland, *Britain's 'Brown Babies': The Stories of Children Born to Black GIs and White Women in the Second World War*, Manchester University Press, Manchester, 2019

8. Home Office 213/926 or HO 213/926, see: https://en.wikipedia.org/wiki/Home_Office_213/926

9. Dan Hancox, 'The Secret Deportations: How Britain Betrayed the Chinese Men Who Served the Country in the War' *Guardian*, 25 May 2021; https://www.theguardian.com/news/2021/may/25/chinese-merchant-seamen-liverpool-deportations

10. Department of Health, 1995; 1999

11. Children Act 1989; Children (Scotland) Act 1995; Children (Northern Ireland) Order 1995

12. Like that of Owen, 2009

13. Selwyn 2008, in Fiona Peters, *Fostering Mixed Race Children: Everyday Experiences of Foster Care*, Palgrave Macmillan, London, 2017

14. Lucille Allain, Principal Lecturer in Social Work, 'An Investigation of how a group of social workers respond to the cultural needs of black, minority ethnic looked after children' 2007, Practice, Vol. 19, Issue DOI: 10.1080/09503150701393650

Chapter 5. Living Our Lives in Full Colour

1. TMZ, 'Rachel Dolezal Embraces British Influencer's Choice to Identify as Korean', 1 July 2021. YouTube: https://www.youtube.com/watch?v=f12Gz_SEc9M&t=6s

Chapter 6. Beauty Standards

1. Tanya Chen, 'A White Teen Is Denying She Is "Posing" As A Black Woman On Instagram After Followers Said They Felt Duped' BuzzFeed.News, 13 November 2018; https://www.buzzfeednews.com/article/tanyachen/white-instagram-teen-emma-hallberg-accused-of-performing-as

2. Karishma Daftary MD, Sneha Poondru BA, Nina Patel MS *et al.*, 'Colorism attitudes and use of skin lightening agents in the United States' *International Journal of Women's Dermatology*, Vol. 9, Issue 3, October 2023 DOI: 10.1097/JW9.000000000000009

3. FDA U.S. Food & Drug Association. See: https://www.fda.gov/media/161034/download#:~:text=The%20FDA%20has%20banned%20the%20use%20of%20mercury%20in%20skin%20lightening%20products.&text=Ingredients%3ALinalool%2C%20Aqua%2C%20Glycerin,PURCHASE%20products%20with%20these%20ingredients

Chapter 7. The 'Tragic Mulatto' Myth

1. J. C. Furnas, *Goodbye to Uncle Tom*, William Sloane Associates, New York, 1956
2. Sky News article 24 November 2021; https://news.sky.com/story/police-officers-who-shared-whatsapp-photos-of-murdered-sisters-bodies-found-guilty-of-gross-misconduct-12477334
3. Barbara Davis, *Daily Mail*, 9 July 2021, updated 10 July 2021; https://www.dailymail.co.uk/news/article-9774161/Sarah-Everards-cousin-recounts-harrowing-months-haunt-family.html
4. AP News article; https://apnews.com/article/a04d7127e7ee746e5bc206287c551a11
5. Zoe Tidman, *Independent*, 24 May 2022; https://www.independent.co.uk/news/uk/crime/teenage-girl-strip-search-met-police-b2085886.html
6. UK Home Office, 'Tacking Violence Against Women and Girls Stategy' 2021: https://www.gov.uk/government/publications/tackling-violence-against-women-and-girls-strategy

Chapter 8. Racism Towards Mixed People in Modern Day

1. Caelainn Hogan, 'In Ireland, Lifting a Veil of Prejudice Against Mixed-Race Children', *The New York Times*, 15 January 2021 [Updated 18 May 2021]
2. Samuel Sinyangwe, 'The Significance of Mixed Race: Public Perceptions of Barack Obama's Race and the Effect of Obama's Race on Favorability', Social Science Research Network, 15 August 2011; https://papers.ssrn.com/sol3/papers.cfm?abstract_id=1910209
3. 'A look back at the "60 Minutes" profile of Barack Obama from February 2007', 60 Minutes; https://www.youtube.com/watch?v=PezB6J-HIJ0, 10 November 2020
4. *Obama: In Pursuit of a More Perfect Union* (3 episodes, 2021) Directed by Peter W. Kunhardt, HBO Documentary Films and Kunhardt Films
5. Karis Campion, '"You think you're Black?" Exploring Black mixed-race experiences of Black rejection', *Ethnic and Racial Studies* Vol. 42, Issue 16, 5 August 2019, pp. 196–213, DOI: 10.1080/01419870.2019.1642503
6. Marrisa G. Muller, 'Meghan Markle Reveals What It's Like to Be a Biracial Woman in Hollywood', *Allure*, 11 December 2017; https://www.allure.com/story/meghan-markle-racism-against-biracial-actresses
7. Lise Funderberg, 'The Changing Face of America', *National Geographic*, October 2013; https://www.nationalgeographic.com/magazine/article/changing-face-america

8. Steve Wyche, 'Colin Kaepernick explains why he sat during national anthem', NFL.com, 27 August 2016; https://bleacherreport.com/ articles/2660568-rodney-harrison-says-colin-kaepernick-is-not-black-amid-49ers-qbs-protest

9. Will Swanton, 'How Japanese is Naomi Osaka?', *The Australian*, 24 July 2021

10. *Naomi Osaka* (3 episodes, 2021) Directed by Garrett Bradley, Film 45 and Uninterrupted

11. Ken Brown, 'Rui Hachimura: 'There's only one race in the world', Olympics.com, 31 July 2020; https://olympics.com/en/news/ rui-hachimura-basketball-race-olympics-nba

12. Carol Lee Kamekona, 'Why Can't Hawaiians Afford to Live in Hawaii?', AJ+ Al Jazeera, YouTube, 20 January 2022; https://youtu.be/ WZvKsfcmO0M?si=394CMK9t6aI-kM9P

Chapter 9. Why We Need to Re-examine the Phrase 'White Passing'

1. The Trevor Project, 'Pronouns Usage Among LGBTQ Youth', 29 July 2020; https://www.thetrevorproject.org/research-briefs/pronouns-usage-among-lgbtq-youth/

2. Rebecca Haithcoat, '20Q Halsey' *Playboy*, 1 September 2017; https:// www.playboy.com/read/20q-halsey

3. Danielle Pergament, 'Halsey Always Breaks the Mold' *Allure*, August 2021; https://www.allure.com/story/halsey-cover-interview-august-2021

4. Georgina Lawton, *Raceless: In Search of Family, Identity, and the Truth About Where I Belong*, Sphere, London, 2021

5. Nikki Khanna and Cathryn Johnson, 'Passing as Black: Racial Identity Work among Biracial Americans' *Social Psychology Quarterly*, Vol. 73, Issue 4, 13 December 2010; https://journals.sagepub.com/ doi/10.1177/0190272510389014

6. Georgina Lawton, *Raceless: In Search of Family, Identity, and the Truth About Where I Belong*, Sphere, London, 2021

7. Meghan Markle, 'I'm More Than An "Other"', *ELLE*, 22 December 2016; https://www.elle.com/uk/life-and-culture/news/a26855/more-than-an-other/

8. Jeremy Clarkson, article about Meghan Markle published in *The Sun*, Friday 17 December 2022

9. Jenna Macfarlane, 'Piers Morgan and Meghan Markle's relationship explained – and the reason they stopped speaking' *The Bucks Herald*, 9

March 2021; https://www.bucksherald.co.uk/read-this/piers-morgan-and-meghan-markles-relationship-explained-and-the-reason-they-stopped-speaking-3159821

10. Piers Morgan, 'Does Harry seem so unhappy because he knows he's been manipulated by a home-wrecker into leaving everything he loved?' *The Sun*, 8 December 2022; https://www.thesun.co.uk/fabulous/20692530/prince-harry-unhappy-manipulated-piers-morgan/

Chapter 10. Everybody Has a Hair Story

1. Emma Dabiri, *Don't Touch My Hair*, Penguin, London, 2020
2. Zainab Kwaw-Swanzy, *A Quick Ting On: The Black Girl Afro*, Jacaranda Books, London, 2022
3. Jacqueline Laurean Yates, 'The Big Debate: Have "Mixed Women" Hijacked the Natural Hair Movement?' Yahoo Life article, 17 June 2017; https://www.yahoo.com/lifestyle/big-debate-mixed-women-hijacked-natural-hair-movement-000120357.html?fr=sycsrp_catchall

Chapter 13. Maggi in Your Shepherd's Pie

1. Michelle Zauner, *Crying in H Mart: A Memoir*, Picador, London, 2021
2. Annaliese Griffin, '"Chefs Table" ditches the boys' club for a triumphant season' *Quartz Magazine*, 22 September 2018; https://qz.com/quartzy/1397550/chefs-table-ditches-the-boys-club-for-a-triumphant-

INDEX